Agencies

Agencies
How Governments do Things Through Semi-Autonomous Organizations

Christopher Pollitt
*Professor of Public Management, Erasmus University Rotterdam,
Scientific Director of the Netherlands Institute of Government*

Colin Talbot
*Professor of Public Policy, University of Nottingham and Director,
Nottingham Policy Centre, UK*

Janice Caulfield
Research Assistant Professor, Hong Kong University

and

Amanda Smullen
Researcher, Erasmus University Rotterdam, The Netherlands

palgrave
macmillan

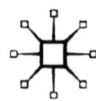

© Christopher Pollitt, Colin Talbot, Janice Caulfield and
Amanda Smullen 2004

All rights reserved. No reproduction, copy or transmission of this
publication may be made without written permission.

No paragraph of this publication may be reproduced, copied or transmitted
save with written permission or in accordance with the provisions of the
Copyright, Designs and Patents Act 1988, or under the terms of any licence
permitting limited copying issued by the Copyright Licensing Agency, 90
Tottenham Court Road, London W1T 4LP.

Any person who does any unauthorized act in relation to this publication
may be liable to criminal prosecution and civil claims for damages.

The authors have asserted their rights to be identified
as the authors of this work in accordance with the Copyright,
Designs and Patents Act 1988.

First published 2004 by
PALGRAVE MACMILLAN
Houndmills, Basingstoke, Hampshire RG21 6XS and
175 Fifth Avenue, New York, N.Y. 10010
Companies and representatives throughout the world.

PALGRAVE MACMILLAN is the global academic imprint of the Palgrave
Macmillan division of St. Martin's Press, LLC and of Palgrave Macmillan Ltd.
Macmillan® is a registered trademark in the United States, United Kingdom
and other countries. Palgrave is a registered trademark in the European
Union and other countries.

ISBN 1–4039–3322–7 hardback

This book is printed on paper suitable for recycling and made from fully
managed and sustained forest sources.

A catalogue record for this book is available from the British Library.

Library of Congress Cataloging-in-Publication Data

    Agencies : how governments do things through semi-autonomous
organizations / Christopher Pollitt ... [et al.]
      p. cm.
    Includes bibliographical references and index.
    ISBN 1–4039–3322–7
      1. Administrative agencies. I. Pollitt, Christopher.

JF1601.A36 2004
352.2′9—dc22   2004052090

10 9 8 7 6 5 4 3 2 1
13 12 11 10 09 08 07 06 05 04

Printed and bound in Great Britain by
Antony Rowe Ltd, Chippenham and Eastbourne.

*To the many long-suffering public servants,
in nine countries and three continents, who helped us so
much with our research*

Contents

List of Tables and Figures	viii
Notes on the Authors	ix
Acknowledgements	x

Part I Setting the Scene — 1

1	Agencies: The Context	3
2	Modern Agencies – The Ideal Type	30

Part II Agencies in Four Countries: A Comparison — 47

3	Finland	49
4	The Netherlands	63
5	Sweden	79
6	The United Kingdom	97

Part III Comparing Tasks — 115

7	Prisons	117
8	Meteorology	147
9	Forestry	183
10	Social Security	216

Part IV Conclusions — 243

11	Conclusions	245

Appendix: The EUROPAIR Research Project	267
Notes	270
References	271
Index	286

List of Tables and Figures

Tables

1.1	Cultural differences	27
2.1	Agency-relevant administrative doctrines	35
3.1	Six country comparison of selected cultural dimensions	51
3.2	Numbers of central administrative units under the direction of the Council of State, Finland	59
4.1	Trust in institutions (2000)	65
4.2	Dutch agencies to 2000	72
8.1	Basic organizational arrangements for Meteorology at time of research (2000–01)	158
9.1	Basic background on four forestry agencies	186
9.2	Organizational arrangements for forestry	190
10.1	Financial and staff resources of selected social security agencies (2000)	222
10.2	Social security agency governance arrangements (2002)	227
11.1	Categories of organizational theory	248

Figures

1.1	Nomenclature	11
1.2	Types of agency by task/work characteristics	26
3.1	State structure and the nature of executive government	50
7.1	Prisoner numbers per 100 000 population	121
7.2	Diversity in prison populations	122

Notes on the Authors

Christopher Pollitt Professor of Public Management at Erasmus University Rotterdam, and Scientific Director, Netherlands Institute of Government. Author of many books and articles on public management issues. Former editor *Public Administration* and former President, European Evaluation Society. Has worked as consultant and adviser for the European Commission, the OECD, the World Bank, the Finnish Ministry of Finance, the Danish Top Executives Forum and the UK National Audit Office.

Colin Talbot Professor of Public Policy, University of Nottingham and Director, Nottingham Policy Center. He has written widely on public management reform policies and has acted in advisory roles to UK government departments, the National Audit Office and the World bank. Adviser to the Parliamentary Select Committee on Public Administration. Member of the Editorial Boards of *Public Administration Review*, *Public Money and Management* and the *International Journal of Public Management*.

Janice Caulfield Research Assistant Professor, University of Hong Kong. Previously Senior Research Fellow at the University of Glamorgan. Current research interests in performance and accountability in both developing and developed countries. Co-editor with Helge O. Larsen of *Local Government at the Crossroads*, 2002, Leske and Budrich.

Amanda Smullen Researcher at the Center for Public Management, Erasmus University Rotterdam. Currently completing her doctoral thesis on the rhetoric of agency reform, a comparative analysis of Australia, the Netherlands and Sweden. Her research interests include public management, discourse analysis and the new institutionalism.

Acknowledgements

In the writing of this book – and more specifically in the EUROPAIR project – our debts to the public servants working in the various organizations in the four countries are huge. Many of them not merely submitted to interview (we carried out more than 90) but also responded generously to subsequent e-mail enquiries and telephone calls beyond number. We cannot name them here – partly because we guaranteed anonymity, but also because the list would simply be too long. Nevertheless, our gratitude is profound. Perhaps the most practical way of signifying our acknowledgement of this extensive, freely offered assistance is simply to list the organizations for whom all these helpful individuals worked:

Finland

The Ministry of Finance
The Ministry of Transport
The Ministry of Agriculture and Forestry
The Ministry of Justice
The State Audit Office (Valtiontalouden Tarkastusvirasto – VTV)
The Finnish Meterological Institute (Ilmatieteen Laitos – FMI)
The Forest Research Institute (METLA)
The Forest and Park Service (Metsähallitus)
The Social Security Office (KELA)
The Criminal Sanctions Agency (Rikosseuraamusvirasto)

The Netherlands

The Ministry of Land, Natural Resources and Fisheries (LNV)
The Ministry of Justice
The National Audit Office (Algemene Rekenkamer)
The Board of Forestry (Staatsbosbeheer)
The Royal Dutch Meteorological Institute (Koninklijk Nederlands Meteorologisch Instituue – KNMI)
The Dutch Prisons Agency (Dienst Justitiële Inrichtingen – DJI)
The Dutch Social Insurance Bank (SVB)
The Board of Supervision of Social Security (CTSV)

Sweden

The Ministry of Finance
The Ministry of Justice
The Ministry of Environment
The Ministry of Industry, Employment and Communications
The Agency for Administrative Development (Statskontoret)
The Swedish Social Security Agency (ABM – Arbeidsmarknadsstyrelssen)
The Swedish Meteorological and Hydrological Institute (Sveriges Meteorologiska och Hydrologiska Institut – SMHI)
The Swedish Forestry Board (Skogsstyrelssen)
The Swedish Prison Administration (Kriminalvard Styrelsen – KVV)

The United Kingdom

The Cabinet Office
The Treasury
The Home Office
The Ministry for Social Security
The Ministry of Defence
The Benefits Agency
The Forestry Commission
Forest Enterprise
Forest Research
The Meteorological Office
H.M. Prison Service (HMPS)

Academic acknowledgements

The breadth and depth of our academic debts should be clear from our list of references. However, there were also some individuals who gave freely of their time to discuss or comment on various aspects of our work. Our thanks in this regard go to Geert Bouckaert, Cesca Gains, Oliver James and Sandra Van Thiel.

Finally, we should acknowledge the excellent editing work undertaken by Mark Freestone of the University of Nottingham. He saved us hours of hard labour.

Part I
Setting the Scene

1
Agencies: The Context

Introduction

Government agencies are tremendously important in the everyday lives of citizens. In a considerable number of countries – the United Kingdom and the United States among them – most of the real work of government is carried on through agencies. It is agencies that may admit you to the country, pay your benefits, register your company, collect your taxes, lock you up when you commit crimes and provide you with your passport when you want to leave. It is agencies that eat up a large slice of the government's total spending and agencies that employ a substantial percentage of the state's employees. It is not at all unusual for them (as in the United Kingdom) to employ far more staff and spend far more money than their parent ministries. In the public sector, agencies are big business.

What is more, agencies seem to be on the increase. A number of countries (Jamaica, Japan, the Netherlands, Tanzania, the United Kingdom) have launched programmes of 'agencification' – of transferring as many government activities as possible into agency-type organizations (Pollitt et al., 2001; Pollitt and Talbot, 2004). Others have embarked upon less programmatic, but nevertheless significant agency creation (e.g. Portugal – Araújo, 2002; Sweden – Pierre, 2004). These innovations, it is said, will increase efficiency, encourage professional management, place services closer to citizens, reduce political meddling, and enable ministers to concentrate on the big policy issues. Agencies are in fashion, and are discussed and analysed in international circles as a major trend (e.g. OECD, 2002b, 2003). Not everyone likes them, however. As more new agencies and other semi-autonomous public bodies have been set up, a chorus of criticism has been heard. Agencies are not sufficiently accountable, anxious politicians in a number of countries have asserted. They are leading to 'hollowed out', fragmented governments, say some academics. They are hampering attempts to provide 'joined-up' policies and 'seamless' services. Their command of technical skills and specialist knowledge may lead to 'captures' where the agency begins to run the ministry, instead of the other way round. Or there may be another kind of capture, where the specialists in a particular agency identify more strongly with the other specialists that they deal with (engineers, let us say, or doctors) than with the citizens they are supposed to serve. Agencies have sometimes been accused of providing well-paid jobs for the cronies of those in power, or, in some countries, of facilitating corruption.

Even the OECD – generally a supporter of agencification – concedes that there are problems:

> Most OECD countries have been creating non-commercial bodies outside the core public service on an *ad hoc* basis, resulting in an administrative 'zoo'. This reduces the transparency of government for the citizen, and may compromise oversight and accountability within government. (OECD, 2003, p. 9)

Such claims and criticisms have waxed and waned in Finland, the Netherlands, New Zealand, Sweden, the United Kingdom and elsewhere. Yet the amount of independent study and analysis of agencies has been modest. Academics have tended to gravitate towards the more glamorous peaks of the state machine – the ministries – rather than spend their time analysing the humble-seeming agency. [There are, of course, some honourable exceptions, which we cite in detail later on.] A few high-profile, but possibly unrepresentative, cases have dominated the debates. Here, therefore, is our first and most important reason for writing this book: we wish to explore a type of organization on which we all have to rely and pay for, and yet which is only rarely the subject for sustained academic enquiry and investigation. This appears to be a task which is both socially and scientifically 'relevant'.

Beyond that, however, there are other reasons. As academics we want to develop and apply theory. We want to build models and apply interpretive *schema*. To us, therefore, the huge *demi-monde* of agencies and semi-autonomous organizations appears as an inviting, under-theorized territory where we might be able to do useful work. Also, third, we have research of our own to report. The four of us have co-operated on one large, multinational piece of research on agencies and, additionally, have worked together in various combinations on a variety of other agency-related projects, in a total of nine countries. Finally, fourth, we must confess to having somewhat fallen for what might be termed the discrete charm of agency life. While ministers are indulging in the competitive rhetoric of the political theatre, and departmental policy advisers are packaging and repackaging their scripts, agencies are getting on with the job. When one goes inside an agency – as we do at some length later in the book – there is a rapid reconnection with the 'real world'. As Erving Goffman once put it, 'all the world is not a stage – certainly the theater isn't entirely. Whether you organize a theater or an aircraft factory, you need to find a place for cars to park and coats to be checked, and these had better be real places, which, incidentally, had better carry real insurance against theft' (Goffman, 1974, p. 1). Agencies do a lot of the car parking for governments, and for the academic researcher there can be sense of relief when their managers start to talk about the concrete daily problems of delivering services in remote locations or paying benefits to more than a million people each day.

The plan of the book

In Chapter 1 we perform a number of scene-setting functions. First, we offer a brief indication of the scope and significance of agencies in contemporary government. Second, we explore the problem of defining agencies. Third, we make a swift, critical overview of the existing theoretical literature relevant to agencies. At the end of this subsection we introduce our own theoretical approach. Fourth, we take a first glance at some of the evidence which has been presented, both in the practitioner and the academic literature. Finally, we discuss this evidence and its implications for our own analysis.

In Chapter 2 we descend from the academic heaven to look more closely at the rationale that practising politicians and officials have offered for recent agency reforms in a number of countries. The different elements of this rationale are disentangled and considered. We interpret this bundle of ideas in terms of an 'ideal type' of modern agency, which can subsequently be used as one kind of pattern against which to assess real agencies. [The 'descent from heaven', by the way, is the Japanese phrase used to denote the practice of finding senior civil servants comfortable jobs in corporate boardrooms after retirement from the hallowed ranks of top bureaucracy. In the first wave of Japanese agencification 50 out of 57 agency chief executive posts went to senior civil servants.] Chapter 2 concludes with a brief introduction to our own, multi-country research project, which was designed to explore the impact on practice of recent reform in a range of agency contexts.

The subsequent Chapters 3–10, form a set. In the first four chapters (3–6) we look at the development of agencies in four countries – Finland and Sweden (where agencies have for many years been a prominent feature of the administrative landscape) and the Netherlands and the United Kingdom (where agencies were seen as 'new', and programmes of agencification were launched in, respectively, 1991 and 1988). This country focus enables us to pick up the distinctive influences of national political and administrative cultures, and of 'starting points' and policies. In the second four chapters (7–10) we examine particular functional tasks, looking at how each task is managed in each of the four countries. This dual perspective enables us to assess the respective contextual influences of, on the one hand, the characteristics of the task and, on the other, national systems and norms.

Finally, in Chapter 11, we return to heaven – or at least to our own Mt Olympus – to look down on all we have assembled and see what general patterns, interpretations or even lessons can be drawn.

Agencies: a brief preview of their scope and significance

The scope of work performed by agencies is very wide indeed. Agencies carry out inspections, issue licenses, pay benefits, run scientific research and development programmes, regulate public utilities, maintain the public infrastructure, develop and operate databases, adjudicate applications, administer museums, safeguard the environment, offer information services, run prisons, collect taxes and many other functions (for a sample of the range, see, Chancellor of the Duchy of Lancaster, 1997 and Pollitt and Talbot, 2004). There is even a UK agency dedicated to training dogs to guard defence establishments.

As for importance, agencies employ more than 75 per cent of the civil service in the United Kingdom, 30 per cent (and rising) in the Netherlands, and perhaps 190 000 out of the 200 000 employed in Swedish central government (Molander *et al.*, pp. 46–7; OECD, 2002b, p. 23). In New Zealand the Crown Entities employ 80 per cent of state sector employees; in Germany 22 per cent of federal public employees work in agencies, and in the United States a large share of the federal civil service works in agencies. At the time of writing, the EU Commission had 14 agencies and it was current policy to increase the 'externalisation' of tasks to these and similar bodies (Vos, 2003). During the last 15 years the programmatic creation of sets of new agencies has been embarked upon by, *inter alia*, the national governments of Canada, Jamaica, Japan, Korea, the Netherlands, New Zealand, Tanzania, Thailand and the United Kingdom, and by the EU Commission. Other countries, including Finland, Sweden and the United States, already used agencies for a very substantial proportion of the administrative work of central government (Pollitt *et al.*, 2001; Pollitt and Talbot, 2004). Although comparative data are notoriously fickle, the OECD recently estimated that 'arm's length bodies in central government now account for between 50 per cent and 75 per cent of public expenditure and public employment in OECD countries' (OECD, 2003, p. 5).

Definitions: what is an agency?

> We believe that one important reason for the shortcomings of international comparative research in this area lies in the use of an ambiguous terminology and the absence of a coherent classification of the variety of organizational forms. (OECD, 2002b, p. 2)

One sympathizes with the author(s) of this OECD paper on *Distributed public governance: agencies, authorities and other government bodies*, although it is a mute point whether the invention of an ungainly new term 'distributed public governance' was a particularly effective solution to the problem. The OECD is far from being alone in its frustration at being unable to develop a classification that is comprehensive, mutually exclusive and applicable internationally. Others have tried and also have been less than wholly successful in defining and standardizing these phenomena (Greve *et al.*, 1999; Peters and Bouckaert, 2004; Pollitt *et al.*, 2001). Peters and Bouckaert state that 'Perhaps the most fundamental problem in this literature is that the participants are often less than clear about what is meant by autonomy, and, indeed, what is meant by an organization' (Peters and Bouckaert, 2004, p. 23). Our own previous effort, focussing on agencies in particular rather than the wider spectrum of all 'distributed' or 'autonomized' public bodies, suggested the following:

- That no universal legal classification can be arrived at, largely because national legal systems differ so profoundly, one from another (e.g. the differences between the 'Napoleonic Code' countries and the British 'common law tradition'). Both 'agencies' and especially (further out from ministries) 'autonomous bodies' exhibit almost every

conceivable combination of public law and private law and mixed public/private status.
- That functional classifications of relationships are also hard to standardize because the 'framing' constitutions and political systems vary, for example, between systems with strong traditions of individual ministerial accountability and those without, or between those systems where appointments to autonomized public bodies are highly party-political, and those where such appointments are significantly less so.

In the light of all this classificatory debate and dissatisfaction, it is perhaps worth asking what we actually *need* of a definition? We need it to be clear, certainly, and to allow us to sort public sector organizations into or out of its 'box'. We also need at last some – preferably most – of the elements of the definition to be amenable to empirical research. However, we probably do not require a box which is 100 per cent precise; we can afford a few borderline cases, so long as we know why they are borderline, and so long as the preponderant majority of public bodies still fall clearly inside or outside.

Such modest goals can perhaps be partly achieved by a process of paring away what agencies (in our sense) *are not*. First, they are not divisions or directorates within ministries or departments of state – they are structurally distinct from the main ministerial hierarchy, even if the *legal* status of this disaggregation varies considerably from country to country (some agencies are statutorily separate from ministries – as in Japan – while others are legally still part of their ministry, as in the United Kingdom and the Netherlands). Second, they are not corporate bodies with primarily commercial purposes. This rules out the state enterprises which are still popular in northern European countries, such as the Finnish Forestry Board (*Metsähallitus*) or the Dutch railway service (*Nationale Spoorweg*). Third, they are not statutorily independent bodies that are free, or almost so, from direct ministerial instruction. Ministers – either individually or collectively – remain responsible for agencies (as we define them). They can, if necessary, alter their operational objectives and/or budgets without having to introduce new legislation. Agencies are therefore 'closer in' to the ministerial/secretary of state core of governments than independent 'quangos' such as (some) Dutch ZBOs or the French *Groupes d'interets publiques*. This third criterion is perhaps the most difficult one to apply, and there are borderline cases in some countries. [For example, there appear to be about 1100 French *établissements publics*, each with its own legal specification. Many of these are sufficiently under the direction of the relevant minister to count, in our definition, as agencies. Others, however, may be more independent – we have not been able to inspect so many statutes.] The same could be said of the large number of New Zealand Crown Entities, some of which are sufficiently 'directable' by ministers as to fall within our definition while others are so protected from ministerial intervention at the operational level as to put them in our 'other/more autonomous bodies' category. Or again, Swedish agencies are famous for their autonomy, but politicians nevertheless have their ways of steering, including political appointments, informal networks of influence and the annual budget allocation (*regleringsbrev*) which define the activities which central government is prepared to fund (Pierre, 2004). Thus we need another, non-agency category, that lies 'beyond' agencies and might be called 'More Autonomous Bodies' or MABs.

Now we move to a more positive identifying characteristic. Agencies are (fourth criterion) *public* bodies: their existence is constituted mainly or entirely in public law (even if the precise status in public law varies, as indicated above). [They are not, therefore, third sector bodies which were originally voluntaristically created to pursue the goals of their membership, but which subsequently became responsible for the delivery of certain public services. Thus bodies such as German sickness funds or Dutch housing associations are not regarded (by us, at any rate) as agencies.]

Fifth, we define agencies as public organizations which have greater autonomy than the 'normal' divisions and directorates in the core of the ministry. This could be greater freedom with respect to finance, personnel, organization or any combination of these. It may not be a big difference, but *some* degree of extra freedom is essential to our concept of an agency. Just how much autonomy, and of what kind has frequently been seen as a crucial variable in discussions of agency performance, but we will pursue that further in Chapter 2.

Notice that we have *not* included as a criterion the idea that the organization in question should have as its main business the carrying out of 'public tasks' (although we did use this in an earlier publication – Pollitt *et al.*, 2001). This now strikes us as a rather weak criterion, because the wider one casts one's research throughout the world the more it becomes clear that, at particular times and in particular places, almost any activity or function can be regarded as 'public' or 'non-public'. Armies, prisons and the police have sometimes been privately run or recruited. Pubs, leisure centres, theatres and even vacuum cleaners have sometimes been organized or delivered by public bodies.

Nor have we thus far said anything about contractual or quasi-contractual relationships between agencies and their parents. Clearly some agencies do have such relationships, and others don't, and the value and appropriateness of this way of structuring relationships has, understandably, been much debated. 'Contractualism' is certainly an important issue, and will be referred to extensively in subsequent chapters, but it is not part of our *definition* of an agency.

To sum up, then, our working definition of an agency is an organization which:

- has its status defined principally or exclusively in public law (though the nature of that law may vary greatly between different national systems)
- is functionally disaggregated from the core of its ministry or department of state
- enjoys *some* degree of autonomy which is not enjoyed by the core ministry
- is nevertheless linked to the ministry/department of state in ways which are close enough to permit ministers/secretaries of state to alter the budgets and main operational goals of the organization
- is therefore not statutorily fully independent of its ministry/department of state
- is not a commercial corporation.

Thus *some* degree of *disaggregation* (structural separation from the core of the ministry) and also *some* degree of *autonomy* (discretion/freedom in use of finance or personnel or organization) are both defining criteria. If an organization has neither of these, then we do not classify it as an agency, whatever it may be called in its local context. By these criteria UK Next Steps agencies, Japanese Independent Administrative Corporations (IACs), Canadian Special Operating Agencies (SOAs), many French *établissements publics* and Dutch *agentschappen* and even some *ZBOs* are agencies, while – for example – many other *ZBOs*, most Nordic public enterprises, German sickness funds and Italian *Autorita amministrative independante* (Independent Administrative Authorities) are not (Allix, 2002). This latter group are disqualified because the opportunity for ministers to fine-tune their annual activities and/or budgets are very small or, to put it the other way, their independence is too great to call them 'agencies'. In our terminology they are MABs.

We would stress that this is an analytic definition, in the sense that it depends on the presence or absence of a specified set of analytic elements. This means that it does not precisely match the organizational and legal categories used in each and every country. Indeed, as we have seen, it cuts partly across the membership of certain categories, such as Dutch ZBOs and French *établissements publics*. While this may seem untidy, it is also inevitable. There simply is not any pre-existing legal or conventional classification which will exclusively but comprehensively embrace the phenomena with which this book is concerned – certainly not across a range of different countries. Hence the construction of the six point definition set out above. It places agencies in a spectrum of public bodies which is set out in Figure 1.1.

One final remark: another disclaimer. It is definitely *not* asserted here that the definitional differences between agencies and other types of autonomous public body are necessarily big influences on the *performance* of the respective types of body, *nor* that we need a special type of theory to deal with agencies and another type to deal with, say, MABs, or state enterprises. *This book is mainly about agencies, but that does not mean that we necessarily consider them to require their own, unique body of theory, quite separate from those theories that are used elsewhere in organizational analysis within public administration.* Indeed, as will become clear, our argument is rather against this line of thinking. For many purposes, factors other than formal classification as an agency will turn out to be of greater theoretical and explanatory significance.

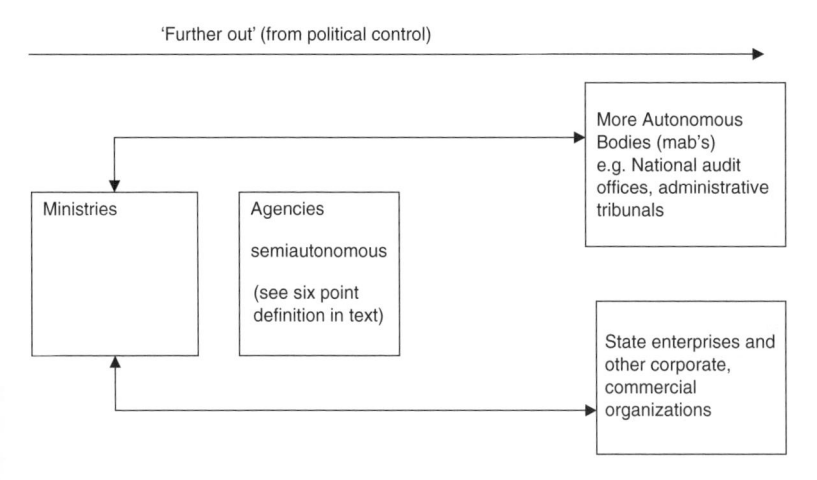

Figure 1.1 Nomenclature

An overview of agency theories

Despite the extent of agencification, academic attempts to analyse and discuss these entities have thus far been inconclusive. Our theoretical models are untidily diverse, yet only loosely related to some of the most pressing questions we want to ask. By and large the scholarly community, instead of developing its own agenda, has limped along behind a variegated and ever-shifting bunch of practitioner concerns. Most of our empirical studies are qualitative treatments of single cases or 'small *n*' sets, and comparative work remains rare. Consultancy reports by academics probably outnumber academic monographs by academics. The Anglophone and Anglo-Saxon biases which inhabit public management generally seem to have taken a particularly virulent hold on this sub-field. There is plenty of official, 'grey literature' on agencies, but most of it is carefully composed to meet reporting requirements or is self-publicizing (we have collected plenty of glossy brochures). These are not the kind of texts in which to look for theory-building, theory-testing or critical discussion of assumptions or data.

So there is much to do. However, we must not exaggerate the parlous state of scientific knowledge in this sub-field. Useful work, even excellent and intriguing work has been accomplished. So, before plunging into our own investigations, we need to describe and assess, according to our literature search, what is already available.

While it is certainly the case that not *every* theory used in the study of agencies has been identified, the references we cite are, to the best of our knowledge, representatively varied and wide. Within this body of literature there are a number of types of theory 'in play'. However, before moving to what those theories are, and how each performs, there is a vital preliminary. Consideration of theories needs to go hand in hand with a consideration of the *questions* they are supposed to address (Pollitt and Talbot, 2004). There is little point in comparing the merits of theory A, designed to answer question X, with theory B, which is designed to answer question Y. In short, there is no 'one best theory' for 'explaining agencies', only particular theories which have strengths and weaknesses in relation to the particular questions to which they were applied.

Furthermore, there are, in principle, an infinity of questions that *could* be asked about agencies – far more than could be dealt with in one chapter, or even a book. We need to confine our analysis to a manageable subset of these. Somewhat arbitrarily, therefore, we have chosen to concentrate on the following three questions, seeing them as among the more general and basic questions about the recent international wave of 'agencification':

- Why has the agency form seemed to become so popular over the past 15 years or so? (Why is it chosen? Why has it spread?)
- How can agencies best be 'steered' by their parent ministries?
- What are the conditions under which agencies perform well (or badly)?

For the moment we confine ourselves to this particular set of questions so that we can proceed to ask which theories have been deployed to deal with them. [Later, we will engage with other questions, beyond this list, but in this first chapter we are staying on the high ground.] From our search of the agency literature we can extract many – perhaps too many – specific theories. To make the discussion manageable these can be grouped into three broad epistemological families, as follows:

1. Economic approaches (including, especially, rational choice theories drawn from the 'New Institutional Economics' or NIE).
2. 'Traditional' social science approaches (including mainstream organization theory and much public administration writing that searches for causes, determining factors, explanatory variables and the like).
3. Interpretive/social constructivist theories (varying from historical institutionalism at the 'conservative' end to out-and-out postmodernist variants at the radical end).

Economic approaches have, of course been widely used in many subfields of politics, public administration and management over the past twenty or so years. Rational choice variants have been particularly popular in the United States, and have also influenced public management practitioners in several countries, most famously New Zealand (Boston *et al.*, 1996). Initial assumptions (particularly the existence of rational, utility maximizing actors – and *only* rational, utility-maximizing actors) are set out very explicitly, and a deductive logic is subsequently pursued. Hypotheses are generated for testing. This body of theory has something to say on all three of our key questions. Agencies are chosen, rational choice theorists suggest, because they are a more efficient form than a traditional bureaucratic/departmental hierarchy. [Why then, one might ask, weren't they chosen a long time ago? Rational choice theories don't really answer this, but macro-economic historians point out that the 1970s and early 1980s witnessed a tightening of many nation states' fiscal positions, under the twin impacts of growing welfare state burdens and global economic upheavals. Such fiscal pressures could easily lead to an intensification of the search for efficient ways of running public services – such as agencies.] Taliercio (2004) offers a good example of a rational choice analysis which explains the choice of the agency form on the grounds that it leads to greater efficiency (in this case, efficiency in revenue collection in developing countries). Dunleavy (1991) sets out a sophisticated general theory which shows why senior civil servants will tend to choose to 'hive off' various kinds of operational function to disaggregated, semi-autonomous bodies. He calls this 'bureau shaping' and sees it as a process which enables senior civil servants to concentrate on the kind of discretionary, high status policy advisory work which they like best. James (2003) deepens this analysis with specific reference to the UK Next Steps agencies. Another instance is Van Thiel's study of Dutch agencies and ZBOs, in which rational choice theory is used to enquire into the recent popularity of these forms (Van Thiel, 2001). In this case it does not perform so convincingly, and the author has to resort to other types of theory in her attempt to explain why Dutch politicians have created so many of these autonomous bodies. Finally, we might mention a more general book about the evaluation of public management reforms against the framework of rational choice theory – Boyne *et al.*, 2003. This work explores at length the suggestion that New Public Management (NPM)-type reforms have led to improvements in efficiency and responsiveness. It concludes that the evidence is suggestive rather than conclusive, but that limited efficiency gains have probably to be balanced against some losses of equity.

With respect to the second question – ways of steering – rational choice theory, and especially principal–agent theory, have quite a lot to say about how agencies should be monitored, and this can be translated into a set of principles for designing contracts (see Lane, 2000 and, more generally, Doumer and Schreuder, 1998). This set of insights also yields useful warnings about the conditions under which agencies may be in danger of performing poorly (those where the principal is unable successfully to monitor the agent, and where the agent's interests are likely to diverge substantially from those of the principal). Molander *et al.* (2002) deploy principal–agent theory to explore why the Government Office in Sweden is having difficulty in steering that country's many agencies. More generally, however, rational choice theorists have perhaps been rather slow to develop models which are sensitive to differing social contexts (e.g. which would show that the incentive structure which well worked in one culture or social context would not work so well in another). Granovetter, in a classic article, refers to this as the problem of the embeddedness of economic action (1985).

For most varieties of rational choice theory much depends on the assumption that agencies (working within well-designed contracts) are indeed a more efficient organizational form than their more bureaucratic and traditional alternatives. We will review how well this assumption stands up when we look at the available empirical evidence in the following section.

We now turn to *traditional social science approaches*. These characteristically concentrate on an initial definition of terms (as in this chapter) followed by a search for influential factors ('independent variables') which will help to explain the phenomenon under study (the creation of an agency, the survival of an agency, the higher performance of an agency, etc.). The hope is that empirical regularities will be found which will permit generalizations, and which will focus the search for underlying causes. The basic assumption is that reality is 'out there' and the job of social scientists is to uncover it by patient observation, classification and measurement. Hypotheses may be tested. Data will be collected. Cases will be analysed. Several works on agencies illustrate the potential richness of this approach. Hogwood *et al.* (2000) search for patterns in the behaviour of MPs towards agencies – why are some agencies constantly in the public eye, while others are seldom heard of – and what are the consequences of these differences for ministry–agency relations? James Q. Wilson, for example, offers a rich analysis of similarities and differences between federal agencies in the United States (Wilson, 1989). Kickert (2001) analyses the differences between public and private organizations and concludes that devolution of authority to semi-autonomous organizations creates a new category of 'hybrid' organizations with which neither private sector management principles nor traditional public sector norms work very well. Pierre (2004) looks for factors which explain the longevity of the Swedish agency system, and, in particular, identifies a range of influences, both formal and informal, which constrain the apparently very large degree of independence which Swedish agencies enjoy.

These approaches have made considerable contributions to each of the three key questions we introduced above. They offer a variety of answers to the 'why agencies?' question, showing how this suited politicians and senior civil servants at particular periods in particular countries (e.g. Boston *et al.*, 1996; Pierre, 2004; Pollitt *et al.*, 2001; Prince, 2000). From this perspective the reasons for creating or reforming agencies might differ considerably from one jurisdiction to another, according to the local menu of political problems and the local balance of political forces. Efficiency might or might not be one of the motives, but seldom would it be the only motive. The answer to the steering question is similarly differentiated – perhaps there are a few general principles, but much will depend on the important particularities of the task in question and the general features of the local administrative and political systems (Pierre, 2004; Prince, 2000; Talbot and Caulfield, 2002; Wilson, 1989). Even in the field of accountancy, where one might suppose that uniformity would be the goal, one can find senior academics arguing for different treatment for different types of agency (Bromwich and Lapsley, 1997). As for the conditions for good agency performance, the same applies: there may be important general principles, such as maintaining adequate supervisory capacity and skills in the parent ministry, setting realistic targets and simultaneously allowing real financial and personnel autonomy to management, but there will also be more task-specific factors, such as the need for high morale and a sense of collective mission for agencies which cannot easily measure or value their performance in terms of standardized outputs (Wilson, 1989).

Interpretive/social constructivist theories. These theories step away from the traditional assumption that reality is out there waiting to be uncovered, classified, measured, predicted and so on. Their adherents maintain that most or all social artefacts (including organizations) are constructed (and perpetually reconstructed) in minds and texts. So there is no single thing called an 'agency' which can be extracted from reality and studied. Instead we must wrestle with a world in which there will always be various competing and shifting perspectives of what agencies are and what they mean. Culture plays an important role here: it furnishes the locally prevalent norms and values, together with a more specific set of stories and symbols and beliefs. These provide the raw materials, so to speak, with which the meanings of specific events or proposals can be constructed (Hood, 1998; Hofstede, 2001). Thus the term 'agency' may travel far and wide, and undergo translation into many languages, but each translation will be imperfect so that certain meanings will be lost and new ones gained (Smullen, 2004). The researcher can track these trajectories of terms, map communities of discourse and deconstruct the constituent parts of official rhetoric, but none of this will reveal some underlying reality, because it isn't there to be revealed.

This body of theory has come rather recently to the field of public administration, and represents something of a challenge to both economic approaches and to traditional social science. It sits a little uneasily with the hitherto largely pragmatic orientation of the field, and with its improvement ethic. Nevertheless, it has yielded a rapidly growing subset of the literature, some of which has been fruitful beyond narrow academic circles. In terms of our three basic questions, social constructivists (at least, those of the 'neo-institutionalist' school) have directed attention to the way in which organizational forms may spread not because of some inherent efficiency, but through various mechanisms of copying and fashion (Pollitt, 2002; Powell and DiMaggio, 1991). The search for legitimacy and normality may be as big an influence on choice as the search for efficiency and effectiveness (Brunsson and Olsen, 1993). Agency–ministry relations may reflect the historically embedded attitudes and norms which characterize a particular ministry – in other words, they be largely path-dependent (Gains, 2004). Equally, however, other social constructivists (it is a broad church) have suggested that this process is not so much cloning or copying as constant adaptation and translation (Sahlin-Anderssen, 2001; Smullen, 2004). Furthermore, studies of the rhetoric of reform indicate that the types of arguments used in favour of agency creation may be part of a wider, but fairly fixed repertoire of administrative proverbs, where choice within the set typically oscillates over time, from one position to another (Hood, 1998; Hood and Jackson, 1991). From this perspective, therefore, the agency form gets chosen and popularized because it is its 'turn' in the endless alternation of fashion and rhetoric between incompatible philosophical positions.

Social constructivists are probably less interested in our second question – how agencies can best be steered – because giving practical advice is not what they are usually about. Indeed, the more radical social constructivists would be likely to argue that general advice on such an issue is impossible – 'good steering' is a notion that will be locally, contextually defined according to the recent history and culture of the jurisdiction in question. What is 'appropriate' will depend on local norms and values (so individual performance related pay, for example, is culturally far more acceptable in US government than in public bodies in the Nordic countries).

Similar comments could be made about the third question – the conditions for good performance by an agency. Social constructivists would be quick to point out that 'good performance' is very much a socially constructed concept, and that the phrase masks a whole array of possible alternative norms and values. Perceptions of performance are negotiated rather than chipped out of some underlying bedrock of hard data (for how widely these perceptions can vary between an agency chief and his minister, see Lewis, 1997). Indeed, talk of 'performance' would itself be a subject for rhetorical and textual analysis: this was not the way public sector organizations were usually talked about in the 1960s and 1970s, so why and how has this kind of vocabulary become so pervasive during the 1980s and 1990s?

Our own approach

Our own theoretical apparatus will be developed, applied and assessed as the book unfolds. However, it may be useful to locate it briefly in general terms now, before we leave the issue of broad theoretical approaches. Although acknowledging their sometime elegance, we are not borrowers from the rational choice/NIE suite of models. Instead we deploy what we term the Task-Specific Path Dependency (TSPD) model. This could be construed as being somewhere on the borderline between a traditional social science approach and social constructivism. Thus we do not assume that organizational change is driven solely, or even mainly, by efficiency considerations (real or imagined). Efficiency may sometimes be the 'big reason', but at other times and places it is not. Nor do we presume that change is always driven principally by the rational self-interest of individual politicians and civil servants (although that self-interest – or self-interests – are surely often a powerful factor). In fact we remain agnostic as to the very existence of an underlying 'real reason' why the agency form has proved increasingly popular. We simply accept that the idea of agency has become fashionable, and that it has acquired powerful advocates, both national and international (Pollitt and Talbot, 2004). The reasons for this may be multifold, and may vary from time to time and place to place. Some of these variations are documented in subsequent chapters.

However, we see the spread and application of these fashionable ideas as being heavily influenced by at least two further sets of factors. First there is the pattern of cultural and institutional norms in a particular jurisdiction (the 'path' of that jurisdiction). Second, there are the requirements and constraints of the particular, primary task of any given organization (issuing licenses, teaching children, etc.). Thus what becomes of the fashionable ideas in practice depends on both the particular history of the jurisdiction in question (the path) and the nature of the actual work to be done (task specificity). Reform ideas are almost always 'edited' or 'translated' to fit path and task.

Empirical evidence: a preliminary overview

Now we can return again to the same three main questions we began with, namely:

- Why has the agency form become so popular?
- How can agencies be best steered?
- Under what conditions do agencies perform best?

The whole of the rest of the book deals with these questions but here, by way of introduction, we will pick out highlights of the evidence from the existing literature. Our own findings will come later.

Why agencification? In the world of official policymaking there seems to be a broadly shared 'official model', but that is not to say that it is applied in any consistent or rigorous way to individual cases, even in those homeland countries from which it originates (New Zealand, the United Kingdom). The official model goes something like this: by structurally separating executive tasks, by giving their managers greater autonomy, and by holding them to account for their performance, improved performance will follow. This is close to what James (2003) refers to as 'the public interest perspective'. It is a normative, practitioner model of what agencies should be – a kind of practitioners' 'ideal type'. Because of its importance we will treat it separately and at length in Chapter 2.

However, when we look at individual agency creations, the literature shows that it may well be that no clear reason has been advanced at all, or, alternatively, multiple and potentially contradictory aims have been stated (for the Dutch case, see Van Thiel, 2001). As we read further, we can see that the list of reasons given by different proponents of agencification has actually been quite long (see, e.g. James, 2003, pp. 17–26; Lane, 2000, chapter 8; OECD, 2002, pp. 6–7; Osborne and Gaebler, 1992; Van Thiel, 2001, Table 1.2). The positive reasons include the following:

1. To lessen political interference, in order to allow the managers to manage, and thereby achieve higher efficiency.
2. To lessen political interference in order to allow regulatory or quasi-judicial decisions to be taken in an impartial way (e.g. the award of benefits to individual applicants).
3. To strengthen political oversight by creating separate, transparent organizations that can be given clear targets.
4. To put public services closer to their users (citizens) so as to increase user-responsiveness.

5. To enhance expertise by allowing specialization (moving away from large, generalist bureaucracies). Enhancing expertise is assumed to increase effectiveness, efficiency or both.
6. To enhance flexibility, by moving out of the 'iron cage' of central civil service rules. Flexibility is assumed to lead to better tailored (higher quality) services for users, and to operating efficiencies.
7. To facilitate partnerships with other public sector bodies and/or with voluntary groups, and/or with commercial companies.
8. To create 'islands of excellence' in otherwise failing or 'backward' public administrations – mainly in developing countries (see Talbot and Caulfield, 2002; Taliercio, 2004).

However, the same, or other studies indicate there may also be other, less noble motives (Dunleavy, 1991; James, 2003; OECD, 2002, p. 7; Pierre, 1995, 2004; Vos, 2003; Yamamoto, 2004). The following have all been identified in the academic literature, and even conceded in some of the official literature:

1. To pay off political allies.
2. To create an institutionalized power base for some party or faction.
3. To distance politicians from awkward or potentially unpopular activities, and enable them to avoid responsibility.
4. To distance senior civil servants from boring, routine (but possible risk-prone) operational work and leave them with more high status 'policy' and 'strategy' work.
5. To massage civil service numbers so as to make it look as though downsizing/economies are being made.
6. To gain legitimacy by imitating an organizational fashion which is seen to be associated with modernization (in Powell and DiMaggio's terms, mimetic isomorphism).
7. To create islands of income generation which can be 'milked' for various purposes (Talbot and Caulfield, 2002).

There are several features to notice about these lists. First, both lists are quite long – a single organizational form, it seems, may be inspired by a wide variety of different motives. Second, the lists contain tensions, or even incoherencies, within themselves. For example, there would appear to be at least a potential tension between the motive of liberating managers to manage and the motive of increasing political steerability. There are also more obvious tensions between some of the motives in the second list (e.g. finding jobs for political allies) and some of those in the first list (e.g. lessening political interference or enhancing expertise). Third, a single agency reform may quite conceivably be fuelled by three or four or more of these motives simultaneously, and may appear to hold advantages for a number of different groups (politicians, senior civil servants, professional experts, etc.). A particular reform may therefore be embarked upon for ambiguous and/or contradictory purposes.

While there is case study evidence for the presence of many of these motives in individual instances (e.g. Araŭjo, 2002; Gains, 1999; Lewis, 1997; Prince, 2000; Vos, 2003), there is no broad-scope research which would enable us to estimate the relative frequency or importance of different motives over a larger number of cases, or over whole programmes of agencification. [There is at least one partial exception. Sandra Van Thiel did try to do this for 545 Dutch quangos and calculated that in 53 per cent of cases no motive at all had been stated! The next most popular reasons given were increased efficiency (18 per cent) and getting closer to the citizen (15 per cent) (Van Thiel, 2001).] So to the question 'why have there been so many agency reforms in so many countries over the past 15 years?', we can only answer, rather weakly, 'there have been lots of different reasons and in many cases we don't have a very clear idea of which were the most influential'. We do know, however, that even the extent to which agencies think and talk about themselves *as agencies* varies, case by case (Smullen, 2004).

How can agencies best be steered? This is a question which has attracted a lot of 'grey literature', but somewhat less academic attention. In the United Kingdom, for example, there has been a long series of official reports examining the ministry/agency relationship – and finding it wanting (Fraser Report, 1991; Office of Public Services Reform, 2002; Trosa Report, 1994). Considerable attention has been given to the kind of performance reporting that should be required of agencies – typically recommendations for good practice (e.g. National Audit Office, 2000). There is also academic work which shows considerable variety, agency by agency. Hogwood *et al.*, found that some agencies with politically sensitive tasks were bombarded with questions from the legislature, and closely monitored by their nervous parent ministry, while other agencies were virtually ignored by politicians (Hogwood *et al.*, 2000). Gains found considerable contrasts in the relationships between various agencies and their ministries, depending on a variety of factors, including the degree of monopoly, the degree of financial independence and the previous history of relationships inside the parent department (path dependency – Gains, 1999, 2004). Overall, it certainly does appear that the balance between active steering (desirable) and micromanagement (undesirable) is hard to find, and to maintain. In the early days in the United Kingdom, there was evidence of too much interference – at least in some cases – but by 2002 the concern had shifted: 'It is the Review team's view that the main problem in achieving more effective performance is that some agencies have become disconnected from their departments' (Office of Public Services Reform, 2002, p. 6).

Similarly, elsewhere in the world, we find quite a few studies which conclude that ministries are either too strong/interfering or too weak/passive. In Latvia, Pollitt found ministries seriously short of the capacity to control their agencies (Pollitt and Talbot, 2004). Elsewhere, however, the balance seems to have swung too far in the opposite direction. In Canada Aucoin argued strongly that the first generation of Special Operating Agencies lacked sufficient autonomy (1996). In Japan Yamamoto believes that the freedom of the Independent Administrative Corporations was seriously circumscribed by Ministry of Finance's insistence on annual reviews of funding, and by the practice of appointing IAC chief executives from the senior civil service (Yamamoto, 2004). In Tanzania the theoretical autonomy of agencies is frequently crippled by cashflow shortages and the tight grip kept by the President and his Secretary General (Talbot and Caulfield, 2002). In Sweden, however, Molander *et al.* (2002) argue that in Swedish central government there are just too few people allocated to the task of monitoring the big, powerful agencies, and that even those that are given this responsibility tend to be too junior and inexperienced. In the Netherlands there has been a lively and persistent concern that ZBOs are insufficiently accountable to the centre, and that even *agentschappen* are not being vigorously steered by their ministries (e.g. Algemene Rekenkamer, 1995; Kickert, 2000, pp. 133–4). In another piece of Dutch research Van Thiel (2001) found some evidence for 'reversal of control' (i.e. autonomized bodies becoming stronger than their ministries), especially where ZBOs had a monopoly in their activity and where they had been created by redefining an organization that was already outside a ministry, rather than being 'hived off' from a ministry. In some cases, however, Kickert argues that 'A number of the new quasi-autonomous executive agencies have found that, as a result of their new status, ministerial control of their policy direction is *stronger* than before' (Kickert, 2001, p. 147 – our emphasis). In fact the case studies in both Kickert's and Van Thiel's researches show a very mixed picture, where in some cases ministries seem weak and in others they seem to interfere too much. Which of these states occurs seems to depend partly on a number of task specific factors, such as the degree of competition, the degree of self-financing, the degree of political sensitivity of the task, and so on. This broadly echoes some of the more in-depth UK research by Gains, Hogwood and James. We will repeatedly return to the importance of these task-specific dimensions.

Under what conditions do agencies perform best? With respect to this third question, it is in some ways easier to say what we do *not* know, rather than parade what we do. We have a series of studies which show that systematic, hard evidence for the increased efficiency of the agency form – in general – is not available. In short, the proposition that turning a function over from a government bureaucracy to an agency *generally* leads to enhanced efficiency is not proven (Bogt, 1999; James, 2003; Molander *et al.*, 2002; Talbot and Caulfield, 2002; Van Thiel, 2001). On the other hand, there seems to be plenty of practitioner evidence that, if a ministry is able to set attainable but demanding targets, agency performance often (though by no means always) responds (Chancellor of the Duchy of Lancaster, 1997; Kraak and van Osteroom, 2002).

From a public administration/organization theory perspective, Wilson offers a complex but persuasive analysis of US agencies (Wilson, 1989). While not by any means dismissing the importance of the organizational form, his main emphasis is placed on the nature of the task and the presence or absence of sufficient cultural homogeneity to give rise to a sense of 'mission'. He also leaves an important space for the play of managerial strategies, although making it clear that the successful strategies tend to be those which take full account of the task characteristics and cultural proclivities of the organization. In another American study, Bardach (1998) sets out down a different track, seeking to identify factors which permit or encourage agencies to co-operate and collaborate with each other. Like Wilson, he arrives at a complex, multi-factorial view of the conditions for 'success'. In the United Kingdom, Gains (1999, 2004) also presents a differentiated picture, arguing that the best relationships tend to result from some kind of balance of needs between ministry and agency. If the agency is very independent (let us say it has high autonomy and can generate much of its own income) then it does not 'need' the ministry. If, on the other hand, the ministry can readily obtain the services, or information the agency provides from alternative sources, then the ministry does not 'need' the agency. The relationship is more likely to be stable and genuinely interactive when both need the other. Finally, using rational choice theory in order to inform a discussion of contracts, Lane (2000) suggests that certain types of task lend themselves to performance contracts better than others; certain types of discretionary, non-standardized human services tasks being among the most difficult to handle through a contractual relationship.

Discussion

One conclusion that can be drawn from the foregoing is that we should not be making *agencies*, or *semi-autonomous public bodies* or even *distributed public bodies*, our main causal or explanatory variable. These are loose terms for families of organizational forms, and, in general, such families seldom serve as no more than one among several intermediate variables in determining the way particular organizations actually perform. What is so noticeable in so many of the in-depth studies is the tremendous *variation* in the way in which agencies work, and in the kinds of relationships they have with their parent departments. A more rewarding focus is therefore likely to be one which directly addresses the characteristics of *both* the processes and the outputs of the service or primary task *and* considers the nature of the prevailing administrative culture *and* examines the management strategy and then works *backwards* from those specific features to examine the appropriateness of the organizational design. This would therefore be an analysis that was constructed mainly of *particularities* rather than *generalities*. By this we mean that, in our reading of the evidence, the particularities of, first, the local administrative culture, second, the operational characteristics of the function in question, and, third, the strategies pursued by management, frequently have far more influence on how a given organization behaves than does the generality of its organizational form. We strongly suspect that the same could be said of MABs and of state enterprises (Figure 1.1), but they are not our main focus here.

This is not at all to say that the formal design of institutions is of no importance. Nor is it to dismiss the assertion of rational choice theorists that the structure of incentives for principals and agents can have a powerful influence on behaviour. But it *is* to argue that it seldom makes sense to discuss either organizational structures or economic incentives in a vacuum, without considering the cultural, managerial and technical/task issues that enable similar organizational structures/incentives to work well in one context and fail or produce perverse outcomes in another. So the crucial questions cease to be the general ones such as 'how much autonomy should agencies have?' or 'how should ministries steer agencies?' and become particular ones such as 'how much autonomy is it appropriate to give the function of running prisons in the particular administrative culture which prevails in country X?', or 'how should a ministry in country Y steer the social security agency?'

When we incorporate these other levels of analysis into the study of agencies, we find complication, but also enrichment. There is a healthy theoretical literature dealing with the importance of task/technical differences (e.g. Abma and Noordegraaf, 2003; Wilson, 1989), with managerial strategies (e.g. Flynn, 2002, p. 114 *et seq*) and with organizational cultures (e.g. Hofstede, 2001; Hood, 1998). This body of theory and evidence is too extensive for it to be summarized here, but at least a couple of indicative illustrations can quickly be given to demonstrate its potential.

The first illustration is taken from James Q. Wilson's *Bureaucracy: what government agencies do and why they do it* (1989). Wilson argues that two particular features of an agency's task have far-reaching effects on what management can do, and therefore on what kind of style of management it is likely to be sensible to adopt. Feature number one is the degree to which the outputs (or, failing that, processes) of an agency can be observed. The issue of driving licenses can be fairly easily observed; the activities of a forest ranger, deep in the forest, or an environmental health inspector, wandering purposefully around his or her 'beat' in the city centre, cannot (or we should say could not – past tense – because new Information and Communication Technologies (ICTs) may be changing this – Bovens and Zouridis, 2002). Feature number two is the degree to which the outcomes (final impacts) of the agency's activities can be observed. The outcomes of a mail delivery agency are reasonably observable (do customers get their mail, securely and on time?). The outcomes of a mental health counselling service are not (clients may be affected – or not – in any part of their lives, either now or over long periods of future time, so it is very hard to keep track of the real impacts of the advice which is offered). Figure 1.2 summarizes the four possible combinations.

One important implication of this analysis is that there is unlikely to be 'one best way' of managing an agency (*and*, we would add, by extension, of steering or supervising an agency). For example, managers in *production* agencies can develop performance indicators systems that register the most important outputs from their staff and systems, and the most important outcomes in the world outside, and connect the two. In principle, this holds open the possibility of quite precise 'steering', and also the possibility of giving some freedom to staff to experiment with new procedures, because both the outputs and the outcomes of any such changes can be monitored.

	Outcomes observable?	
	Yes	No
Outputs observable? Yes	Production organizations e.g. a mail service; tax collection agencies	Procedural organizations e.g. a mental health counselling service
Outputs observable? No	Craft organizations e.g. field inspection agencies	Coping organizations e.g. a diplomatic service; certain types of education

Figure 1.2 Types of agency by task/work characteristics
Source: Derived from Wilson, 1989, pp. 158–71.

For *procedural* organizations, however:

> If the manager cannot justify on the grounds of results leaving operators alone to run things as they see fit, the manager will have to convince political superiors that the rules governing government work are being faithfully followed. (Wilson, 1989, p. 164)

In this type of organization Standard Operating Procedures (SOPs) therefore become of great importance. It isn't surprising that armed forces tend to lay great emphasis on following procedural rules ('by numbers!') since, during peacetime they are the classic example of the procedural type (outcomes only becoming visible once actual conflict begins). Note, however, that technological change can sometimes render the previously invisible visible. New ICTs may suddenly enable management to track the forest ranger, police constable or environmental health inspector on every step of their complicated and discretionary itineraries (Bovens and Zouridis, 2002).

Each cell in Figure 1.2 also carries its own pitfalls and pathologies. Where some outputs are measurable and some are not, for example, there may be a tendency to slide towards focusing on the measurable, even if the unruly, unmeasurable aspects of the task are of greater significance for the outcomes.

Wilson acknowledges that this fourfold typology is crude, and encourages others to elaborate it further (Wilson, 1989, p. 159, footnote). In our own work we have begun to try to do that, for example by distinguishing between more and less politically sensitive tasks, and also by distinguishing between agencies which are substantially self-funding from those which are largely or wholly dependent on their parent departments for budget allocations. This kind of analysis obviously makes the picture more complex, and the number of possibilities much greater, but, as we shall see in later chapters, it can still yield pointers towards what are likely to be more or less appropriate management strategies.

Our second illustration shows the influence of institutional culture. We refer here to Geert Hofstede's work, *Culture's consequences: comparing values, behaviors, institutions and organizations across nations* (2001). So here we are not concerned with the specifics of task but rather with the background 'cultural climate'. Hofstede examines variations in values and organizational norms across 50 countries. Unusually for a cultural analyst, he actually quantifies his variables, using six principle dimensional measures. There is no space to go into them all here, but suffice it to say that some are of considerable significance for inter- and intra-organizational relations. For example, Hofstede's first measure is a power distance index, which concerns norms about boss–subordinate relations, and the extent to which inequality is accepted ('the boss is the boss'). Another of his measures is individualism versus collectivism, where 'individualism stands for a society in which the ties between individuals are loose ... Collectivism stands for a society in which people from birth onwards are integrated into strong, cohesive in-groups, which throughout people's lifetimes continue to protect them in exchange for unquestioning loyalty' (Hofstede, 2001, p. 225). To see some of the variations between countries with respect to these two dimensions (power–distance and individualism–collectivism) see Table 1.1.

Now consider what the implications of this might be for agency management. How would the appointment of a chief executive with a powerful, autocratic style go down in, say, Finland (Power–distance index (PDI) = 33) as compared with France (PDI = 68, i.e. much higher acceptance of power differences)? Alternatively, what implications might big

Table 1.1 Cultural differences

Country	Power–distance index	Individualism–collectivism
Finland	33	63
France	68	71
Italy	50	76
Netherlands	38	80
Sweden	31	71
United States	40	91

Source: Selected from Hofstede, 2001, p. 500.

differences in the PDI hold for the likelihood that an agency chief would feel entitled to act without necessarily consulting the parent minister, or might be prepared to express a slightly different opinion on issues of public policy? Or again, would the chances of a highly individualistic style of management – going one's own way with little regard for collective norms and informal ties and traditions – be the same in the United States (individualism score of 91) as in Sweden (71) or Finland (63)? Of course, one has to be careful in applying this sort of cultural analysis. Cultures differ between sectors and organizations and different social groups, and it can be dangerous to apply national 'averages' to particular situations. Nevertheless, the basic point about the significance of cultural factors holds, and tools exist for identifying and measuring its main parameters.

These were short illustrations of the fact that the existing literature is rich in possibilities for sorting and weighing the various contextual influences on the behaviours of ministries, agencies and their staffs. The main burden of this discussion is that cultural, managerial and task/technical variables are frequently likely to be crucial either for scientifically *understanding* what is going on in agencies, or practically for *managing* them. By contrast, approaches which extract the formal, structural forms of agency–ministry relations from these contexts and treat them in some general, abstracted way, are likely to be just that: general and abstract.

The foregoing discussion suggests that there is not, and cannot be, one best theory for explaining agency behaviour, anywhere, any time. In the marriage between theory and agencies one partner – the agency – is much too weak to sustain the weight of the relationship alone. For agencies, even when defined as restrictively as we have attempted to do here, vary tremendously. They have no single, strong and stable personality. Somewhat jelly-like, their behaviours assume new shapes according to the pressures of administrative cultures, management strategies and task requirements. A better way to understand them is to direct attention to these pressures as well as to the organizational form itself. If we can identify, classify and sometimes measure the main pressures, then we have some chance of formulating at least some middle-range generalizations about how the jelly is likely to wobble.

This chapter has lightly sketched one way of beginning to map the key pressures – an approach which positions itself on the boundary between the 'traditional social science' camp and social constructivism, borrowing elements of both. It has reasoned that we need to develop analyses which take account of the cultural environment, managerial strategies and the nature of the primary task. Two examples of such approaches have been summarized, but these were intended to be no more than illustrative. We are not saying that one must use Wilson's typology to analyse tasks, or Hofstede's particular approach to cultures. Rather we are arguing that we need to develop *some* way of characterizing tasks and *some* way of characterizing cultures.

In Chapter 2 we shall put academic theory on the back-burner for a while in order to examine recent practitioner ideas about agencies: the 'ideal type' of a modern agency that has come to play such a prominent part in many countries' reform programmes.

2
Modern Agencies – The Ideal Type

> In order to provide bodies with: i) a differentiated governance structure; and/or, ii) a differentiated control environment; and/or iii) some management autonomy, governments throughout the OECD area have created bodies with certain degrees of separateness from traditional, vertically integrated ministries.
>
> (OECD, 2002b, p. 6)

Introduction

While Chapter 1 introduced the main body of academic theory pertaining to agencies, this chapter analyses what we suggest has become an 'ideal type' for practitioners – the dominant improvement model in many recent public management reforms. We call this the Tripod Model, for reasons that will soon become apparent.

The tripod model is not entirely divorced or distinct from the various academic theories introduced in Chapter 1, but it is not exclusively identified with any one of those theories either. Indeed, one of its advantages for politicians and officials is that it can be allied with quite a few of the long list of positive reasons listed on p. 27. The connections between the worlds of academic theorizing and practitioner model-building are both complex and slippery, and we will examine them in some detail as the book unfolds. However, we consider the (predominantly practitioner) Tripod Model to be sufficiently important in its own right to merit examination here. It personifies the 'new age agency'.

Agencies: the old and the new

In what is probably one of the classic texts on bureaucracy, James Q. Wilson adopts the term 'agency' to 'tag' government organizations

(1989). Writing from a US perspective, it is hardly surprising that this is what he saw as bureaucracy. The idea of organizing state activities – whether tax collection, policing or social services – in more or less autonomous and separate agencies is nothing new in the United States. Important US federal functions, such as forestry, posts and food and drug administration fought for, and won, substantial autonomy over both operations and policy in the early years of the twentieth century. This was consolidated in the governmental expansions of the New Deal, the Second World War and in the big post-war expansion of public services (Carpenter, 2001).

In Europe on the other hand, most of the classical writers on the organizations of the state would have assumed that 'bureaucracy' referred not to separate, autonomous organizations so much as to homogenous, unified, very large scale integrated organizations – the 'Ministry' of popular understanding.

In truth of course both Europe and America have long had both 'Ministry' and 'Agency' type organizations. In Europe the equivalent to US agencies would more usually be called 'boards' and there have been many of these, usually limited to specific functions, for example tax and customs collection – two of the only substantial 'statutory boards' in UK government are the Inland Revenue and Customs & Excise. Sweden's central services have nearly all been organized as constitutionally defined boards (see Chapter 5).

In fact, the history of state organization almost everywhere has usually contained some mix of these two forms of organization – unified ministry and autonomous boards – and many intermediary forms of quasi-autonomous organization.

So why has the idea of the 'agency' form of organization of government activities become a subject of reform programmes in dozens of countries in the past decade and a half – the so-called 'unbundling of government' (Pollitt and Talbot, 2004)? To be sure, the initiatives which can be grouped together under this label are diverse: from reforming pre-existing agencies (the United States, Sweden, Finland) through creating new, only moderately autonomous, organizations (the United Kingdom, Netherlands) and finally to fairly radical separating out of a new 'class' of organizations with extensive autonomy (New Zealand, Jamaica, Latvia).

This chapter seeks to explore this modern 'agency' phenomenon as a prelude to a more detailed analysis of four countries (Finland, Netherlands, Sweden and the United Kingdom) and four functions (social security, forests, meteorology, prisons). It will provide a wider perspective within which these more detailed analyses can be located.

The dominant 'short-hand' explanation of the agency movement is simple enough: government got big, very big, in the post-Second World War expansion, to produce what has become commonly known as the Welfare State. Huge ministries were built employing millions of people producing standardized products and services for a (at first) grateful population. These bureaucratic monoliths became gradually more cumbersome, rule-bound, inflexible, inefficient and unresponsive. And of course they became too expensive in an age where voters were demanding more services for less taxes and the state began to feel the fiscal crunch at the end of the long-boom of the 1950s and 1960s (O'Connor, 1973).

As the apparent crisis of big government deepened into the 1980s and 1990s one solution which became fashionable was to 'unbundle government': to break up these large ministries into smaller, more manageable, less rule bound, more flexible and responsive agencies. These new agencies, in this narrative, fit better than ministries with the consumer choice dominated, flexible, post-bureaucratic world of today. And they are cheaper – they can be contract-managed to produce more for less and their greater flexibility allows managers to get the most out of them by applying 'modern management methods', to quote one UK Minister, and by which of course he meant private sector modern management methods.

Central government organizations were not the only ones to which various forms of agencification were applied, or at least some of the components which we describe below (disaggregating large organizations into smaller units; granting them greater, or at any rate changed, autonomy over various management decisions; putting in place some sort of contractual or quasi-contractual arrangements, linked to performance). Schools, hospitals, universities and colleges, museums – all sorts of public bodies were moved from being officially just part of the Ministry to being in some way separate and subject to recreated institutional settings. But it is quite clear that 'agencies' have come to be seen as a distinctive programme of central government reform, espoused by national Governments and international bodies like the World Bank (Pollitt and Talbot, 2004).

An uncharted process of international policy transfer has been taking place with British Civil Service reformers studying Swedish agencies as early as 1968 (Fulton Committee, 1968) and 20 years later implementing a wholesale programme at least in part allegedly based on this model. In the meantime, Hong Kong (a British Colony) experimented with the 'Swedish Model' in the 1970s (shortly after Fulton which may or may not be a coincidence). In the wake of (some would say in tandem with) the big UK reform programme Canada, the Netherlands and many other countries started various agency-type reforms, and still later the United States and Japan joined the 'movement' with their own separate and unique takes on 'agencies'. Finally, many developing and transitional countries (Pollitt and Talbot, 2004; Talbot and Caulfield, 2002) have opted for agency type reforms in a process of what might be called mimetic and coercive isomorphism (the coercive part being played by international donor organizations, bilateral and multilateral).

So the agency movement is real, it represents an international (but certainly not global) trend and there is at least a degree of commonality in the rhetoric of its proponents, if not necessarily in the detailed decisions and actions. In short, we know that there is some kind of movement towards something called 'agencies', but how can this trend be isolated and studied effectively? The answer is, of course: not easily. The first task is to try to delineate what the factors involved in any agency-like reforms might consist of (and of course how these differ from other reforms). We have already intimated that we have developed a 'tripod' model which isolates three factors, but before we turn to explaining that and giving some concrete examples of what we mean it is just worth taking a slight detour to look at some other possible ways of both isolating and bundling-together the combination of changes which are distinctively 'agency' transformations.

Agency doctrines: administrative DNA?

The most straightforward way of looking at the practitioner doctrines which lie behind the recent construction of new forms of agencies in many different countries is simply to examine the statements made by politicians and officials at the time that the main organizational decisions were made. In the specific countries and cases examined later in the book we do indeed adopt this approach. But by itself this tends to leave the collector of such statements with only a weak and superficial grasp of the deeper interconnections. What can strengthen analysis is the construction of some wider classificatory framework of ideas, which will enable specific reasons given at specific times and places to be located, like with like, and which will show up the continuities and tensions which exist beneath the ever-changing fashions for particular terms or phrases.

Just such a framework was put forward more than a decade ago by two English scholars, Hood and Jackson (1991). This work identified a long list of 'doctrines' – ninety-nine in all – which they termed 'administrative DNA'. In fact these 99 group together into only 26 choice areas about the shape of administrations. Not all of these are relevant to our study of 'agencies' but it is useful to look at some to see if they help to reduce the dimensions of 'agencification' to something manageable and useful. We can identify four such areas, although there are others which might also be relevant. These are the decision areas for control, for independence, for specialization and for decision. (The numbers refer to Hood and Jackson's numbering – see pp. 34–5.)

The first choice area is for how public bodies are controlled and it has several variants, but these can be grouped into two broadly antithetical sets of options: the first variant combines two doctrines, Fcontrol by input (X1) and process (X2); the second consists of the control by outputs doctrine (X3) and several sub-variants, including control by outcomes (X3.2). The second choice area covers the degree of independence of public organizations – how much are they to be under the direct control and integrated with Ministerial offices – what Hood and Jackson call classic bureaucracy (A1); or whether they are to be separated (usually but not always statutorily) and independent from ministerial or executive offices (A2). A third choice area is specialization which decides, among other things, if a public body should be formed on the basis of a separation of policy and operations (J1.2) or consolidated in single structures (J2). The fourth and final choice area concerns whether decision-making should be exercised by various forms of discretion (K2) or by rule and rote (K1). If these four choice areas are applied to classical ideal-type ministries and boards and the new 'agency' model we shall find an interesting morphology.

This classification of doctrines chimes quite closely (though not entirely) with our own analysis of the rationales given for agency creation. Our analysis has suggested that there are three important dimensions to practitioner doctrines about 'agencification', although there are also a whole host of more-or-less closely associated changes. We have called this tripod of doctrines disaggregation, autonomization and contractualization (Talbot, 2004).

Disaggregation – organizational divorce?

> In my view by breaking down areas of responsibility in the Civil Service into tailor-made, discrete and clear-cut services, and moving away from a more amorphous body, we are likely to have a more effective civil service which will be of benefit to the government of the day and the public. (The Rt.Hon Richard Luce, then Minister for the Civil Service, in response to questions from the Parliamentary

Treasury and Civil Service Committee, 10 July 1990: Treasury and Civil Service Committee, 1990, p. 52)

Seperateness coupled with a differentiated governance structure allows specialization of functions and a better focus on client needs.
(OECD, 2002b, p. 6)

For some functions (such as the allocation of grants or benefits, economic regulation, professional oversight of some professions, or when the government's actions are subject to the jurisdiction of the body) and in some institutional settings, differentiating organizational form can help increase independence from on-going political or bureaucratic influence, and signal change. (OECD, 2002b, p. 6)

Disaggregation is very similar to the 'independence' cluster of administrative DNA (Hood and Jackson, 1991 – and see Table 2.1, above) but with a very important difference. The term 'independence' can be, like the other ill-treated term 'autonomy', misleading if used inappropriately.

Table 2.1 Agency-relevant administrative doctrines (selectively derived from Hood and Jackson, 1991)

Administrative doctrines – choice areas	'Ministries'	New style 'Agencies'	Traditional 'Boards'
Control	Control exercised principally by levers of inputs (budgets) or processes.	Control exercised primarily through outputs or outcomes.	Control exercised principally by levers of inputs (budgets) or processes.
Independence	Direct control by ministers in integrated classical bureaucracy.	Direct control by ministers through a mixture of direction and legal or quasi-legal frameworks.	Formally and legally independent 'boards' with no direct ministerial control.
Specialization	Integration of policy and operations.	Separation of policymaking and operational implementation functions.	Integration of policy and operations.
Decision-making	Decisions made principally by rule and rote.	Mostly local discretion with some general rules.	Mostly externally imposed rules with some local discretion.

Independence implies autonomy over a whole range of choices about how an agency or other arms-length body organizes itself internally. Both 'independence' and 'autonomy' tend to run together two different dimensions: (a) how far is an organization formally separated out from its 'parent' body and clearly delimited as a separate entity and (b) how far is the organization free to make its own choices about internal arrangements or how far are these externally imposed upon it? These are what we separate out as 'disaggregation' and 'autonomization'.

Traditional public sector Boards were often highly disaggregated, and even quite independent about some policy and strategy issues, while at the same time being tightly regulated by external government actors on a range of personnel, financial, purchasing and other matters (Carpenter, 2001; Graham and Roberts, 2004). Indiscriminate use of concepts like 'independence' or 'autonomy' tends to elide these important differences.

It is, of course, possible to argue that because formally separate organizations are subject to regulation by other organizations they are not truly separate or different. This line of argument has led at least one scholar into suggesting that 'all organizations are public' because they are all regulated to a greater of lesser degree by government (Bozeman, 1987). This is a one-dimensional argument and is easily recognizable as failing to capture the complexities of the real situation, but it does highlight the difficulties of producing models with sufficient complexity to capture 'real life' agencies while remaining simple enough to be useable.

Divorce, as many ex-couples know, can easily mean separation but not independence. While a divorced couple are clearly no longer 'together' (they have been 'disaggregated' in our terminology) it does not mean there are not still important elements of dependence between them. Often this is resource dependence but it may include other forms of mutually dependent interactions (e.g. over access rights to children). No one mistakes this for them still being together, but it is clearly not full 'independence' or 'autonomy' either.

To continue to use the marital analogy, agencies may lie at almost any point between 'trial separation' and complete legally sanctioned divorce. United Kingdom and Dutch agencies have, in most cases, been subject to formula which sees them as separate entities but still part of their parent Ministries. In the United Kingdom in particular, because neither ministries nor agencies have any formal legal basis (in most cases – see Harden, 1992) then the separation is real but not in any sense legally binding (a bit like an informal separation of a couple in British matrimonial law). At the other extreme, in Sweden and the United

States agencies are legally and formally separated bodies (constitutionally in the Swedish case), making them well and truly divorced. (Actually, US agencies are sometimes singles who were never married.)

There are a series of factors which may establish separation. Is the agency in some way formally, legally or constitutionally separated out from other (usually parent) bodies? If it has been separated from another body, how far is that separation seen as permanent or temporary and possibly subject to reversal? Does the organization have a clearly separate and separately accounted for budget? Does the organization have a formal mandate which sets out its policy framework, aims and objectives? Does it have formally imposed governance and accountability arrangements? Do the latter clearly distinguish between the rights and duties of the organization and those of its sponsors or parent bodies? How far does it 'own' its own resources (e.g. capital assets) and have rights of disposal over them? Does the organization own risks it takes or would someone else pick up the bill if its risk taking went wrong? How far does the separate organization have a clear self-identity? We could go on but it should by now be clear that the notion of disaggregation or separation in a public sector context is a problematic one. Simply saying an organization has been separated or 'hived-off', to use one popular idiom, actually tells us very little. Only a careful and detailed analysis of an actual organization's degrees of separation across a range of factors can tell us just how 'separate' it really is. And even then the formal story may not be the whole picture – we know from the history of nationalized industries that formally separate organizations can be subjected to all sorts of informal controls.

Autonomization

> The Government's reply ... emphasized as one of the key ingredients the need for Departments and Agencies to use to the full the managerial freedoms and incentives they are getting and delegate to the lowest appropriate level their operation to local management. (Memorandum submitted to the Treasury and Civil Service Committee by the Project Manager of the Next Steps programme, June 1990: Treasury and Civil Service Committee, 1990, p. 2)
>
> Managerial autonomy, coupled in some cases with a differentiated governance structure, allows the development of a more managerialist culture and a better focus on outputs and outcomes. (OECD, 2002b, p. 6)

Autonomization in our model is very similar to 'decision-making' in Hood and Jackson's administrative DNA. It essentially addresses the same issue – how much discretion do organizations or individuals have in making decisions and how much are they circumscribed by specific rules or even just 'standard operating procedures' which are the norm? But we apply this idea specifically to the issue of regulation inside government – that is, how far should a separated-out, disaggregated, organization be subject to decision-making by externally imposed rules and how far left to make discretionary decisions itself?

Regulation *within* government is a curiously under-researched phenomena at the organizational level, given the perennial prominence afforded to criticisms of bureaucratic 'red tape' (Light, 1997). Most of the rhetorical and normative literature on reform of public services addressed this issue as simply deregulation of public bureaucracies (DiIulio, 1994). More recently the issue of re-regulation and even of simply changed regulation has surfaced, especially in a pioneering work on 'regulation inside government' in the United Kingdom (Hood *et al.*, 1999). As the US example shows, it is perfectly possible to have formally very separate public bodies which remain subject to fairly tight external regulatory regimes (Graham and Roberts, 2004). This is one important reason why we find it necessary to treat disaggregation as a separate dimension from autonomization. What the Hood *et al.*, study showed was that changes to organizational status (in this case not just Executive Agencies in the Civil Service but a host of other disaggregatory reforms) can be accompanied by a changed, and sometimes even increased, regulatory burden. In short, where hierarchical managerial control is removed through disaggregation it is often replaced by external rule imposition (Hood *et al.*, 1999). This is, of course, not necessarily the case and even where there has been some new external regulation there may also have been increased freedoms over specific areas of decision-making.

It should be stressed that there can be a difference between the rhetorical, formal, position of rule making and the reality. Within formally quite strict regulatory environments it is nevertheless possible that individuals may find tremendous scope for discretion, as the classic study of 'street level bureaucrats' demonstrated (Lipsky, 1980). The same may be true at the organizational level – the pathology of public bureaucracies in developing countries is a good illustration of where escalating regulation paradoxically produces greater and greater scope for unofficial discretion (often connected with corrupt practices) (de Soto, 2000).

Contractualization – my principals and your agency?

> We are moving from a hierarchical system to a system in which the minister and chief executive are in a quasi-contractual position ... . (Peter – later Sir Peter – Kemp, Project Manager for the Next Steps projects, answering questions from the Parliamentary Treasury and Civil Service Committee, 10 July 1990: Treasury and Civil Service Committee, 1990, p. 51)

> In both countries [the UK and the Netherlands] agency formation was expected to lead to more goal-oriented steering by the ministry, more business-like functioning of the implementing organization and a stronger orientation towards the users (clients). (Report to the Dutch Ministry of Transport and Water, 2002: Ministerie van Verkeer en Waterstaat, 2002, p. 3 – translation by the authors from 'In beide landen wordt agentschapvorming geacht te leiden tot een meer prestatiegerichte sturing door het ministerie, bedrijfsmatiger functioneren van de uitvoeringsorganisatie en een groetere oriëntatie op de gebruikers (klanten)')

> Many of these bodies [agencies and other 'distributed' entities] have a quasi- or fully contractual relationship with their line ministry/ minister. Targets are set jointly by the line ministry and the chief executive and boards (where they exist), and chief executives report on, and are accountable for the achievement of these targets. (OECD, 2002b, p. 5)

The idea of putting relationships within the public sector, whether between purchasers and providers, parent departments and agencies, or Ministers and Chief Executives, on some sort of contractual or quasi-contractual basis, usually linked to performance, has become very fashionable (Fortin and Van Hassel, 2000; Harden, 1992; Harrison, 1993; Jordan, 1992; Lane, 2000; OECD–PUMA, 1999).

The general idea has often been derived from principal–agent theory and varieties of the new institutional economics, and has been applied, *inter alia*, to the creation of internal markets and the introduction of other market-type mechanisms within the public sector (Cowen and Parker, 1997; Le Grand and Bartlett, 1993; Pollitt and Bouckaert, 2000). It has been very explicitly linked to agency-type reforms by reformers themselves (as in New Zealand – Boston, Martin *et al.*, 1996) or inferred from the nature of the reform process without being explicitly employed by reformers (as in the United Kingdom – Greer, 1994).

There are, however, some important differences between the way that principal–agent type contracting models can be deployed in the public sector from those in the private sector.

In the raw version of principal–agency contracting it is assumed that the partners are legally equal and that contracts can be placed on a legal footing if necessary (although in some intra-firm cases they will not be). One constraint and difference with the public sector is that such contractual arrangements are more usually not founded in law, and certainly not tort when internal to public services. In the United Kingdom nearly all such contracts have no legal standing at all (Harden, 1992) while elsewhere they may be based on public administrative law, but more usually on less formal bases (OECD–PUMA, 1999).

This general lack of a legal basis produces some interesting anomalies. Inequalities in principal–agent relationships are usually attributed to informational asymmetries. However in public sector internal contracting there are also power inequalities related to formal authority, public accountability and resources which make these 'contracts' often very one-sided. While the principals can often vary the contract at will – adding new demands, changing policies and reshaping services – there is no corresponding right of the agent (agency) to demand additional resources. Even in the most explicitly contracted system this has caused major problems. With what may have been unintentional irony, the matter was beautifully summed up by the Project Manager for the Next Steps project, while giving evidence to a parliamentary select committee:

> Framework agreements are meant to be durable but they can be changed at any time. (Peter Kemp, in Treasury and Civil Service Committee, 1990, p. 22)

An important element in contractualization is performance. In a memorandum submitted to a 1990 parliamentary enquiry by HM Treasury the point was firmly put: 'It is a basic requirement that Agencies are set up with a clear view of their objectives, and challenging performance targets' (Treasury and Civil Service Committee, 1990, p. 22). In any contract-like arrangement it is obviously important that the principal has information about how well the agent is producing the contracted-for services. It could be expected, therefore, that any form of contracting within government would include a substantial element of performance reporting. However, this is not always, or at least not substantially, the case (OECD–PUMA, 1999).

Performance reporting has also, however, been widely introduced to government for reasons other than, or supplementary to, contracting arrangements (OECD–PUMA, 1997; Talbot et al., 2001). It is not therefore always clear when performance reporting for disaggregated public bodies has been introduced for wider reasons (public accountability, steering, etc.) and how much for contract management purposes. The Government Performance and Results Act (GPRA) in the United States represents just such a mixed system – part performance contracting, part public accountability system, part strategic steering mechanism.

The fact that performance systems are often dissociated from other organizational systems, including quasi-contractual arrangements (Talbot, 1996), makes it even more difficult in such cases to see what the actual function of performance information may be.

The dog that didn't bark: separating policy and operations

In Hood and Jackson's catalogue of administrative doctrines the group which covers specialization includes the issue of policy and operations integration or separation. In many accounts of the agency movement it is suggested that this includes a split between policymaking and policy implementation (operations). It is not at all clear, however, that such a separation actually is a fundamental part of the agency idea and agency practice.

At the level of ideas, some proponents of agencification do not see the fundamental split as being between policy and operations but between purchasing and providing, and provision may include not just services but even policy advice itself (Boston et al., 1996; Carpenter, 2001; Kemp, 1993, 1996). Nor has it been the case that policy-operations splits have formed a crucial part of agency practices. In Sweden agencies and ministries both play important roles in policymaking. In the United States, many agencies, have gained a great deal of policy autonomy (Carpenter, 2001). In the United Kingdom the split has varied – in the largest five agencies, three were both policy and service delivery agencies (Prisons, Inland Revenue and Customs & Excise) one was service delivery only (Benefits) and one was mixed (Employment) (Talbot, 2004). There were even agencies largely concerned with policy, such as the National Weights and Measures Laboratory (Common et al., 1992).

It seems inadvisable therefore to include the policy-operations split as a fundamental part of the ideal type of agencification as there are both doctrinal and practical examples of where the split forms no part of the agency movement and others where it does. This suggests that it is not fundamental but may rather represent a sub-variant within the agency trend.

The whole three yards?

So the ideal-type model for modern agencies is: where an organization has been clearly and probably formally separated from any other public organization; where it has some degree of discretion over internal rule setting (e.g. over personnel, finance and other arrangements); and where it is subjected to some sort of contractual or quasi-contractual arrangements including reporting of its performance. These appear to us to constitute the most fundamental doctrinal building blocks upon which many recent agency reforms have been justified.

The alleged strength of the modern agency idea comes not from these individual elements – all of which have existed independently or in pairs before – but in the synthesis of these different components. The agency is supposed to be steerable through its contractual arrangements, autonomous enough to organize itself in the best ways possible for delivering and focussed enough by its organizational separation to concentrate on its core tasks.

So how far do real agencies meet this simple template? As we will see, it all depends. This is not mealy-mouthed academic equivocation – 'on the other hand X, but on the other hand Y'. Real agencies carrying out real tasks in real countries are far more complex than this simple normative model suggests.

First, every specific agency and public task has a history – a history specific to itself (how was it organized before?) and to its context (how does it fit into the wider public sector landscape?).

Thus in countries where the tasks organized into agencies have always, or nearly always been organized in this way, then agency-type changes may have little real effect on the degree of separation (e.g. the United States, Sweden). Indeed, we will find examples in our cases of where agency-type changes have brought about a reduction in the degree of organizational separation of some functions and tasks. In other cases the changes to unbundled agencies has been truly dramatic (e.g. United Kingdom, Tanzania, Latvia).

Similarly, in a context where a form of performance contracting is already widespread within existing structures (e.g. the United States) it is difficult to see what substantive difference agency-type contracting introduces (which is not to say that changes like the United States's 'performance-based organization' initiative introduce no such changes) (Graham and Roberts, 2004).

Second, the degree of real change (whatever the formal transformations) seems to be at least partially related to the ease of introducing the changes. This in turn seems to be linked by the nature of the tasks which are being reformed. Some such tasks are more susceptible to performance measurement than others (Wilson, 1989). Some tasks are more easily separable and delineated than others depending on the complexity of the task itself and the context of the task (e.g. the number of other actors who need to collaborate for its successful completion). Some are more susceptible to political controversy and therefore, more likely to be contested in their design, resources, processes and performance. One of our task-based cases – prisons – is often highly contentious, whereas others rarely produce a blip on the political radar. All of these factors suggest there may be something about the nature of the task itself which can affect the reality of agencification and its success or otherwise.

One further issue needs to be mentioned – the focus in our discussion so far has been almost exclusively on agencies themselves or the functions which are, or can be, transformed into agencies. However agencies exist within larger political-administrative systems. Where the system has always been built around some sort of agency type arrangements (the United States and Sweden) then the impact of agency reforms on the central apparatus (central ministries, finance ministries, civil service commissions, supreme audit bodies and other regulatory bodies and of course parliamentary/legislative bodies) could be expected to be small. Where the model was more 'Whitehall'-like, large scale creation of agencies could have a much more dramatic impact, as some have argued (Campbell and Wilson, 1995). So agencies have to be understood in their political-administrative context as well as in themselves.

We will return to these issues in the conclusions to our analysis after we have had a closer look at some real countries' reforms and some real agencies.

Researching the real world of agencies

A great deal of analysis of public sector reform processes is conducted at the level of dissecting reform pronouncements and official accounts of their successes (there are rarely accounts of their failures) (Pollitt and Bouckaert, 2000). This is understandable. Even in a single country, it is far easier to analyse policy changes at the level of official documentation. All that is required is a researcher and access to the relevant documents and background information. Such research can be conducted without leaving one's office or at most by visiting a few officials to elucidate a little further what was intended.

Getting beneath the skin of official pronouncements to understand what detailed changes have been enacted is more difficult. The detailed personnel rules, standard operating procedures, frameworks, laws, financial arrangements, property allocations and so, on often tell a different story to the official policy rhetoric. These are difficult to access, both because governments tend to be more secretive about this type of internal information and also simply because it is usually more diffuse, complex and difficult to understand, and there is a huge amount of this sort of 'grey literature'.

Finally, understanding what has actually changed at the 'front-line' is even more messy and expensive. Burrowing down into the management and operations of individual agencies, understanding both their formal status and the processes of interaction between them and their sponsors, stakeholders and regulators as well, as the reality of how these formal systems actually run in practice requires detailed and forensic investigation, which sometimes feels more like investigative reporting or detective work than research. Clues have to be found and interpreted, leads followed-up and evidence collated.

These problems are multiplied when research is extended across national borders – the scope for cultural and linguistic confusion is vast. We will not dwell on these problems here, they have often been rehearsed elsewhere (Heady, 2001; Pollitt and Bouckaert, 2000). While recognizing the problems we see comparative work across national boundaries (and indeed within them) as a very powerful tool. There is a biblical injunction that it is foolish to comment on the mote in someone else's eye while failing to see the beam in one's own. It is only in seeing both the mote and the beam that we can understand their relative significance. Comparative research may be difficult, but it can highlight both motes and beams and help us to understand the difference between the two.

The following chapters are partly based on a specific piece of research and partly on a series of overlapping research, advisory and consultancy exercises which we have, jointly and severally, engaged in over the past decade or more. The core of our work is described below.

First, we reasoned that the trend towards agencies could best be understood by a detailed comparison across several countries. These should include countries where strong forms of agencies had existed for some time (we chose Sweden and Finland) and where agencies were fairly new (we chose the United Kingdom and the Netherlands). In all cases there should have been some substantial debate and at least some reforms in recent years (i.e. we were not just dealing with historical legacies but also with contemporary reforms).

Second, besides comparing agencification at a national level (overall programmes and policies for whole countries) we thought that by studying similar functions in different countries we might be able to highlight where there were similarities and differences in the handling of particular types of task. Thus we decided to choose several functions where there were (as far as possible) apparently similar arrangements in the chosen group of countries. After a great deal of searching and debate we settled on four functions – prisons, social security benefits, meteorology and forests. These were arrived at partly by elimination (e.g. one or more countries did not operate the given function in a semi-autonomized form) and partly by a desire to find a useful spread of quite different types of task (service delivery versus research-based; coercive versus voluntary with respect to [*beneficial towards*] clients; large versus small; etc.). Interestingly, finding four tasks that reorganized in roughly the same way across four north-western European countries turned out to be less than easy. In the end we had to make do with approximate similarities rather than exact institutional equivalents.

Originally we felt that selecting similar agencies would highlight differences between our selected countries by minimizing the variables. We had a hunch that perhaps the nature of the different types of tasks organized into agencies could affect how agency status worked in practice. This has turned into a third dimension of the research: how far do similar functions end up being organized similarly?

So our basic research design was to compare four countries (Finland, Netherlands, Sweden and the United Kingdom) and four comparable sets of public sector tasks which were delivered through agencies or more-autonomized bodies (MABs) – prisons, social security benefits, meteorology and forestry. Our aim was to see how these agencies were organized and how they fitted into national patterns of political/administrative structures and agencification. We were also particularly interested in how formally autonomous and performance managed they were. In the four countries we gained access to 25 organizations (agencies, ministries and central ministries), conducted over 80 face-to-face interviews with more than 100 public servants, exchanged many emails with helpful officials and collected very extensive documentary evidence. More details of our methods are given in Appendix 1.

In addition, and in parallel, we carried out field visits to three developing and transitional countries (Jamaica, Latvia, Tanzania) as part of another research project which has been reported elsewhere (Pollitt and Talbot, 2004; Talbot and Caulfield, 2002), as well as making informal visits to several other countries where 'agencies' reforms were being implemented (e.g. Canada, United States, Japan, etc.).

Thus the main part of the book is structured to take a double look at agencies: the first from a country perspective (Part II) and the second from a task perspective. We believe that this cross-cutting approach extends the discussion in these first two chapters in at least two ways. First, it yields new insights concerning the adequacy – and inadequacy – of current academic theories for explaining why agencies behave as they do. Second, it casts a strong light on the realities – and unrealities – behind the reformers' vision, which we have characterized as a 'tripod', of a modern executive agency.

Part II
Agencies in Four Countries: A Comparison

3
Finland

Background: the political system

Finland is a unitary state, though with a strong tradition of relatively autonomous municipal government, protected by the constitution (like Sweden). The basic pieces of legislation are the Constitution Act (1919) and the Parliament Act (1928). A new constitution came into force at the beginning of 2000. There is a multi-party political system and governments are usually stable coalitions. The Cabinet acts collegially, with the Prime Minister having less personal prominence than in the 'Westminster' systems of the United Kingdom and New Zealand. Nevertheless, recent years have seen some increase in the Prime Minister's role (confirmed in the 2000 constitution) especially in relation to EU affairs. Formally, the power of execution lies with a Council of State, consisting of government ministers and the Chancellor of Justice. There is a President, who is elected every six years, retains some responsibility for foreign policy and is Commander-in-Chief of the armed forces. However, s/he no longer nominates the government, this authority having passed, by the most recent constitutional amendments, to the parliament. In general it might be said that the Finnish President, while considerably more active and politically powerful than his/her German counterpart, is also nothing like as dominant as the French President. During the last decade it is the Prime Minister's Office that has tended to gain new responsibilities and powers, while the President's Office has not (see Bouckaert *et al.*, 2000). At the time the first draft of this chapter was written Finland was unusual in that both President and Prime Minister were women. [According to comparative cultural studies, Finland has a fairly low score on an indicator which measures perceived differences between the roles of men and women – see Hofstede, 2001, p. 500, which shows the following

	Nature of executive government		
	Majoritarian ←	Intermediate	→ Consensual
Centralized (unitary)	The United Kingdom	France	Italy Netherlands
Intermediate	Sweden		Finland
Decentralized (federal)	United States		

Figure 3.1 State structure and the nature of executive government (loosely adapted from Lijphart, 1984, p. 219 and 1999, pp. 110–11 and 248)

index scores: Finland = 26; Netherlands = 14; Sweden = 5; the United Kingdom = 66. By comparison Germany = 66, Italy = 70, the United States = 62] By the time the book was handed over to the publisher, however, the woman Prime Minister (Mrs Jäätteenmäki) had resigned, following a scandal, and a man (Mr Vanhanen) had taken over.

The legislature (*Eduskunta*) is unicameral, with 200 seats. Eighty per cent of MPs tend also to be municipal politicians – so the interests of the municipalities are strongly represented at the centre. The three big parties in recent years have been the Social Democrats, the National Coalition (conservatives) and the Centre Party (originally an agrarian party). The reforming coalitions since the late 1980s have been led by the National Coalition (Holkeri, 1987–91), the Centre Party (Aho, 1991–95), the Social Democrats (Lipponen's 'Rainbow Coalition', 1995–99 and 1999–2003) and now the Centre Party (Jäätteenmäki, 2003; Vanhanen, 2003–). The Communist Party was a significant political force during the 1960s and 1970s, but has since lost most of its strength.

A leading contemporary comparative political scientist classifies Finland as a highly consensualist system, and in an intermediate position with regard to centralization/decentralization (Lijphart, 1984, p. 219, 1999, pp. 110–11 and 248). Figure 3.1 shows this, and also positions the other three countries covered in our book on the same dimensions.

The politico-administrative culture

Culturally, the Finnish approach to government and administration tends to be 'pragmatic/technocratic' (Puoskari, 1996) – and it is also still quite legalistic. While it is, of course, dangerous to rely heavily on general stereotypes there does seem to be a good deal of support for a view of the Finnish culture as one which values technical competence combined with a consensual, fairly egalitarian approach (which is sometimes said by Finns themselves to be connected to the absence of any native monarchy or aristocracy). The parties forming a government have to be brought to agreement. At the same time there is dislike, or suspicion of highly egotistical or individualistic behaviour, and a quiet pride for all that Finland has accomplished, in the face of larger and more powerful neighbours (and a less than helpful climate). 'Little Napoleons' and flamboyant gurus are not appreciated. Politicians who indulge in strong doctrinal politics, or sharp personal attacks are unlikely to be well-regarded – this is not the kind of behaviour which will build agreements within the coalition. Table 3.1 shows one attempt to measure key cultural dimensions or norms. Hofstede's individualism/collectivism index (second column) measures the extent to which people from birth are socialized into strong groups and expect those groups to support them, in return for continuing loyalty (collectivism). The alternative (individualism) is a society in which ties between individuals are loose, and most people expect to have to look after themselves. Hofstede's power–distance index (third column) gives a measure of the difference between the extent to which a boss can determine the behaviour of a subordinate and the extent to which a subordinate can determine the behaviour of a boss. It is thus closely connected with cultural tolerance for inequality, at least in the workplace. Table 3.1 shows Finland's position relative to our other three countries, with France, Italy and the United States thrown in for additional comparisons.

Table 3.1 Six country comparison of selected cultural dimensions

Country	Individualism/collectivism (the higher the score, the more individualistic the culture)	Power distance index (the higher the score, the greater tolerance for power differentials)
Finland	63	33
France	71	68
Netherlands	80	38
Italy	76	50
Sweden	71	31
The United Kingdom	89	35
United States	91	40

Source: Selected from Hofstede, 2001, p. 500.

It can be seen that Finland has a low individualism/high collectivism score, and also a fairly low tolerance of interpersonal power differentials.

It is also important to remember that Finland is (in population terms) a small and relatively homogenous country, so the elite is correspondingly small and everyone tends to know everyone else.

The administrative system

For many years Finland, like Sweden, had an administrative system consisting of three main levels. First, there were ministries. Then there were national-level boards (sometimes translated into English as 'agencies') with considerable powers of rule-making and detailed intervention. Last, but not least, there were the municipalities. [It should be noted that, although this book is focused principally on the central state, Finnish local (municipal) government employs roughly four-fifths of the public sector workforce.] In the mid-1990s the board/agency level was subject to fairly fundamental reform, shrinking its size and numbers and reorienting its role away from detailed regulation and towards research and development or support activities for ministries.

The population of central ministries has been fairly stable over the past two decades. Since the early 1990s there have usually been 12 ministries and the Prime Minister's Office, which itself has the status of a ministry (Prime Minister's Office and Ministries, 1995 – see www.mmm.fi for the latest state of play). The Ministries of Finance and the Interior are the two with the most important responsibilities for administrative reform. Much of the writing about reform (at least in English) has come from the Public Management Department of the Ministry of Finance (see references), which has employed or contracted a number of academic-minded individuals (see, e.g. Holkeri and Nuurmi, 2002; Summa, 1995) as well as contracting out research into management reform (e.g. Bouckaert *et al.*, 2000; Kiviniemi *et al.*, 1995; Ministry of Finance, 1997). 'Pure' academic debate about the public management reforms (from the Finnish universities) has certainly taken place, but has been limited in quantity and has seldom been conducted on strong theoretical lines.

Traditionally each ministry has independent responsibility for implementation and control of laws and policies within their own sphere so, although the Ministry of Finance is, in some general sense, the most 'powerful' ministry, it usually cannot impose its own programmes on other ministries to the degree that has occasionally been possible in more centralized systems such as that in France, New Zealand or the

United Kingdom. However, by the beginning of the new century, concern about this relative lack of co-ordination was growing, and a commissioned report drew attention to the need for better integration across government (Bouckaert *et al.*, 2000). The strengthening of the Prime Minister's Office, especially but not exclusively with respect to EU co-ordination, was one consequence of this debate.

There is a career civil service, and political and 'mandarin' careers are usually separate. However, some of the top three levels of civil service appointment go to known sympathizers with particular political parties, according to a kind of informal 'quota' system (Tiihonen, 1996, p. 40). In the past senior Finnish civil servants were mainly lawyers, but this balance has shifted over the past generation, with more people with a training in economics or the social sciences being recruited into senior posts. Public management reform has been mainly an 'insider' process, with senior civil servants playing a crucial role. External consultants, although used for certain purposes, have not been as influential as in, say, the United Kingdom or the United States (Ministry of Finance, 1997, p. 74).

Finland has been an active member of many international organizations, both governmental and academic (e.g. PUMA, European Group for Public Administration). In that sense it has been open to and acquainted with the full range of contemporary management concepts and techniques as applied to the public sector. However, it has not slavishly followed fashions but rather carefully selected and piloted those ideas considered suitable for Finnish needs. To take two examples, TQM and ISO 9000 approaches to service quality improvement were widely adopted in Finnish local government (Association of Finnish Local Authorities, 1995a, 1995b) and, in central government, accruals accounting practices in other countries were closely studied but then only partly adopted. What has been notable, however, is that Finnish central government has not made intensive use of management consultants to *implement* reform (in the way that occurred in, say, the United Kingdom). Consultants have been used to gather information, and a number of foreign academics have been used as advisers, but actual implementation has remained, for the most part, firmly in the hands of civil servants.

Reforms have been mainly the work of a fairly small elite of senior civil servants and a few politicians. Media interest in the reforms has not been particularly strong (Ministry of Finance, 1997, pp. 73 and 81). Finland did not experience strongly ideological governments with strong views about changing the role of the state in the way that the United States did under President Reagan or the United Kingdom under Prime Minister Thatcher.

Public management reform: the decision-making process

The process by which Finnish reforms came into being was quite drawn-out and cautious. It was not a matter of a few individuals passionately advocating specific 'solutions' (which would be unusual anyway within the Finnish politico-administrative culture), but rather the gradual, consensual formation of a set of proposals for streamlining the state apparatus. Then, from 1991, there was the powerful additional impetus of an economic crisis, which helped to crystallize the need for urgent action to trim the state apparatus and tighten control over spending (Selovuori, 1999, pp. 228–9). Within this overall process some central themes were the lightening of the bureaucratic 'weight' of central government (especially by reforming the national-level agencies); a shift from input budgeting to a stronger focus on results; a parallel shift to frame (block) budgeting for central transfers to municipalities; a commitment to service quality improvement and some measure of decentralization.

At the highest level the co-ordination of the reform programme was ensured by the creation of a ministerial committee on which all the main political parties in government were represented (Ministry of Finance, 1997, p. 69). Stability was also enhanced by the long-term participation of a small number of senior civil servants from the Ministry of Finance and the Ministry of the Interior. One Finnish commentator went so far as to term the Finnish approach 'technocratic' (Puoskari, 1996, p. 105).

From the late 1990s there was some thinking by ministers and senior civil servants about the possibility of a second wave of reform. This would have involved a fairly comprehensive restructuring of central government into different relational categories (e.g. organizations where the government was principally exercising the interests of an owner, organizations where the government's interest was as a direct service provider, and so on). This then became coupled to a wider agenda, embracing improved steering by ministries, e-governance and strengthened citizen participation. Under the second Lipponen administration (1999–2003) ministers again became more directly and actively interested in management reform, especially the strengthening of the Prime Minister's Office, the improvement of horizontal co-ordination between ministries and attempts to stem the perceived loss of citizens' trust in the state machine.

The substance of the reforms

There was much internal discussion on reform during the early and mid-1980s, but the first major initiatives came with the arrival in office of the Holkeri government in 1987. The subsequent decade was then a busy one, with several main lines of reform unfolding simultaneously or in sequence. The two changes of government (1991 and 1995) did not appear to make any dramatic difference to the general thrust of the reforms, although possibly it could be said that the level of political interest in management reform (never overwhelmingly high among the majority of politicians) declined somewhat after 1994, but then revived from the beginning of the second Lipponen administration in 1999.

The main lines of the first wave of reform were as follows (see the pamphlet *Government decision in principle on reforms in central and regional government*, 1993):

- Results-oriented budgeting was piloted from 1987 and rolled out to the whole government by 1994. This required a number of potentially important changes including the definition of results indicators for agencies (to enable their performance to be assessed more explicitly by their 'parent' ministries) and the creation of unified running costs budgets for ministries and agencies. The pilot projects appeared to show that significant running cost savings could be achieved, but that some ministries were slow to take up the challenge of using indicators as an active form of performance management (Ministry of Finance, 1992). There was concern that 'in practically all cases the link between money and the level of performance was missing' (Summa, 1995, p. 158).
- An Administrative Development Agency (later retitled the Finnish Institute of Public Management) was set up in 1987 to provide training and consultancy to support reform. The Agency/Institute has been obliged to operate along increasingly commercial/self-financing lines. A first attempt to sell it off failed, but in 2002 it was corporatized with 40 per cent of its shares being sold to a private sector consultancy company.
- The transformation of a number of agencies with commercial functions into, first, State Enterprises (12 were created 1989–97) and in some cases, subsequently State-Owned Companies. The law enabling the creation of State Enterprises was passed in 1988. The further transformation to state-owned joint stock companies included Post and Telecommunications and Railways (Kiviniemi *et al.*, 1995).
- The introduction from 1993 of a framework budgeting system to control central government aid to municipalities. This was partly a decentralization measure, aimed at reducing the amount of detailed central intervention in municipal decision-making, but it was also a

way of gaining firm control of the *totals* of municipal spending at a time of great budgetary pressure, and of delegating painful decisions about spending priorities down to municipal leaders. The total aid going to a given municipality was henceforth calculated as a lump sum based on the values taken by certain indicators, such as the number and age structure of the population. Later, framework management was developed into 'a central procedure steering the preparation of the State budget by the government' (*High quality services, good governance and a responsible civic society*, Ministry of Finance, 1998, p. 10).

- A restructuring of the central agencies. This was also a decentralization measure. The agencies with commercial functions were turned into State Enterprises (see earlier). Others were merged or downsized, and their role was changed from that of regulation to one of providing research and development and evaluation to the ministries. Their internal governance structures were also changed – usually away from collegial forms towards more managerial and/or monocratic arrangements (Savolainen, 1999).
- Government data collection streamlined and barriers to data transfer between different parts of the state reduced.
- Provincial state administration unified and lightened. The offices of different ministries at the provincial level were combined.
- Human Resource Management reforms, including provision for performance-related pay and for more decentralized management of staff. The main decisions and announcements here were made during the Aho administration (1991–95) but subsequent implementation has been quite slow.
- In 1998 it was announced that 'The quality as well as the citizen- and customer-orientation of the services will be developed by means of a new type of Service Charters to be given to the customers' [*sic*] (*High quality services, good governance and a responsible civic society*, 1998, p. 15).

Thus the balance of the reforms leant towards decentralization, simplification and tighter control of spending (Ministry of Finance, 1993; Puoskari, 1996). There was no great enthusiasm for widespread privatization, although the Finnish governments were quite prepared to privatize selectively, when it seemed to make sense on its own terms (e.g. the government printing company). More use was made of commercial forms that stopped short of full privatization, such as state enterprises and state-owned companies.

In the late 1990s a second wave of reform began. Considerable emphasis was placed on improving the quality of public services, and on encouraging citizen participation (Holkeri and Nurmi, 2002). To support this and other goals, a sophisticated national electronic portal on the public sector was developed and opened in 2002 (Romakkaniemi, 2001). There was also an attempt to tidy up some of the 'unfinished business' from the first wave of reforms, particularly the slowness of ministries to engage in active, performance-oriented steering of their agencies (Joustie, 2001).

Overall, the implementation process has been gradual and deliberate, with pilot projects and extensive training programmes to ensure the smoothest possible implementation. One does not get the sense of the hectic pace and urgency which undoubtedly prevailed during, say, 1986–92 in New Zealand or 1987–97 in the United Kingdom.

The Finnish government has supported a programme of evaluations of its reforms (Holkeri and Summa, 1996). It is not clear that these evaluations (e.g. Ministry of Finance, 1997) have had any clear and direct effect on subsequent decisions, but the evaluation function has now been firmly established in Finland as an on-going component of modern public management.

Finally, some interesting reflections on the reforms of the 1987–97 period appeared in the 1998 Government Resolution *High quality services, good governance and a responsible civic society* (Ministry of Finance, 1998):

> there are still problems in performance management. The members of Parliament have considered it to have weakened the budgetary powers of Parliament. Several agencies have considered it to be still too largely managed from above and to restrict their initiative. The evaluation of its effects and the development of effects indicators are only just beginning. (p. 13)

There were also concerns that:

> As functions that were earlier dealt with on the national level are transferred to the international level, the forms of political decision-making must change. The shrinking of national sovereignty may weaken the trust of citizens in political decision makers, because the decisions of the Government have an increasingly indirect effect on their lives. (p. 28)

In subsequent years this concern with citizens and legitimacy was intensified, and became one of the themes of reform (Holkeri and Nurmi, 2002; Romakkaniemi, 2001).

Finnish agencies in the twenty-first century

As indicated above, during the mid-1990s the Finnish system of national boards (agencies) underwent what was said at the time to be a fundamental reform. These boards had come to be seen, by central government reformers, as part of the 'old ways': heavy, bureaucratic, duplicatory of decisions taken within ministries, and interfering in detail in the affairs of municipalities. So, unlike the bright new 'Next Steps' agencies which were at the very same time being set up in the United Kingdom, Finnish agencies had to be slimmed down reduced, confined to a more limited role. This was 1990s agency reform, Finnish style.

Accordingly, a number of big national boards were formally abolished or re-designated with more limited roles. One popular model was that these agencies, instead of being rule-makers and regulators, should become the eyes and ears of their parent ministries. They would gather data, undertake research, amass expertise and policy-relevant knowledge. They would not issue detailed regulations or interpose themselves as central government's representatives to local authorities. This was a much more 'upwards-looking' role than the 'downwards' regulating, interfering life of the past.

However, things did not work out entirely according to the script. Finland is unique (as far as we are aware) in sponsoring an official administrative history, under the auspices of the 1986-founded Commission on the History of Central Administration in Finland. The products of this admirable enterprise make our task much easier (e.g. Selovuori, 1999). The view of the national experts is that:

> Although the system of national boards has been dismantled in the 1990s, both through closures and by setting up state enterprises and state-owned joint-stock companies, personnel savings have been slight. The greatest single reason for this has been the implementation of reforms by simply dressing the old administration in new clothes. Although some national boards have been closed their staff have for the most part merely been transferred into the ministries or into new offices or agencies set up to replace the boards. The biggest ostensible saving has been achieved by categorising the new state enterprises and state-owned joint-stock companies as belonging to the private sector. (Savolianen, 1999, p. 144)

Indeed, 'new offices and agencies sprout from the ruins of the national boards' (Savolainen, 1999, p. 132). Many examples can be given. When

Table 3.2 Numbers of central administrative units under the direction of the Council of State, Finland

1960s	1970s	1980s	1990–95	1995–99
61	69	71	68	70

the National Board of Trade and Consumer Affairs was brought to an end it was succeeded by three new agencies – the National Consumer Administration, the National Food Administration and the National Consumer Research Centre. When the National Board of Agriculture was reformed in 1993, some functions went to the Ministry, but others were passed to more new bodies reporting to the Ministry, including the Information Centre of the Ministry of Agriculture and Forestry, the Plant Production Inspection Centre and the National Veterinary and Food Research Institute. And so on – the overall picture does not indicate a big reduction in complexity.

This sceptical note is not intended to suggest that everything has remained the same. Roles and relationships have been altered. The squadrons of new, specialized agencies and institutes are the creatures of their ministries, unlike the powerful, multi-purpose national boards of old. Nevertheless, the original idea that there would simply be two levels of government, the ministries and the municipalities, looks rather optimistic.

The above mainly concerns national boards which had administrative, social or regulatory tasks. Those which were principally engaged with commercial functions were treated rather differently. A 1988 Act enabled the government to create state enterprises and, within seven years, 14 bodies had been 'translated' into this new status (and many of them had been propelled even further, into the category of state-owned joint stock companies). For example, the National Board of Posts and Telecommunications became a state enterprise in 1990 and then a state-owned company in 1994. The state railways, similarly, became a state enterprise and then (in 1995) a state-owned company. One of the organizations we examine in this book – what had previously been the Forest and Park Service – became an off-budget state enterprise in 1993. One advantage of such changes of legal status for the hard-pressed Finnish government of the early- and mid-1990s was indeed that both the staff and most of the expenditures of state enterprises were moved outside the official state budget.

Alongside changes in organizational status and structure came new forms of steering. From the early 1990s the Finnish government laid great emphasis on the development of a system of 'results-oriented budgeting'. Each ministry was supposed to draw up a 'contract' with each of its agencies, incorporating a set of performance targets (Summa, 1995, p. 150). Yet what is noticeable from the official Finnish literature is a continuing concern that this system is not working very well (e.g. Joustie, 2001; Ministry of Finance, 1992). Evidently ministries often lack either the will or the expertise (or both) to set challenging targets and hold the agencies to their achievement. Thus, in 2001 senior Ministry of Finance officials were still expressing dissatisfaction with the degree of real performance-orientation that had been achieved:

> After different analyses we have made several observations of weak points in our system. We understand that more clear requirements of accountability are badly needed. Poor results do not cause the necessary reactions in the machinery today ... The strategic touch should be strengthened in the government as a whole and in the ministries as individual negotiators and contracting parties. (Joustie, p. 19)

This is a topic we shall certainly return to in the later chapters where we look at particular functions.

Conclusions: some key issues concerning Finnish agencies

In Chapter 2 we introduced the idea that there were three principal dimensions within the new concept of executive agencies which has emerged in the OECD world since the mid-1980s. These were, first, structural disaggregation; second, the granting of management autonomy and, third, the shaping of the relationship between agency and parent ministry into a contract-like set of procedures and arrangements. We will now use these same 'tripod' dimensions to frame the 'agency story' in Finland, and to identify some key issues for further attention later in the book.

In some ways the Finnish case may sound similar to that of the United Kingdom. Agencies with non-commercial tasks are set up to deal with operational issues, provide expertise on technical matters and conduct research and development. They are to be steered by ministries on the basis of results expressed through sets of performance indicators. In other ways, however, Finland and the United Kingdom are very different. It is not only that the constitutional assumption of individual ministerial responsibility is much less prominent in a coalition government – which clearly affects agency/ministry relations. Nor is it that the Finnish political culture is gradualist and consensualist, whereas that of the United Kingdom is aggressively majoritarian – important though that also seems to be. It is most fundamental that *the concept of an 'agency' itself starts from a different place.* It begins with the powerful national boards that were set up soon after Finnish independence in 1917, and which were partly dismantled by the reforms of the 1990s. As in Sweden, large 'agencies' were part of old-style government, rather than the novelties they were portrayed as being in the United Kingdom and the Netherlands. So in many ways the agency reform of the 1990s, far from being an act of disaggregation, was one of *re-aggregation*. In some cases activities were actually taken back into ministries, and in others they were re-assigned to new agencies which were probably smaller and more dependent on their parent ministry than the big, old-style national boards. One purpose here was to increase the capacity for 'democratic' steering by ministers, another to reduce bureaucracy and complexity. One key question, therefore, is whether these aims were achieved. Are the new agencies subject to active steering and, if so, how does that work? Has the (alleged) old bureaucratic culture been dissolved, and a more responsive set of organizations been created?

Second, we should consider the issue of *management autonomy*. The degree of structural disaggregation may be a poor guide to the degree of real management autonomy. Management authority may be decentralized or centralized *within* a ministry, just as it may be centralized or decentralized *across* a relationship between a ministry and its satellite bodies. So the mere fact that, structurally, an activity may have been drawn back from a National Board to a new style ministerial agency does not tell us – or certainly does not tell us for sure – whether managerial autonomy has shrunk, grown or stayed much the same. This must be investigated directly, and this is what we will do in the four 'functional' chapters later on. There we will examine the Finnish agencies for prisons, meteorology, and social security, and the state enterprise for forestry. To anticipate that later discussion slightly, it seems that autonomy can be influenced by characteristics of the particular function, so not all agencies have the same degree of autonomy. There may also be an element of path dependency, in the sense that current autonomy is related to what that activity enjoyed before, in its previous organizational incarnation. A third influence seems to be the general politico-administrative culture, including the consensual, small-elite characteristics already alluded to.

Finally, we come to the attempt to *contractualize* relationships between ministries, on the one hand, and agencies and state enterprises on the other. Certainly we see that the Finns have put the apparatus in place. Results-oriented budgeting, targets, performance-related remuneration for chief executives – all this and more has featured in the management reforms of the past 15 years. Yet there seems to be a persistent dissatisfaction with what has been achieved – at least as far as the Ministry of Finance is concerned. They seem to believe that ministries are not really pushing their agencies and state enterprises, that the relationships are too cosy. The questions here are thus whether this picture is true and, if so, why it is so? Perhaps this is no more than the perpetual, genetic suspicion that all ministries of finance direct towards spending ministries? Or perhaps it is simply that, in a consensual culture, ministries don't like to act in a demanding and combative way? Or is it that there is some kind of community of interest between ministries and agencies which the Ministry of Finance cannot break? Or, finally, is there something else here: could there be reasons why, even if ministries *do* try to operate the relationship like a performance contract, agencies can nonetheless resist or avoid the sharper edges of the negotiation? In the later chapters we will be able to see what view our selected agencies take of contracts, targets and the Ministry of Finance.

4
The Netherlands

Background: the political system

> The Netherlands is a unitary, but decentralised state: 'traditionally, the Dutch state ... has always resisted centralisation of state authority'.
>
> (Kickert and In 't Veld, 1995, p. 45)

The political system is consociational, consensual, multi-party and corporatist (Lijphart, 1984; 1999 – see Figure 3.1 in Chapter 3, above). Elections take place according to a system of proportional representation. In the recent period the main parties have been Christian Democrat (a 1980s merger of previously separate Christian parties – CDA), a Liberal Party (conservative – VVD), a Social-Democrat party (PvdA) and a small Progressive Liberal Party (D66). There are also a number of other small parties. The Christian parties were continuously in government from the First World War until 1994, allied to various groupings of other parties. Through the 1970s the governing coalitions were centre left, in the 1980s centre right. Unusually, in 1994 and 1998, *'purple'* (left–right) coalitions were formed *without* Christian Democrat participation. However, from the late 1990s the party system became more volatile, with the rapid emergence, and then equally rapid decline, of Pim Fortuyn's anti-establishment LPF party. After the elections of May 2002 and January 2003 (and after Pim Fortuyn's assassination) the Christian Democrats, under Balkende's leadership, returned to government. They formed a coalition with the VVD and D66.

The Dutch tendency to talk round the table can scarcely be exaggerated:

> In the Netherlands almost every sector of government policy consists of a myriad of consultative and advisory councils, which are deeply

interwined with government and form an 'iron ring' around the ministerial departments ... Deliberation, consultation, and pursuit of compromise and consensus form the deeply rooted basic traits of Dutch political culture. (Kickert and In 't Veld, 1995, p. 53)

... the Dutch ministries are relatively open organisations. They are not only populated by career civil servants, but also by many external consultants and scientists who contribute enthusiastically to policy making in general. (Kickert and In 't Veld, 1995, p. 56)

Yet there is also a component of individualism. '*Ministerial responsibility* is the cornerstone of our system' (Kickert and In 't Veld, 1995, p. 46). Ministers are responsible politically, in criminal and in civil law. [Also, in the so-called 'dual system', they are not members of parliament, ceasing to be so once they accept ministerial office.] Nevertheless, the collectivity is dominant. Collective decision-making takes place in the weekly council of ministers. The Prime Minister is not as strong a coordinating and centralizing force as in the UK system – indeed, various attempts during the 1980s and 1990s to strengthen the PM's Office have been rejected or dropped or implemented only weakly. S/he remains *primus inter pares*, and is certainly not presidential.

The politico-administrative culture

The Dutch culture contains several paradoxes. One is the theoretical stress on individual freedom, yet the practice of consensual decision-making. In Hofstede's work (see Table 3.1 in Chapter 3) the Dutch index score is 80 for individualism, compared with 63 for Finland and 71 for Sweden. Another paradox is the emphasis on openness, combined with the practice of corporatist deals in 'smoke-filled rooms' (except they are not so smoky nowadays – most Dutch public buildings have a no-smoking policy).

While there is a popular suspicion that 'the bureaucracy' is inefficient, and while public service seems to have become a less attractive career for young people, Dutch public opinion nevertheless, does not support the strongly anti-government attitudes which have been quite popular in the United States and, to a lesser extent, in Australia, New Zealand and the United Kingdom. Indeed, relative to other European countries – and certainly to the United States – public opinion in the Netherlands has a positive attitude towards the government. Dutch public opinion also gives relatively high trust ratings to institutions such as Parliament, social security, health care and education (see Table 4.1).

Table 4.1 Trust in institutions (2000) [all figures = % of respondents expressing trust]

Sector	Finland	France	The Netherlands	Sweden	The United Kingdom
Parliament	43.7	40.6	55.3	51.1	35.5
Civil service	40.9	45.9	37.5	48.8	45.9
Social security	50.9	66.9	64.4	50.9	36.4
Health care system	84.4	77.4	75.1	76.3	58.7

Sources: Figures drawn from Halman, L. (2001) *The European values Study: a Third Wave: Source Book of the 1999–2000 European Values Study Surveys*, Tilburg, WORC, Tilburg University.

In Table 4.1 one can see that the 'odd man out' in our set of four countries is actually the United Kingdom, which has very low levels of citizen trust in parliament and the civil service. Interestingly, the Dutch seem to show more trust in their parliament than their civil service. It should be noted, however, that the 37.5 per cent figure for trust in the civil service represents a sharp recent fall – the corresponding figures in previous surveys were 46 per cent (1990) and 44.5 per cent (1981). Still more recently, a study by the Social and Cultural Planning Bureau appears to show falling public satisfaction with government (www.scp.nl, accessed September 2003).

One might also mention that many Dutch have a certain cultural aversion to public figures 'showing off', and this may have meant that the potential popular appeal of politicians with bold, doctrinaire programmes (such as Thatcher in the United Kingdom, Reagan in the United States, or Howard in Australia) is less in the Netherlands than in some other countries. However, the meteoric rise of Pim Fortuyn and his party in 2001 (until his murder in 2002) somewhat dented this image of Dutch 'steadiness', as did the prolonged and ultimately failed negotiations between the CDA and the PvDA trying to form a coalition government in 2003.

Thus, confidence in the administrative and political system, though substantial, has been under pressure. In 2001 a fireworks store exploded in Enschede with 20 killed and many injured, resulting in questions on procedures related to permits and inspections. There was the 2002 murder of Pim Fortuyn which also caused a parliamentary commission to look hard at the responsibilities and levels of accountability of different administrative and political actors involved. Also in 2002 a large scale fraud was uncovered, involving large sums of public money for road, bridge and house construction. This led to discussions of the importance of ethical standards in public sector reform. All these incidents combined to raise the question of whether the characteristic Dutch 'cosy consensualism' had gone too far. Dutch politicians and media debated whether the 'Polders model' should be abandoned in favour of a tougher, more results-oriented style (e.g. De Boer and Peeperkorn, 2003). Disquiet grew over *gedogen* – the lax enforcement regime that tolerated the bending of rules and regulations (Economist, 2002).

It should also be noted that the Netherlands, relative to its size, has one of the largest community of public administration academics in western Europe. Many professors played some part in advising government on administrative reform. During the 1980s open systems approaches and network theories provided alternative perspectives to business management approaches and, during the 1990s, the Dutch academic community played an important part in developing the 'new steering model' of governance (Kickert and In 't Veld, 1995, pp. 59–60; Kickert, 2000, pp. 79–82). The culture is thus inclusive of, rather than exclusive of, academic opinion.

The administrative system

In the late 1990s there were 13 ministries (the number has varied over time, e.g. in 1982 the new government abolished the Ministry of Public Health and Environment and transferred its functions to two new ministries). Because of the absence of a strong central power each has considerable autonomy – more so than would be the case in the United Kingdom. The highest civil servant in each ministry is the Secretary General, and ministries are generally divided into directorates general. In 1995 the ABD (*Algemene Bestuursdienst*) was created (Senior Executive Service) which numbered, at the end of 2000, 628 civil servants.

The civil service is not partisan, and civil service and political careers are separate. As noted above, Ministries are fairly open organizations, at least in the sense that they frequently bring outside experts into the processes of policy deliberation. According to OECD figures, 74.2 per cent of Dutch public employment was at central government level in 1999. This is a relatively high figure (compared with 23.4 per cent in Finland, less than 20 per cent in Sweden and 47.6 per cent in the United Kingdom) but includes the staff of ZBOs and other central organizations as well as the ministries themselves (OECD, Summary of the PSPE data analysis, www.oecd.org, accessed October 2003). One might say that the Dutch system has a large centre, but quite a fragmented one.

Nevertheless, the provincial and municipal levels are highly significant in terms of services and expenditure. There are 12 provinces and about 490 municipalities (recently down from well over 600, due to amalgamations). These sub-national tiers are responsible for most of the expensive, labour-intensive welfare state services (municipalities account for roughly one-third of public expenditure, though much of this is financed by central government). Many of the cutbacks of the 1980s were directed at these levels.

Public management reform: the decision-making process

The contents of the reform package developed over time, with shifts in the coalition government, and with changes in the fortunes of the Dutch economy. The aforementioned system of consultative and advisory councils afforded many channels for both business-based and academic ideas to enter public administration. In this respect, therefore, the Netherlands is dissimilar to more closed, *rechsstaat*-type regimes such as Germany or France. Among our four countries it is more similar to the United Kingdom than, say, Finland. During the 1980s and 1990s specific reform ideas came from a number of other countries, especially Sweden, the United Kingdom and the United States.

As in many other countries, during the 1980s notions of comprehensive planning were in rapid retreat, and business-origin management ideas increasingly penetrated the public sector (Kickert, 2000). However, in the Netherlands, the drive for efficiency and savings did not carry a sharp anti-government ideological edge. As a leading Dutch professor put it:

> Extreme neo-liberal 'new right' ideologies like 'Reaganonomics' in the United States and 'Thatcherism' in Great Britain, cannot become dominant in a typical consensus model of democracy like ours.
> (Kickert, 2000, p. 131)

A longstanding feature of Dutch decision-making is its sectoralization (*verkokering*), which Kickert (2000, p. 87) dubs 'notorious'. Many reports have drawn attention to this, and various attempts have been made, especially since 1990, to alleviate the fragmentation. However, neither the installation of governing boards (*bestuursraad* – bringing top civil servants together in boards), nor the 1995 formation of a unified senior public service, nor experimentation with 'integral management' seem yet to have transformed the culture (Kickert, 2000, pp. 87–91). This is of significance for agencies in several ways, one being that no overarching regime of accountability, performance measurement or reporting has been developed for all agencies (or, indeed, ZBOs):

> Contrary to the British civil service where administrative reform is centrally guided by the Cabinet Office [authors' note – Prof. Kickert might have added 'and the Treasury'], in the Netherlands there is no central director of the stage. Each ministry is free to choose its own way of reform, resulting in more variety. (Kickert, 2000, p. 101)

Another significant feature of the decision-making process was the generally low level of political interest in management issues *per se* (although, of course political interest leapt upwards whenever scandals were revealed or disasters occurred). Ministers, of course, would become interested in organizational changes that seemed likely to affect their 'patch', but:

> Parliament has hardly ever discussed the management reforms, and, if so, mainly as a financial subject in the parliamentary sub-committee for financial affairs. With a few occasional exceptions, no political interference has disturbed the pathway of departmental reforms.
> (Kickert, 2000, p. 131)

The corollary to this, of course, is that senior officials themselves have enjoyed considerable freedom to develop their own ideas and schemes for administrative reform.

The substance of the reforms

In general terms it might be said that the package appeared most radical in the early and mid-1980s, especially under the 'Lubbers 1' centre-right coalition of 1982–86. Privatization was a prominent theme, but the scope for returning state bodies to private ownership was less than in, say, the United Kingdom, because the extent of pre-existing state ownership was more modest. [Also, it should be noted that the Dutch have often tended to use the term privatization (*privatisering*) much more loosely and extensively than the British. Thus, for example, hiving out functions to a wholly publicly owned, public law, non-profit ZBO has sometimes been termed *privatisering*.] Nevertheless, the Postbank (10 500 staff), Posts and Telecommunications (95 000 staff), the Royal Mint, the state mines and the state fishery – the main state companies – were either corporatized or wholly or partly sold off.

The 'Lubbers 1' administration announced a series of 'large operations'. These comprized privatization, measures to trim central government spending, the decentralization of activities to lower levels of government and the simplification of legal and bureaucratic procedures.

The 1980s was also a period in which many new ZBOs (self-steering public organizations, free of direct ministerial responsibility) were created. A survey by the national audit office showed that, by 1992, 18 per cent of total state expenditure passed through these semi-autonomous bodies. Some were long established (e.g. the state universities) but more than 40 per cent dated from after 1980 – although some of these represented amalgamations of pre-existing bodies (Algemene Rekenkamer, 1995).

After the cuts of the 1980s the emphasis moved towards a greater concern with efficiency – and even effectiveness. Three main lines were followed (Kickert, 2000, p. 84):

- Promoting results-oriented management (which was also popular at that time in Finland and Sweden – see Chapters 3 and 5).
- Introducing accruals accounting (which was particularly important for agencies – see later).
- Introducing market-type-mechanisms (MTMs) to encourage a competitive approach.

One important manifestation of this orientation was the 'Great Efficiency Operation' which the government launched in 1990. This became a foundation for the programme of agencification, because many departments responded with proposals for autonomizing functions.

By the mid-1990s the fiscal pressures had slackened, and academics were even beginning to write of the 'Dutch economic miracle' (Visser and Hemerijk, 1997). Management reforms could afford to be less draconian than during the mid-1980s. By 2002, however, the world economic slowdown meant that cuts were back on top of the political agenda.

In the 1990s the departmental agency, rather than the ZBO, became the fashionable format for decentralizing administrative authority. Between 1991 and 2002 the number of agencies went up to 24 and the number of ZBOs fell from the 545 recorded by the national audit office in 1993 to 431 – but mainly because of definitional changes (Ministerie van Financiën, 2002; Van Thiel and Van Buuren, 2001). Agencies included for example, Meteorology, Immigration and Naturalization, Defence Telematics and the Government Buildings Service. Nevertheless, despite the 'primacy of politics' and the dubious reputation of the ZBO as far as public accountability was concerned, research has shown that the creation of new ZBOs went steadily on (Van Thiel and Van Buuren, 2001).

In Human Resource Management/personnel management there was a gradual shift towards the 'normalisation' of the terms of public service, bringing them more in line with private sector labour conditions. The Netherlands, along with many other countries in this study, experienced a tension between the desire to use HRM to build a more skilled and highly-motivated workforce, and the desire to shed jobs and economize (Korsten and Van der Krogt, 1995).

Finally, in 2001, performance budgeting (VBTB) was legally implemented: the format of the budget bill became outcome-oriented and policy objectives and performance measures were integrated in the explanatory memorandum. In 2000 the Ministry of Finance also proposed the extension of the accrual budgeting system from the agencies to the departments, though at the time of writing it seemed unlikely that this would be fully accepted and implemented.

In many, perhaps most countries, the rhetoric of public management reform outdistances the actual changes in practice. This has certainly been true for the Netherlands during the period since 1980. The implementation of decentralization is a good example:

> the decentralisation process in the 1980s and 1990s became largely a power struggle. Spending departments often held out resolutely (and with success) against the transfer of power to provinces and municipalities. Decentralisation only began to assume any importance when spending cuts and decentralisation were brought together in a single context: municipalities were permitted to take over certain tasks if they were prepared to accept 90% funding; the 10% contraction was (without much evidence) justified as 'efficiency gains'.
> (Derksen and Korsten, 1995, p. 83)

Another example, as we will see later, is the promises that were made with respect to agencies, and, in particular, their measurable performance, which were far from universally fulfilled.

Dutch agencies in the twenty-first century

The tale of Dutch agencies shows how a single organizational form – in this case the agency – can come to stand for several different ideas or purposes, and how these can vary over time – sometimes over quite short periods. When the first agencies were set up, in 1994, Dutch politicians were beginning to worry about the loss of control and accountability which had accompanied the creation of so many autonomous ZBOs during the previous decade or so (Algemene Rekenkamer, 1995; Van Thiel, 2001, p. 207). There was a desire to reassert 'the primacy of politics'. So agencies, rather than standing for radical new freedoms, were to some extent a safer substitute for more highly autonomous organizational forms. As the Ministry of Transport and Water put it recently:

> At first Dutch agencies represented and were seen as an alternative to the *external* autonomization of government functions. (Ministerie van Verkeer en Waterstaat, 2002, p. 14 [italics added]. Quotation translated by the author from the original: *Agentschappen werden in Nederland aanvankelijk gepresenteerd en gezien als een alternatief voor externe verzelfstandiging van overheidstaken*)

Thus agencies were relatively 'safe', but they would also have special freedoms. Prime among these was financial freedom, including especially the use of accruals accounting. In fact, in this first phase, these aspects seem to have been much more developed than performance frameworks or personnel freedoms (unlike, say, the UK position– see Chapter 6). In practice, agencification was 'run' by the Ministry of Finance, and had a predominantly financial character (Smullen *et al.*, 2001; Smullen, 2004). The theory was that, in order to qualify for agency status, an organization had to demonstrate that it could measure both the price and the quantity of the service it produced. Note, though, that from a strictly juridical perspective, virtually nothing had changed. Unlike ZBOs – each one of which had its own statute defining its autonomy – *agentschappen* had no separate legal personality, and so the minister remained wholly responsible for their acts and omissions.

Table 4.2 lists the agencies of the 'first wave'. This is a manifestly mixed bunch (Smullen and Van Thiel, 2002). There are large (by Dutch standards) organizations, such as the prison service, and small ones, such as the Information Government Personnel office. There are politically highly sensitive activities (immigration and naturalization) and normally uncontroversial ones (the meteorological institute, the state archives). There is high science (medical testing, defence telematics) and pure bureaucracy (archives, core personnel administration). Most sectors are represented, but a few significant ones are missing (foreign affairs, finance).

Table 4.2 Dutch agencies to 2000

Agency	Ministry	Expenditure (Millions of Euros, 1999)	Date of creation
Centre for Propogation of Imports from Developing Countries	Home Affairs	10.6	1998
Immigration and Naturalisation Office	Justice	237.4	1994
Prison Service	Justice	1069.6	1995
Judicial Incasso Service	Justice	29.3	1996
National Police Services	Justice	205.4	1998
Information Government Personnel	Home Affairs	9.4	1995
Core Administration Personnel Information and Travel Documents	Home Affairs	26.2	1998
IT Organization	Home Affairs	90.5	1998
State Archive Service	Education and Science	24.5	1996
Defence Telematics Organization	Defence	221.1	1998
Building, Works and Terrain Office	Defence	76.0	1996
State Building Office	Housing and Environment	844.0	1999
Royal Meteorological Institute (KNMI)	Transport Public Works	39.2	1995
State Service Radio-Communication	Transport Public Works	28.6	1996
SENTER	Economic Affairs	36.8	1994
Plant Disease Service	Agriculture and Nature	14.7	1994
Levies Office	Agriculture and Nature	30.7	1998
LASER	Agriculture and Nature	63.1	1999
Medicine Test Council	Health, Welfare, Sports	11.6	1996
Public Health Protection	Health, Welfare, Sports	58.7	2000

Source: Adapted from Kickert, 2000, Table 5.5, p. 99.

Rather as happened in the United Kingdom, the creation of agencies provoked or at least ran alongside a reconsideration of the role of the rump ministries. In Den Haag a debate arose about the concept of 'core departments': what they should contain and what they should do (Kickert, 2000, pp. 102–4). It is not clear that this debate led to many clear, concrete outcomes, and it suffered not merely from coming partly *after* the commitment to agencification, but also from the fact that it was overtaken by a series of financial cutbacks that apparently bore no relation to any coherent vision of the roles of the respective departments.

The burst of creative activity during the early and mid-1990s was followed by a much quieter period, in which the attractiveness of agency status seemed to fluctuate. Almost immediately, in 1994, an important advisory committee produced a report which set out quite elaborate conditions for autonomizing, and was interpreted as a cautious note, especially with respect to 'external' autonomization (i.e. ZBOs – Sint, 1994). Later, in 2000, accruals accounting provisions were extended, so that an organization did not actually have to be an agency in order to acquire this 'privilege'. The tax service (Belastingstdienst), for example, took the freedom but avoided the title *agentschap*, in part so as to avoid confusion with another, pre-existing body within the Ministry of Finance. During the same period, the possibilities for agencies to engage in commercial activities shrank. Anxieties were expressed concerning the dangers of cross-subsidization, and the difficulties of detecting it. Following pressure from the Dutch employers' organization (itself responding to lobbying from medium and small businesses) a new government-wide doctrine emerged to the effect that agencies must not compete with the private sector, and should sell off activities which were potentially profitable (Cohen Committee, 1997). As we shall see in a later chapter, this directly affected the Dutch meteorological office (KNMI). All in all, being an agency ceased to be very 'sexy'.

Early in the twenty-first century, however, agencies made something of a 'comeback'. A new generation of agency proposals came forward for active consideration (see, e.g. Ministerie van Verkeer en Waterstaat, 2002). At the time of writing approximately 20 new agency proposals are in circulation, and it is estimated that eventually 70–80 per cent of civil servants may be working in *agentschappen*. Politically, agencies seem to have regained their attractiveness for a mixture of reasons. The continuing critique of ZBOs, and the increasingly elaborate regulation of ZBO-creation probably helped to make that form less tempting. At the same time the stalling of the proposal to extend accruals accounting to ministries themselves refreshed the financial autonomy of agencies (see Kraak and Osteroom, 2002). In 2002 an evaluation by the Ministry of Finance was modestly positive, indicating that there was a general tendency for agency status to lead to an increasing goal-and-results orientation (Ministrie van Financiën, 2002). Yet the traffic was not all one-way. In the social security field, as we shall see in Chapter 9, certain autonomous and semi-autonomous bodies were pulled back more closely into the orbit of the relevant ministry. ZBOs have become agencies, and some agency functions have been re-absorbed into ministries, though, like the United Kingdom, not on a large scale. Furthermore extensive dissatisfaction began to be expressed over the increasingly cumbersome regulations of the agencification process (see, e.g. Ministry of Finance, 2001).

After more than a decade of agency creation, and more than two decades of expansion in the population of ZBOs, we may ask what assessments the Dutch have made of these semi-autonomous and more autonomous organizational forms. The Netherlands is a country where programme and policy evaluation has been fairly widely practised (a 1991 survey recorded 300 evaluations being undertaken across 14 ministries) but relatively little of this effort seems to have been focussed upon management reforms *per se*. For example, many ZBOs were created during the 1980s, but, writing in the mid-1990s, one Dutch expert considered that their performance was a blind spot (Leeuw, 1995). Certainly there does not seem to have been any overall evaluation of the reforms or even of significant sections of them, such as the 'great operations' of the Lubbers I and II administrations. There have, however, been a few academic assessments (e.g. Van Thiel, 2001). Some questioning of the reforms has certainly come from the national court of audit (Algemene Rekenkamer). In particular, they published a 1995 report which was highly critical of the lack of public accountability of some ZBOs. For example, the report indicated that only 22 per cent of the ZBOs surveyed produced performance indicator data for their parent ministries. Financial control procedures were often weak and in some cases the legal basis for certain tasks was not clear (Algemene Rekenkamer, 1995). This contributed to the 'primacy of politics' debate referred to above.

More recently the Ministry of Finance sponsored at least two assessments of the programme of creating agencies (Ministerie van Financien, 1998, 2002). Despite the original promise that agencies would all have clearly measurable and costable products, the quantitative analysis in these two evaluations is limited. In brief, no evidence is shown that, for a majority of the organizations concerned, agency status has led to greater measurable efficiency. However, the 1998 evaluation claimed that measured efficiency increases had taken place at 7 of the 14 agencies reviewed, and that all possessed performance indicator sets (although possession is not necessarily active use, as we shall see). It also acknowledged that training staff to cope with the new systems of financial management and accounting was a major task. In its conclusions, it argued that the original preconditions for agency status had been insufficient, and suggested that three new conditions should henceforth be applied:

- The activities of the organization should be separated out into definable products and services.
- There must be a clear indication of how efficiency improvements would be tracked and measured. A basic formulation would be unit cost per product plus a quality measure.
- There must be an external result-oriented planning and control system (Kickert, 2000, p. 100).

The 2002 evaluation indicated that agency status usually encourages a greater goal-orientation – a rather 'softer' claim than the enthusiasts originally made for the agency format, a decade previously. It mainly consisted of a systematic check on what management practices were or were not in place in each agency, but no direct measurement of efficiency changes.

Conclusions: some key issues concerning Dutch agencies

The story of the Dutch agency is greatly complicated by the parallel story of the more autonomous Dutch ZBO. As a proportion of central government activity, the Dutch agency programme is much more modest than the UK Next Steps programme, but that is partly because it has always proceeded in the shadow of an unprogrammatic, yet extensive 'ZBO-ization'. The steady, piecemeal creation of hundreds of ZBOs has 'autonomized' more money and staff than agencies yet have. ZBOs have been mentioned here (and will be mentioned further later, because one of our set of Dutch case studies is a ZBO) because it is important to 'read' the two stories side by side. Read together, it can be seen that Dutch central government has been very willing to put 'at arm's length' a very substantial number and range of public activities (Van Thiel and Van Buuren, 2001; Van Thiel, 2004). Most of the debate has been about just how far to go, not about the direction of travel.

A second salient feature of the Dutch agency programme is that, in practice if not in theory, it has developed in a narrower way than either the Finnish or the UK agency reforms. Specifically, non-financial performance measurement, though definitely present, does not seem to have 'soaked in' to the same extent. The 1998 evaluation indicated that quality indicators were frequently lacking. Agencification, Dutch-style, has been mainly about financial and accounting flexibilities (Smullen, 2004). The full development of this point must await the later chapters on specific functions, but suffice it to say here that the performance indicator culture has put down much deeper roots in the United Kingdom than in the Netherlands.

A third feature of the Dutch programme is that it has developed at a relatively modest pace. At the time of writing it is roughly ten years since the programme began. Roughly 30 per cent of Dutch civil servants now work in agencies, and the debate about performance indicator frameworks, although quite sophisticated, has yet to result in a major, publicly accessible databank on service quality and performance. Agencies have been in and out of fashion. Compare that to Next Steps in the United Kingdom, where, after 10 years, more than 75 per cent of civil servants worked in agencies, and there was a comprehensive annual report to Parliament on hundreds of performance indicators. Even in Finland (Chapter 3) the agency reforms of 1994–96 were quite drastic and rapid, involving the large scale downsizing and re-tasking of a number of major national boards. And in Sweden, well over 90 per cent of civil servants work in agencies rather than in ministries. If current proposals in Den Haag all come to fruition, then the scale of Dutch agencification will soon leap ahead, but consideration of the history of Dutch reform proposals should caution us to wait and see what is actually implemented.

Finally, we can try to summarize the Dutch story using the conceptual framework developed in Chapter 2. There we characterized the recent international enthusiasm for executive agencies as being constructed along three dimensions – structural disaggregation, management autonomy and performance 'contracting'. How does the Dutch trajectory appear with respect to these three components?

First, Dutch agencies are structurally disaggregated. They have their own titles and chief executives, their own organization charts, buildings and logos (though some, like the royal meteorological institute, also had these *before* agency status). However, unlike ZBOs, this disaggregation has virtually no basis in law – it is just an administrative convenience, of no particular constitutional significance. In this respect the

Netherlands is like the United Kingdom but unlike Sweden (see Chapter 5).

Second, the degree of autonomization – of delegated authority and discretion – is real but not huge. It has been most marked in the financial sphere. With respect to personnel freedoms, agencies have not proceeded much faster than general civil service reforms, and could not be described as possessing much greater autonomy than their parent ministries. Unlike ZBO staff, agency employees have the same legal status as civil servants. Agencies also have significant freedom with respect to their internal organizational structures – they can adopt new forms of organization without having to check every detail with the parent ministry. To sum up, the overall autonomy of Dutch agencies could be said to be somewhat less than most UK Next Steps agencies, and much less than Swedish agencies. They have not travelled far from their ministerial 'homes'. On the other hand, this 'finding' has to be read in conjunction with other considerations. One is that, as in other countries, there is considerable variance between different agencies – something we will explore in depth in later chapters. Another is that, as has been said above, Dutch agencies exist in the shadow of Dutch ZBOs – many of which have enjoyed very considerable autonomy indeed.

Third, there is the issue of performance contracting (or quasi-contracting). As in Finland (Chapter 3), what we find here is that performance contracting and results steering are all there in theory, but often turn out to be lacklustre or ritualistic in practice. The Ministry of Finance evaluations do not show all or most Dutch agencies operating within a vibrant, constantly self-improving regime of target setting and seeking. Neither Finnish nor Dutch ministries seem keen (or perhaps capable) to engage their agencies in a demanding performance dialogue. Certainly there *are* targets (and these are changed and refined) but the question is: what status do these have and how are they used in ministry/agency relations? Cultural change seems slow in coming, and the emphasis of the current Balkende coalition on results must be judged by just that – results – rather than by popular rhetoric. At present there is no strong, overarching framework of the kind that exists in the United Kingdom, and which has been re-enforced under the Labour administration since 1997 (by the advent of Public Service Agreements and other measures). Again, though, there is considerable variation between agencies, and we will pursue this issue more deeply in later chapters.

All in all, one might say that, considered against the 'tripod' model, Dutch agencies appear to have three half legs! They are structurally disaggregated, but this disaggregation has no legal or constitutional reinforcement. They have additional operational autonomy, but mainly on the narrow – if important – front of accounting and fiscal freedoms. They have all the paraphernalia of performance indicators and agreements, but there is at least a suspicion that hitherto these have been more for decoration than for active steering by parent ministries.

5
Sweden

Introduction

The Swedish national context offers a distinctive case from which to view the trajectory of agency reform. This is because organizational separation between implementing and making policy has long characterized the administrative features of the Swedish State. Swedish agencies have not been recently created, but rather have had a long history as structurally separate and independent bodies from Swedish *departementen*. Far from justifications about efficiency or performance, this characteristic of the Swedish administration has evolved from historical events and political arguments about the separation of powers, bureaucratic neutrality and state continuity (Andersson, 2001). Even the term 'agency' is not exactly an accurate translation of the Swedish title of these independent bodies. Rather, this title *myndigheter* is more akin to the English term 'authority'[1] – though even Swedish commentators have adopted the term 'agency' in their (recent) contributions to international discussions (Larsson, 2001; OECD, 2002b; Pierre, 1995).

In spite of these important distinctive features of agencies in Sweden, there have also been a number of recent reform initiatives that attend to issues quite familiar to general international discussions about agencies and their attributes. In particular, financial reforms and the formalization of a number of political expectations about agency performance have been features of the agency reform trajectory in Sweden. Legislation and the budget have been the primary means by which these expectations have been made more explicit. In this chapter we will describe the political and administrative context in Sweden, the debates and character of recent reforms, as well as the dimensions of Swedish agencies.

The Swedish context

The political system

The political system in Sweden has been widely described as collective and consensual (Larsson, 1995; Lijphart, 1999, Pollitt and Bouckaert, 2000). This characterization is based upon formal elements of the Swedish constitution that prescribe collective decision-making within the government, and thus almost totally exclude individual ministerial rule and responsibility (Larrson, 1995, p. 50). Some (Swedish) commentators have gone so far as to state that the 'principle of ministerial rule is regarded as something negative, even reprehensible in Sweden' (Larsson, 1995, p. 50). This is reflected in the term '*ministerstyre*', which has been used negatively to describe a minister who is too active in directing the administration, and has been deemed unconstitutional by some (SOU, 1983, pp. 39, 99). The role of Prime Minister in Sweden also has a more collective character about it, since, unlike in the United Kingdom, it is much less about taking hard decisions alone or putting a personal stamp on political direction, and more about coordinating one's team and getting the best out of them. Consensus in the Swedish political system is apparent in the use of proportional representation to elect members of parliament, the committee system of law-making and the informal relations that have been found to characterize the policy-making process (ESV, 1999, p. 19).

In the terminology of political scientists Sweden is a unitary decentralized state (Lijphart, 1999). There is a strong local government tradition, and the local level has been permitted to pursue its own political and policy agendas. It has a constitutional monarch, but this role is almost exclusively ceremonial. The Swedish Parliament has been unicameral since 1970 and presently has 349 seats. As in Finland, many of the Riksdag members are also active at the local level, and bring attention to municipal interests at the national level. The Social Democratic party in Sweden is the largest political party and has with it the longest experience in governing, however, there are seven other political parties represented in the Riksdag today. The most important of these are the Conservatives, the Liberals and the Christian Democrats. The role of review in Swedish politics is generally undertaken by committees and parliamentary auditors appointed by the Parliament.

The politico-administrative culture

As in Finland there is a strong technocratic administrative culture in Sweden, as well as a tendency to be quite legalistic. While recognizing the dangers of pigeonholing any nationality, there is evidence to suggest that the Swedes take a very rational approach to administration with great efforts being taken to use extensive and objective information in decision-making processes (Anton, 1980, viii). Historical analyses and – at the least the emulation of – scientific methods are typical of the ways discussions about good administration, planning and policy are conducted (Premfors, 1983). This is not a context in which verbosity and flamboyance is appropriate but rather a place where the emphasis is upon getting things done. Instrumental and pragmatic approaches – or at least the appearance of these – dominate the administrative culture.

There is also a fairly egalitarian and consensual approach to administration, at least compared to the United Kingdom, although some commentators have suggested that consensus has been on the decline in Sweden (Premfors, 1981, 1983). Like in Finland, Sweden remains a fairly homogeneous society where administrative elites are generally well acquainted with one another. This promotes an element of informality throughout both the political and administrative system, and informal contacts have been found to be an important means of getting things done in Sweden. With respect to Swedish agencies, Pierre (2004) has argued that their informal relations with ministries have provided a kind of coping mechanism for their traditional independence. In Hofstede's scheme we have already seen that Sweden rates relatively low on individualism, although higher than Finland (see Table 3.1), and also quite low with respect to the power differential. Hierarchy is something to be avoided in Sweden.

The administrative system

The Swedish administration is composed of ten government *departementen* as well as a government office. There are also some 300 state agencies responsible for the administration of government policy. Some of these agencies have branches at the regional level, and there is also an administrative apparatus at the municipal level. Most observers of Sweden's administrative system point to two distinctive features: its dual structure of small policy-making ministries and numerous agencies, and the extensive decentralization of responsibility to local and regional levels (Larsson, 1995; Pierre, 1995). The dual administrative structure in Sweden can hardly be exaggerated – in 2002 there were a total of 220 000 employees working in central agencies in Sweden and just 5000 employees working in the ministries.[2] The personnel ratio between ministries and agencies has actually declined substantially over the last ten years with just 3500 employees working in the ministries and 361 000 employees working in agencies in 1992. At the municipal level there are approximately 734 000 employees (OECD, 1997). Without wishing to downplay the substantial role that the municipal level clearly has in the Swedish administration, we will focus primarily upon the central level in this chapter.

Agencies in Sweden are separate from ministries by virtue of the Swedish Constitution. This recognizes both the structural separation of administrative agencies from ministries, as well as prescribing them some independence. Indeed, the Swedish Constitution grants administrative agencies the same rights of judicial review as the courts. This is expressed in what is sometimes referred to as the 'independence principle' or rather *själfständighetsprincipen*, which states:

> Neither any public authority, nor the Riksdag, nor the decision making body of a local government commune may determine how an administrative authority shall make its decision in a particular case concerning the exercise of public authority against a private subject or against a commune, or concerning the application of law.
> (Larsson, 1995, p. 58)

The government can set the framework within which administrative independence takes place through such instruments as government ordinances which may define aspects of how the law should be interpreted or the goals of particular agencies. Despite collective rule and the 'independence principle', the responsibility for supervising and financing administrative agencies is distributed functionally among individual ministries. It can be said, however, that there is a more diluted sense of ministerial ownership of agencies in Sweden compared with the United Kingdom for example, where agencies are considered very much a part of the Ministry empire.

Agencies dominate the administrative scene at the national level although at least two other kinds of organizational forms, public enterprises and state companies, can also be observed in the public sector. A distinction is made in Sweden between civil service work (*centrala ämbetsverk*) and public service enterprises (*central affärsverk*), where civil service work is primarily occupied with public tasks and goals while enterprises combine public goals with commercial activities.[3] All the agencies that we have examined in this research have been occupied with civil service work although the Swedish Meteorological Institute has an exceptional status (see Chapter 8). Public enterprises or *Affärsverk* are a dying breed in Sweden with most of them, including Swedish Post, being reorganized into State Companies or privatized during the 90's. Today, only three *Affärsverk* continue to exist, including the Civil Aviation Service and the Electricity Grid. The demise of this organizational type would seem to be part of an attempt by Swedish government to 'cultivate' the public sector through applying a rationale that distinguishes strictly between organizations with commercial goals and those without (Premfors, 1999, p. 161). Finally, there are also 59 State Companies or *Statliga Bolag* in Sweden. These are mandated under the Swedish Limited Liability Incorporation Act. The majority of state companies are entirely state owned, although there are some exceptions where state shares are as small as 9.5 per cent.

There is a strong tradition of administrative law in Sweden and it has been classified as a *rechtstaat* (Loughlin and Peters, 1997; Pollitt and Boukaert, 2000, p. 53). This is apparent from the integrating role that the State has played in Swedish society, particularly in its heyday of 'social planning' after the Second World War (Anton, 1980; Davidson, 1989). In addition, *Rechtstaat* principles are evident in the widespread use of the law to define the roles of different state actors, and also to restrain them from abuses of power. The constitutional recognition of administrative independence, for example, has been interpreted as protecting administrative agencies from political interference in the realm of applying the law (see Lundell, 1994, p. 118), and is one indication of the way respect for the law has been institutionalized in the Swedish administration. 'Equality before the law' also remains an important concept in discussions about public administration in Sweden and is an argument for maintaining administrative independence (SOU, 1983, p. 39).

Another way in which the legal character of Swedish administration manifests itself is in the educational background of civil servants. In the past a majority of civil servants have had legal training, and this still remains prominent, though not dominant, in the profiles of many Swedish '*ambetsmannen*'. As in Finland, there is a career civil service with political and mandarin careers usually kept separate. Political appointees within the departments include the senior secretary, information officials and some spokesmen (Pierre, 1995, p. 143). There has been extensive discussion about political appointments at the agency level as a means to assert government control over agencies (SOU, 1985, p. 40). Directors of agencies and members of agency boards are to be appointed by the Government, although the extent to which this has happened, particularly in the case of boards, is not clear. During the late 1970s/early 1980s there was some concern that the civil service had become too dominated by Social Democratic supporters and that this obstructed the introduction of the then non-socialist government's policies. Today, one suspects that the civil service in Sweden is far less politically homogeneous than it may have been in the past.

A final note to make about the administrative system in Sweden is that the responsibility for reform initiatives has become much more the terrain of the Ministry of Finance and more specifically its budget unit. In the early 1980s the social democratic government had established a new department, *Civildepartementet*, to coordinate and develop policies concerning the public sector but this was reorganized and dismantled within quite a short period of time. Also the Swedish Agency for Public Management, which had been reporting to the *Civildepartementet*, has now become answerable to the Ministry of Finance. There tends to be quite a slow process in introducing public sector reforms, at least compared with the United Kingdom, since new initiatives or evaluation of perceived problems in the current system go through the commission system which involves a number of actors and substantial time.

Reforming Swedish agencies

Since agencies are the primary way in which policies are implemented at the central level of government, most public sector reform debate has been about and directed at them. We, like many others, will begin our account of the reform period with the 1976 election of the first government for 40 years without Social Democratic participation. By pointing to 'troublesome and unnecessary bureaucracy', this government put public sector effectiveness and savings high upon the political agenda (Sundström, 2001, p. 9; Tarschys, 1983). A number of commissions were instigated to articulate the bureaucracy problem, not least the commission reports *Renewal through reexamination* (SOU, 1979, p. 61), and *Political Steering and Administrative Independence* (SOU, 1983, p. 39). These reports set the framework for debate about public sector reform and also for defining the bureaucracy problem in terms of automatism in the budget, a shift in decision-making powers from the political sphere to the bureaucracy, and barriers to steering the Swedish State (SOU, 1979, p. 61, 1983, p. 39). Far from very focussed analyses about management techniques, it was arguments about democracy that were being used in these reports to identify the most appropriate trajectory of reform.

Indeed, in order to address the issues of budgetary automatism, the shift in decision-making powers and barriers to steering – all matters that were documented in the reports – an analysis of the Constitution was conducted in order to define the appropriate roles of state actors. More specifically, a reconsideration of the Constitution was required because in Sweden, the prominent view that the administration was constitutionally prescribed as independent contradicted political attempts to control or reform it. *Political Control and Administrative Independence* produced the conclusion that the government was empowered to steer the administration, even in aspects of law, because the Constitution stated that 'central authorities and administrative work is subordinate to the government' (SOU, 1983, pp. 39, 45). It also found that the Parliament should be more active in its role to require the Government to report upon its activities within the administration (SOU, 1983, pp. 39, 98–100). Although hardly a closed matter, since many actors later refuted this finding, the administrative independence of agencies was found not to preclude them from 'democratic steering', which meant they should conform to the intentions of government as defined in the political sphere, as well as be responsive to citizens.

As a consequence of these reports, three potential trajectories of reform were identified and these were all proposed to improve the steering of agencies. The three trajectories were:

- Return decision-making to the political sphere and strengthen its capacity for steering.
- Increase political control over agencies through political appointment to leading positions and/or by decentralizing these organizations to the commune level.
- Increase market steering and stimulate responsiveness to customers.

By the early 1980s the Social Democrats had returned to government and were also keen to show their commitment to public sector reform. They did this by introducing their own *Renewal Programme* in 1985. Though pursuing reforms that fitted into all three of the above strategies, they were principally against privatization, keeping 'market strategies' to ideas of being more customer orientated or using voucher schemes. Also, they focussed primarily upon increasing political control and decentralization (Premfors, 1991, p. 85).

It should be noted that while the discourse of the 'Renewal Programme' also maintained a strong link between notions of democracy and public sector reform, it did this in a somewhat different way to that which occurred in earlier commission reports. The emphasis was now much more upon involving the users of public services in defining service requirements, and the catch phrase became 'from authority culture towards a service culture'. Some strategies to increase political control of the bureaucracy were also pursued, ordinances relating to the appointment of agency directors were introduced, as well as rules about agency board types and the selection of their members, and attempts to specify agency goals.

Changes to the budget were also initiated in 1988 when the budget law was changed to introduce three-year budgets. This initiative followed a period of testing a detailed three-year budget on 20 agencies (Brunsson, 1995, p. 11). The budget change followed earlier attempts at Programme Budgeting, and was one of the most significant changes of the period, since it established what is now the common practice in Sweden of using the budget to maintain political and financial control over agencies. With regard to earlier debates about the Constitution, the budget was also a convenient instrument of political control, since it was explicitly recognized in the Constitution as a power belonging to the government and the parliament. There was no Constitutional confusion about the ability of the government to reform budgetary arrangements.

Although the detailed three-year budget was already being dismantled in the early 1990s, as financial crisis was taking hold (Fortin, 1996), many of the conventions created with the detailed three-year budget remained. For example, they still set three-year limits to total expenditure in Sweden; however, many aspects of the proposal for a detailed budget such as a revolving three-year cycle for each agency were not continued. In addition, although the budget appropriations for different agencies had long been presented to the parliament in the *regleringsbrevet* (government letter), with the three-year budget this had also become the medium in which political objectives and reporting requirements could be communicated to agencies (RRV, 1998, p. 93). It was no longer merely a financial document but became a means by which governments could steer agencies, even after the dismantling of the detailed three-year budget. In addition, agencies were required to report back some performance measures relating to the objectives in the following budget year, and a 2 per cent savings standard had been set (Brunsson, 1995, p. 114). These aspects also remained institutionalized in the budget process, with annual reports being required as part of the budget process from 1992. Saving requests brought a new strain of automatism in the budget up to the present day. The term 'results steering' (*resultatstyrning*) had also entered the reform vocabulary after 1992.

As in the Netherlands, reform of agencies became very financially orientated, at least after the 1988 budgetary reforms and was no doubt stimulated by the financial crisis (Premfors, 1998, p. 151). Of course, there were other kinds of reforms going on after this time such as the 'privatisation' of some 13 agencies into public companies (Pollitt and Boukaert, 2000, p. 254), but the financial theme was most prominent. The *Civildepartement* – which had been created during the Renewal period and given responsibilities to co-ordinate public sector reforms – was reorganized and the Ministry of Finance took over their role in initiating and promoting reforms. In addition, accrual accounting was introduced in 1993 and a number of 'financial freedoms' regarding savings and investment decisions were delegated to agency managers (ESV, 2001). Periodic financial reporting was also refined and the requirements for financial reporting on both monthly and six monthly basis were made more explicit (Prop. 1996–97, p. 150).

The budget continued to be a central object of reform and attained a much more top-down character from 1996 (Blondell, 1998). This was quite revolutionary in consensus-orientated Sweden. The fiscal year was changed to correspond with the calendar year and a very clear formal procedure was put in place, with each step in the process being explicitly associated with an appropriate time frame and particular documents (see Brunsson, 1995, 2002). Agencies were required to supply their annual reports and budgetary requests before the end of January, and were to receive their yearly directives (in the *regleringsbrevet*) for the coming year in early December. The top-down character of this new budget format was expressed in at least two ways. First, a three-year ceiling for the entire budget was introduced and was to be proposed by the cabinet in early March. This proposal was then decided on by the parliament. They also set corresponding limits for each expenditure area, which were then to be voted upon in Parliament. This reduced the capacity of different agencies to negotiate their appropriations since many of them had only just made their requests when these negotiations were taking place. It also meant that any negotiations about appropriations could be restrained, since they would have to be fought out within expenditure areas. Although there remained expectations about good performance with this change in the budget, it became apparent that there was always going to be a limit to the kinds of (financial) rewards that could be offered for good performance.

More recently, the budget unit of the Ministry of Finance has made further proposals for a more integrated performance budgeting system in Sweden. These proposals have emerged from a workgroup entitled VESTA (in Swedish this stands for 'instrument for economic steering of the state') which included (sometimes less enthusiastic) representatives from other ministries (see Ehn, 2001). Their proposals included identifying a number of objectives in the political arena for policy areas, programme areas and then sub-programmes which concerns those activities conducted within individual agencies. The budget unit envisions goal setting that will tie the activity goals of particular agencies with wider objectives at the programme and policy levels (Ministry of Finance, 2001; DS, 2000). Their ambition is to put the national budgetary accounts on the same footing as those of the accounts of agencies, by moving the budget to full accruals (Ministry of Finance, 2001). Some movement towards introducing the recommendations of VESTA was seen in the budget bill of 2001 when 47 policy areas were distinguished.

Although the exchange of performance information has clearly been a significant part of Sweden's budgetary reforms, there is only sparse evidence suggesting that it is actually being used to make resource decisions, or in political debate. The impetus for the VESTA project was after all, the limited role that agency reporting has had upon budgetary decisions (Ministry of Finance, 2001). Brunsson has also argued that annual reports have been perceived as documents required purely for auditors rather than for assisting in political decision-making. She has also noted that '(O)nly rarely have Members of Parliament explicitly employed the information on agency accomplishments that the Government has provided in the budget bills.' Further, she has found that, in a period of ten years, only 22 references to annual reports have been made during legislation procedures, even though there was a total of 30 229 private bills initiated during this time (Brunsson, 2002, p. 95). We might be able to give good accounts of the kinds of reforms that have been initiated in Sweden but their effects are still quite questionable.

Swedish agencies in the twenty-first century

In Chapter 2 we mentioned three dimensions – structural disaggregation, performance contracting and management autonomization – that have characterized the agency reform debate in different countries. We also suggested that national agency reforms may often have only embraced one or two of these dimensions, and that the trajectory of agency reform may be different in different countries. In Sweden, we can already say that the trajectory of agency reform is distinct from that in the Netherlands and the United Kingdom, because strong structural disaggregation has long characterized the administration. Indeed, as discussed in the previous section, most of the reforms affecting agencies have been intended to tighten the surveillance of agencies and even curb their administrative independence. To get a glimpse into how Swedish agencies are steered and managed in the present century, it is useful to revisit our three dimensions, and discuss their relevance in Sweden.

Structural disaggregation

The 'independence principle' in the Swedish Constitution and its recognition of an organizational split between the government offices (ministries) and the central administration (agencies) is the primary way in which structural disaggregation has characterized central government–agency relations in Sweden. However, debates about the 'democratic deficit' in the early 1980s and the concern that independent agencies were out of reach of both politicians and citizens, gave greater impetus to establishing more political control over agencies. This has led to a greater formalization of the separation between agencies and the government through government ordinances. The controversies over the constitutional independence of agencies seems to be have been left somewhat aside, and greater clarity about the role of agencies has been pursued by passing a Government ordinance that defines the main objectives of individual agencies, as well as the values they should seek to uphold.

Two kinds of Government ordinances have been created in order to clarify the political expectations that are required of administrative agencies. There is a general ordinance which identifies a framework of criteria that all agencies should comply to, and a more specific ordinance for each agency, where their goals and tasks are identified with reference to this framework (Molander *et al.*, 2002, pp. 73–4; SFS, 1987, p. 1100; SFS, 1995, p. 1332). These ordinances identify rather general goals such as avoiding unnecessary increases in costs, guaranteeing co-operation with other agencies to promote benefits to the government as a whole, and ensuring that contact with the general public and other parties is characterized by good service and accessibility. While it may be that these ordinances have involved greater political clarification about the expected role of agencies, they are hardly very precisely worded or focussed documents. As others have noted:

> (A)gency instructions point out the broad direction of agency activities, and they provide a large set of boundary restrictions but it is obvious they do not provide a basis for accountability enforcement. (Molander *et al.*, 2002, p. 75)

Another way in which the structural disaggregation of Swedish agencies has become more formalized is with respect to political decision-making about board types and board composition. Most agencies in Sweden have a board and Government ordinances have now also been used to clarify what board type is appropriate for a particular agency. Larsson (2000, p. 138) distinguishes three types of governing boards in Sweden: the one-man rule, and two different board principles. When the one-man rule (*enrådighetsmodellen*) applies, the head of the agency makes all the decisions of the agency but often appoints an advisory committee to assist in making these decisions and offering insight into the agency's performance. The most common arrangement regarding board principles is a 'limited responsibility' board (*collegiale modellen*), which is chaired by the Director General (DG) and includes other members that have been appointed for a period of three years. Alternatively, there are also boards with 'extended responsibility' where the DG is not the chairperson of the board, although she may be a member, and the members have a one-year mandate (*lekmannastyrelsen*). The members of this board are generally individuals recruited outside of the agency. It should be noted that both board members and Directors of agencies in Sweden are political appointments, and have also been seen as a way to ensure the compliance of agencies, although expertise is also essential (Pierre, 2004).

A final point to make about the structural separation between agencies and ministries is that attempts to formalize the arrangement have not eroded the wealth of informal relationships that exist across this divide. The informal relationships between agencies and ministries have long been documented in Sweden (Anton, 1980) and may be interpreted as a kind of coping mechanism for the traditional independence of Swedish agencies. Pierre (2004) has argued that these informal contacts have been instrumental to successful policymaking and implementation. In our interviews, it became apparent that most of our agencies had quite regular contact with staff in the ministries. This was not primarily with respect to performance issues but policy matters more generally. As one interviewee stated, 'I mean I am having contact with the Ministry once or twice a week.' The interviews in the ministries also tended to confirm regular contact with the agencies, although the interest from the ministries did seem to be greater the bigger and more politically significant the agency. Social security inspired far more interest than meteorology or forestry. Leaving aside the variation in contact between different agencies and their ministry, it might be said that informal contacts in Sweden act to reduce structural disaggregation.

Performance contracting

Recent budget reforms in Sweden would also indicate that there has been some movement along the dimension of performance contracting. However, it should be said that the term 'contract' has not appeared very frequently, if at all, in Swedish discussions about agency reform (see DS, 2000, p. 63; SOU, 1985, p. 40). Instead, descriptions of setting objectives or reporting requirements, tend to adopt such terms as steering, result steering, management by objectives or performance budgeting. In personal correspondence with Swedish observers of public sector reform, the absence of the term 'contract' is generally explained with respect to the Constitutional status of Swedish agencies. On the one hand, it is argued that the idea of a contract within government is only appropriate where the agency is part of the ministry, but since the Swedish Constitution defines agencies as organizationally separate from Ministries/the Minister, a contract is not relevant. On the other hand, it has been suggested that the term 'contract' to describe relations between ministries/government and agencies would be too provocative in Sweden because it would imply that the *independence principle* of Swedish agencies was being ignored and that ministers were indulging in *ministerstyre* (see Blondell, 2001, p. 15). This argument would suggest that the validity of political control of the administration still remains questionable in Sweden.

Leaving aside the term 'contract', we have observed that agencies are required to follow a clearly defined budgetary process with clearly defined documents, produced at clearly defined times (Brunsson, 1995, 2002). This process includes the written communication of objectives and performance requirements as well as a follow-up procedure. The government letter of appropriation or *regleringsbrevet* which is sent to agencies at the beginning of the budget year (currently end December) has been described as the most important document for the government to steer Swedish agencies (RRV, 1993, p. 22). Ministries are responsible for preparing this document, although informally, agencies also contribute to its contents. While improvements in directives have been noted over the years (RRV, 1994, pp. 34, 31), in general they have been characterized as vague, unsuitable for measurement, or general goals without an indication of how they should be reported (Molander *et al.*, 2001, p. 79).

Our research would also suggest that the performance goals tended to be articulated in very broad political priorities and with limited specificity. Indeed, there seemed to be the view among agencies that the *regleringsbrevet* was not designed to set specific targets but was more about establishing broader political priorities. This is illustrated by the following interviewee response, 'The government makes more vague requests, they give us a framework and we make the details.' Or

> (T)here are policy goals and economic goals that we get from parliament and the government but then our board must interpret these into sector goals, we have to integrate them into the practice. The goals that we get given from government are not measurable we must interpret them.

Among the different functions we examined, there was quite some variation in the precision with which performance measures were requested, with AMS, the social insurance agency, being subject to the most stringent regime of measures (see Chapter 10). A broader conceptualization of the idea of performance was also evident with respect to personnel issues. Most respondents rejected the appropriateness of performance pay in the Swedish public sector, and considered training and a good working environment as more conducive to better performance. This emphasis was also reflected in the collection of a wealth of statistics about personnel, and reporting back about such matters as gender distribution and training. We might conclude from these observations that performance tends to have much wider connotations in Sweden (the exception being financial performance – see below) than the more focussed agenda setting that takes place in the United Kingdom (see Chapter 6).

The 'reporting back' of agency performance is presented in the agency annual reports (Brunsson, 1995; RRV, 1994; Wilks, 1995). These have also been in use since 1992 and they should be submitted to Government by January each year (Regeringskansliet, 2000). The information in the annual reports should not only relate to the directives, but is also guided by an ordinance that identifies a standardized information list of what agencies should report (SFS, 1996, p. 882). This information includes time series about personnel, productivity, cost per unit and quality of service (Brunsson, 1995, p. 112), and requires some comment upon the internal and external factors that have affected organizational performance (OECD, 2002b, p. 53). The annual reports are required by law to be audited and these audit reports are submitted to government. Related to the quality of requests in the *regleringsbrevet*, the National Audit Office has at different times expressed concern about the quality of the performance information in the annual reports (OECD, 2001, p. 54).

To complement the financial figures that are reported in the annual report, there is also regular financial reporting between the agency and the Swedish Financial Management Authority (ESV). Every month a list of standard financial information such as the use of appropriations, the collection of income and types of expenditures are sent electronically to ESV (ESV, 2001, p. 8). They compile and analyse this information and then transfer it to the ministries and other agencies such as the National Institute for Economic Research. Quarterly and half-yearly financial reports are also submitted to ESV covering respectively the articles in the National Accounts and the same financial figures required for the annual report (ESV, 2001, p. 8). It was clear in all the agencies visited in Sweden that this financial reporting was supported by quite extensive investments in information technology. In some cases this enabled all unit managers within agencies to have immediate access to the most recently reported figures, as well as figures from the recent past, and to compare these between the regional offices of a particular agency.

Another way in which follow-up of agency performance occurs, and which seems to be rarely discussed in the literature about Swedish agencies, is through the formal yearly dialogue between Agency directors and the Minister, or the Secretary of State in some cases. This dialogue has been referred to as the 'objectives and results dialogue' (Hajlmarsson, 2001, p. 9). It is a structured meeting where a checklist drafted by the Ministry of Finance is meant to guide the issues discussed. In addition, the Directors of agencies have the opportunity to bring up issues regarding the past year, issues affecting the agency and the particular situation of the Director. In the interviews we conducted, there seemed to be quite diverse experiences relayed about these dialogues, while some informants described a routine, 'not very hard' even 'just 30 minutes' talk, others gave indications of a quite sharp and intense discussion. In all cases, it was apparent that this dialogue was seen by agencies as an opportunity to be able to make a plea for a greater slice of the budget.

So far we have described the performance relationship in Sweden as characterized by informal negotiations over the criteria to be reported upon, as well as being quite commodious when it comes to performance definitions. If we are going to talk about a 'performance contract' in Sweden, we need to clarify that this is more an open agreement about the supply of information across wide ranging terrain. It includes some collection of information about specific output and quality of production, but also refers to less tangible political goals, and personnel policies that promote equality of sexes, training and flexibility.

Management autonomy

The reforms of the 1980s and 1990s have also included some movement along the third dimension of management autonomy. This has been most visible in areas of finance and personnel. Since 1988 a total 'frame budget' was allocated annually to agencies; this gave agency managers the ability to make most of their own internal financial decisions (DS, 2000, p. 63). In addition, with the introduction of accrual accounting in 1993, each agency has become its own independent accounting unit, with the ability to carry over 3–5 per cent of the total appropriation at the year's end and to loan from following years. Office space has also become an internal management responsibility, without any central regulations. Indeed, the agency that was previously responsible for agency buildings was transformed into a limited company, and the agencies were given the right to rent premises from any property owner (Murray, 8). Funds collected from commercial activities appeared, in contrast, to be quite stringently regulated (see Chapters 8 and 10). There was a wealth of regulations about keeping commercial finances separate from government accounts, about price setting and competition, as well as many watchdogs to keep an eye on this.

Since 1985 legislation aiming to simplify, decentralize and adapt government staffing policies to market conditions has been introduced. In 1987 an Administrative Act was passed clearly delegating responsibility for employment policy to Agency directors (Ministry of Justice, 2000; SFS, 1987, p. 1100). At this time these delegated responsibilities included decisions about the supply of staff, skills development, and conditions for pay and employment. These changes were made in the spirit of making agency work more amenable to the local context in which they worked. However, the degree to which this delegation effected flexibility in employment policy, particularly with respect to pay and employment conditions, is questionable because of the continuing role of collective bargaining in setting the boundaries within which negotiations can take place. Also, the system where posts were positioned in salary grades was not dismantled until 1990 (www.arbetsgivarverket.se). Currently, individual salaries are negotiated between agency management and individual employees, but this occurs within a context of collective local agreements and also collective union agreements at the central level.

It should be noted that although employment policies have clearly become more deregulated in Sweden there are still a number of government initiatives that aim to effect and regulate the employment policies of agencies. In particular, there is a government ordinance identifying agency responsibility for implementing integration policy. This requires agencies to have an equal opportunity policy promoting gender equality and the position of people with disabilities in the workplace (Ministry of Justice, 2000). Other initiatives that affect the employment policies of all agencies include policies that obligate agencies to promote the training and competence of their individual employees.

A third area in which agency directors would appear to have a great deal of discretion is with regard to organizational design. This said, we have been unable to find any official reference to delegation of organizational design to agency managers, rather we have only observed that most of our agencies referred to recent reorganizations that were initiated by agency directors. In the three agencies that were responsible for supervising and monitoring regional offices (Forestry, Prisons and Social Insurance Agency) there had been organizational changes to make these regional areas bigger. This preference for bigger units would appear to be related to the performance systems that were being adopted in the agencies, since it promoted standardization throughout the organization. The exception to management discretion in organizational design was with respect to commercial activities, since requirements to keep these activities financially separate usually meant that they were also conducted within a separate organizational unit.

Conclusion: some key issues concerning Swedish agencies

Agency reforms in Sweden have generally been pursued under the guise of democratic renewal, although financial considerations also played an important role, particularly from the late 1980s. In the early 1980s, there was the view that independent agencies had been far removed from both community and political influences for too long, and that they needed to be made more answerable to government and to citizens. To this extent agency reform in Sweden has not been about creating a distance between ministries and agencies, but rather reducing this distance.

Second, there is a tendency in Sweden to conceptualize performance in terms of democratic values like equality of the sexes, openness or co-operation, and not just in relation to specific outputs or service quality. Of course, there are requests for more production of information about output volumes or even some outcomes, but these are also accompanied by more general requests about the democratic contribution of agencies to government and society. Perhaps these kinds of performance requests lend themselves less to the kind of specific terms of reference we might expect in a contract-like relationship.

A final note to make about agency reform in Sweden is that it is likely to continue to rely upon informal relationships between agency and ministry staff. This means that any contractual relationship is supported by ongoing exchanges about what can be expected from agencies, and agency expertise. In this way, agencies continue to maintain substantial independence from their small ministerial counterparts.

6
The United Kingdom

The political system

The United Kingdom is the only purely majoritarian system among our four countries. It is also highly centralized (see Figure 3.1, p. 50). This gives the whole political process a significantly different cast from the Dutch, Finnish and Swedish systems. It begins with the electoral system. This has a simple 'whichever individual gets the largest vote in each constituency wins' principle, which has tended to produce dramatic swings in the make-up of the Parliament on the basis of only relatively small swings in voting. Thus the Conservatives won four general elections between 1979 and 1992 with only an average of 44 per cent of the vote while the two New Labour governments elected since 1997 have enjoyed huge majorities in Parliament on only 43 per cent of the vote (in 1997 and 2001). This situation has tended to vary with two factors: the size of 'third party' voting and shifting politico-demographic patterns.

In the United Kingdom there has been an effective two-party system for many years: during most of the nineteenth century it was the Liberals and Conservatives and during most of the twentieth century, the Labour Party and Conservatives after the collapse of the Liberals. Apart from periods of national emergency (during the Great Depression of the 1930s or the Second World War) this has led to majority governments of one party and during most of the twentieth century, it was the Conservatives. In the second half of the century, from 1950 to 2000, the Conservatives ruled for 35 out of 50 years and won 8 out of 13 general Elections.

There are of course other parties and these have sometimes contributed to spectacular results: Labour won a landslide victory in 1945 with a Parliamentary majority of 146 seats on 48.8 per cent of the vote but lost the 1951 Election with 49.4 per cent. This was more than the Tories who only received 47.8 per cent of the vote but who nevertheless won with 26 more seats than Labour. The crucial factors in these two Elections was the collapse of the Liberal vote to the Tories (they fell from 9.2 per cent in 1945 to only 2.6 per cent in 1951) and the geographical distributions of the votes (Labour tended to pile up huge majorities in a minority of seats whereas the Tories vote was more evenly spread across the country). Thus Labour could lose with a higher vote than the Tories and an even higher than in their 1945 landslide victory.

By the start of the twenty-first century these factors had changed – now the Conservatives are more geographically limited and the third-party challenge (the Liberal Democrats) is much stronger (averaging 18 per cent in 1997 and 2001).

The political system would therefore seem to be very adversarial and majoritarian. It certainly has given, coupled with the peculiar constitutional arrangements of the United Kingdom, the Government of the day very strong executive powers to make changes to laws, public finances and organizational arrangements. The paradox of this system is that actually, despite this strong adversarialism in electoral politics, from the Second World War until the election in 1979 of Margaret Thatcher the policies of governments towards the public sector remained largely consensual.

What became known as the 'post-War consensus' actually emerged during the Second World War as a set of planned reforms to welfare policies usually known as the Beveridge reforms (Timmins, 2001). The consensus which emerged during wartime was that the state had to address, and manage, the so-called 'Five Giants': Want, Disease, Ignorance, Squalor and Idleness. Through a mixture of national insurance, taxation, and rents the state would provide for benefits, health services, education, and housing and create employment opportunities. While there were some disagreements about precisely how these were to be achieved there was a broad political consensus that they had to be dealt with by Government – indeed on some fronts the Conservatives and Labour competed in the 1950s over who would provide the biggest benefits (e.g. housing) (Timmins, 2001). Most political controversy focussed not on these welfare issues but on economic management, state intervention (or not) in industry, industrial relations and workers' rights, regulation, defence and foreign affairs.

The Welfare State was politically uncontroversial until 1979 and Margaret Thatcher's commitment to 'roll back the frontiers of the state' and substantially reduce government spending on welfare. How far she succeeded is another issue, but part of the Conservative Government's agenda was the reform of public services, including the Civil Service, to make them more economical, efficient and effective (the so-called 3 E's), although the emphasis was on the first two. We will return later to this reform agenda.

The Constitution

When addressing international audiences we (the authors of this book who come from the United Kingdom) are frequently asked 'can you point us to the legislation on which the creation of Executive Agencies is based please?' Our questioners are usually shocked and somewhat bewildered when we reply that there isn't any. 'How can a government fundamentally change the organization of the Civil Service and create dozens of new public bodies without legislation?' they not unreasonably ask. The reasons are complex and require a quick detour into the murky world of the British Constitution, or rather the lack of one.

Until very recently the United Kingdom had only a single, bi-cameral, Parliament for the whole of the United Kingdom and Northern Ireland with a fully elected House of Commons and an un-elected House of Lords (filled by a mixture of hereditary and appointed Peers). There have been major changes since 1997 with the introduction of a Scottish Parliament and Welsh and Northern Ireland Assemblies and removal from the House of Lords of most hereditary Peers. However the UK Parliament remains the sovereign body, with some very important reservations.

The United Kingdom is often described as a 'constitutional monarchy' which can be misleading. The United Kingdom does not have a written Constitution and thus constitutional arrangements are made up of a mix of laws, common law, conventions and customary practices which are often obscure – one constitutional historian famously described them as the 'hidden wiring' (Hennessy, 1995). This affects the formal position of executive government and the civil service and hence the executive agencies which we examine below.

The Government is conventionally accountable to parliament but is actually appointed not by parliament at all but by the monarch who chooses the prime minister who in turn appoints the cabinet and other ministers. Conventionally the Monarch chooses as the Prime Minister the leader of the largest party in parliament, but this is only a convention and could, in theory, be deviated from (e.g. in the case of a coalition government of two minority parties). What this means is, very importantly, that the Prime Minister and other ministers are actually able to exercise the powers of 'the Crown in Parliament' or what is known as 'Crown Prerogative'. They are accountable to Parliament in one sense, but they also exercise enormous Crown powers (e.g. British prime ministers can declare war or sign treaties without seeking Parliament's approval, although they usually, but not always, do).

A consequence of these arrangements is that the civil service has no formal constitutional or legal basis other than exercising the powers of the Crown through ministers (Harden, 1992; Harden and Lewis, 1986; Hennessy, 1990; Hennessy, 1991). It is not formally accountable to Parliament (although there are accountability arrangements) nor formally independent of Government. This was most strongly expressed in a 1985 Memorandum by the then Head of the Civil Service Sir Robert Armstrong which set out the 'Duties of Civil Servants in Relation to Ministers'. In this Memorandum he wrote: 'Civil Servants are servants of the Crown. For all practical purposes the Crown in this context means and is represented by the Government of the day.' He went on to say 'the Civil Service as such has no constitutional personality or responsibility separate from the duly elected Government of the day'. We will discuss later in this chapter how far this is true in practice, but it does have important constitutional, legal and organizational consequences.

As civil servants have always been seen as 'servants of the Crown' the civil service has never been constituted on a formal legal basis. As a result ministries, agencies, and departments have no formal independent standing in law and the prime minister, and in some cases ministers, can often change the structure and functions of government bodies without recourse to legislation or parliament (Pollitt, 1984). This is why prime ministers can merge, disband, or create new ministries at will and why the creation of executive agencies within the civil service required no legislation or even secondary legislation to do so.

The only legislation which has been passed, covering a small minority of cases, is of two types. Some government bodies are formally set up through legislation: HM Customs & Excise and the Inland Revenue are the most obvious examples.* Both are based on specific Acts of Parliament and as a result any changes affecting their overall status (e.g. the merging of the Contributions Agency into the Inland Revenue) do require legislation. The other example is Trading Fund agencies, where specific generic legislation was introduced in order to give these bodies a separate legal existence so they could trade with commercial organizations. No more than about one in ten agencies ever had this status.

Political-administrative culture

In terms of the very broad cultural categories used by Hofstede, the United Kingdom scores fairly high on individualism (89, where Finland = 63, the Netherlands = 80 and Sweden = 71). On the 'power-distance index' it scores 35 (Finland = 33; the Netherlands = 38; Sweden = 35), putting it in the middle of the fairly egalitarian countries, but well below the more hierarchically conscious French (68) and Italians (50) (see Table 3.1, p. 51). It is a culture where colourful and idiosyncratic politicians are at least tolerated (and sometimes highly regarded as 'national treasures' – one thinks of Lloyd George, Tony Benn and even Margaret Thatcher). However, it is also an environment in which the demands for individual accountability seem to be more insistent than in some of the more consensual/collective polities. Furthermore, it is a political culture which is still centred on an almost medieval notion of dyadic combat – of constant duals between party leaders and between government and opposition. It is these conflicts – sometimes ritualistic, sometimes real – that the mass media focuses on and amplifies, often to an almost obsessive extent. Agencies can be drawn into these tournaments, as we shall see, and when they are 'business as usual' often goes out of the window. We were struck, for example, by how prisons policy seemed to be portrayed in a far more adversarial and dramatic way in the United Kingdom than in Finland or Sweden (see Chapter 7).

More specifically, the constitutional position of relations between government and administration (the civil service) may appear to suggest that the latter is completely dominated by the former: 'the Civil Service as such has no constitutional personality or responsibility separate from the duly elected Government of the day.' In practice the roles have sometimes seemed reversed and the power of the civil service to influence ministers has been a highly controversial issue. The highly successful TV series 'Yes, minister' and 'Yes, prime minister' of the 1980s depicted a hapless minister (and later prime minister) being thoroughly out-manoeuvred by a highly intelligent and urbane Civil Servant Sir Humphrey Appleby. So successful was this image that the term 'Sir Humphrey' has entered popular language in the United Kingdom as a synonym for 'senior Civil Servant.'

While Sir Humphrey may have been a caricature it was based on a widely held view that the Civil Service wielded far too much power. A succession of ex-ministers from the 1960s onwards, of both main Parties, complained about the power of the Whitehall 'Mandarins' (Hennessy, 1990). The supposed power of civil servants in the United

Kingdom is often attributed to longevity – ministers come and go, at an average rate of a couple of years in ministerial office, while the civil servants remain in post (Campbell and Wilson, 1995). Hence the top civil servant in a department is called a 'Permanent Secretary' (as opposed to minister who, as secretary of state, is temporary).

The truth is more complicated – top civil servants rotate their posts almost as quickly as ministers and moreover the UK Civil Service is renowned for having a 'generalist' senior civil service with little specialist training in law, economics or even politics (Ridley, 1968). The results can be that:

> What we get ... is a two-tier dilettantism. It may well happen that both the Permanent Secretary and the Minister arrive simultaneously at a new department. Neither of them has made an intensive study of the problems with which they have to deal ... How purposive positive policy can be formed under these conditions is a mystery, or rather it would be a mystery if purposive policy were formed.
> Thomas Balogh, 1959 (cited in Hennessy, 1990, p. 169)

It is more likely that the feeling of helplessness experienced by some ministers is a combination of occasional individual usurpation by civil servants, civil service systems (which do provide for some continuity) and the simple inertia of a very large system of government programmes which are difficult to change (Rose and Davies, 1994).

Another important issue in UK political-administrative culture is the role of the Treasury. As a combined economics and finance ministry, the Treasury has, until very recently, wielded enormous power within the UK system. This too has probably contributed to ministers' sense of relative powerlessness as the Treasury held tight control of spending allowed to ministries and intervened in policy choices about what money could be spent on (Chapman, 1997; Deakin and Parry, 2000; Pliatzky, 1989; Thain and Wright, 1996).

The administrative system

The so-called 'Whitehall model' of managing the relationship between politics and administration has been defined as 'cabinet government supported by a high-status civil service':

> British governments had the institutional unity, thanks to the combination of legislative and executive leadership in the cabinet, to

implement Keynesian economic policies, whereas hopelessly fragmented American institutions could not. The professional civil service provided politicians with both fearless advice, thanks to a security of tenure comparable to that of university professors, and a smoothly running machine for implementing decisions once they had been made. A career bureaucracy was willing 'to speak truth to power' in a way that American political appointees were not, and, imbued with a strong sense of serving the public interest, was able to overcome the tendencies for the self-interest of individual agencies, so common in the United States, to block the adoption of good public policy. The cabinet and its committees provided a mechanism for reconciling conflicting policy views, goals and departmental interests that countries with political systems other than the Westminster model could only envy. (Campbell and Wilson, 1995)

We will leave aside the Cabinet Government part of this account as it is not especially relevant to our investigation, but suffice it to say that this view is not uncontroversial (Burch, 1995; Hennessy, 1991; Performance and Innovation Unit, 2000a; Weller *et al.*, 1997). We will concentrate on the high status, career, 'speaking truth unto power', public interest serving Civil Service. We have already noted some of the criticisms of this model, or rather its perceived reality.

The civil service is a small, but extremely powerful, part of the UK public service – on average over the past 20–30 years the civil service has only accounted for about one in ten public servants. Varying from a high point of over three-quarters of a million and reducing under the Conservative Governments to around half-a-million, the civil service was nevertheless a large body. Because of the lack of a constitutional position for lower tiers of government (local authorities exist at the discretion of Parliament) and its extensive controls over other parts of public services (the National Health Service, public corporations, quangos, etc.) the central administration disposes of disproportionate powers compared to its relative size (and compared to federal or less centralized systems).

In fact even this can be misleading, as it is only the central parts of Government – the Headquarters of Ministries, Treasury and Cabinet Office – which exercise real power, and these employ probably about one-tenth of civil servants. Most civil servants work in service delivery type organizations (prisons, benefits, taxation, passports, etc.). It is only in the so-called 'Whitehall Village' (Heclo and Wildavsky, 1981) or what has since become known as the 'Senior Civil Service' (Prime Minister and Minister for the Civil Service, 1994, 1995), that budgetary and policy decisions get made.

Within the Whitehall Village a very particular culture operates, with civil servants 'playing the game' of identifying strongly with their (current) ministry but recognizing that because of their generalist nature and the high mobility of their posts they could, for example, just as easily be on the opposite side of the table in the next round of spending negotiations. This creates a strong sense that senior civil servants' role is to take care of 'their' minister and 'their' ministry, especially in relation to other ministries, parliament and the public.

This culture of 'gifted amateurism' and generalism, coupled with an almost symbiotic relationship with the 'government of the day' as suggested by the Armstrong Memorandum, has exposed the Civil Service to sustained criticism over the years. The most frequent such criticism has focussed on lack of managerial ability, failure to understand implementation issues in public policy, failure to evaluate policies and to manage services effectively (Fry, 1981; Fry, 1993; Fulton Committee, 1968; Garrett, 1972; Keeling, 1972; Ponting, 1986).

Within the Whitehall Village then there is a culture of what could be called 'exclusive-collegialism' or what the organizational theorist William Ouchi calls a 'clan culture' (Ouchi, 1981). Within the Village there is a sense that everyone knows everyone else, people play the roles which are (temporarily) assigned to them but recognize the wider need for collective solidarity, especially against the major outside players: Parliament, the public, the rest of the public sector and so on. This has been cemented by the famous lack of Whitehall transparency which creates a space in which issues can be fought over and resolved behind closed doors before being revealed to the world as a complete product. Most emblematic of this is the budget process (Heclo and Wildavsky, 1981; Thain and Wright, 1996) which remains highly secretive and is simply rubber-stamped by Parliament (contrast the role of the US Congress in the budget process (Rubin, 2000; Wildavsky, 1992)).

Public management reform: decision making

The Thatcher governments (1979–90) are credited with introducing a much more centralized, less collegial, style of executive government. While this is arguable in some policy areas, when it came to the reform of public sector institutions and the Civil Service it certainly appears to be true (Flynn, 2002; Metcalfe and Richards, 1990). A series of managerialist reforms to various parts of the public services followed one another over the years (Talbot, 2001b). Reforms of the civil service were the very first to be attempted. When Thatcher came to power in 1979 she immediately introduced a system of 'efficiency scrutinies' within the Civil Service, headed by her Efficiency Adviser, Derek Rayner (a retail executive). These were followed by the Financial Management Initiative (FMI) and still later (1988) by the Next Steps programme of creating executive agencies.

The 'Rayner Scrutinies' are important for our analysis not so much for what they did, but to how they did it. The typical 'scrutiny' model was to gather a small group of young 'fast-track' (i.e. destined for the top) civil servants from several ministries, led by a slightly more experienced person, and give them 90 days to study and report on a problem or issue (Metcalfe and Richards, 1990; Richards, 1997). Over 130 such reviews were conducted but what is most interesting is the way this methodology was extended to other, policy-making, areas such as the Poll Tax (Butler *et al.*, 1994) and, most importantly for us, in the inception of the Next Steps agency reforms (Hennessy, 1990).

Most, if not all, the major reforms to the Civil Service during the period 1979–97 were conceived behind closed doors, usually by relatively small groups of civil servants and advisers, and implemented without any legislation or even in most cases debate in parliament.

The substance of the reforms

The overall public management reform agenda in the run-up to the agency creation drive (1979–88) can be summarized as: if possible move all or parts of public services into the private sector; if that is not possible, introduce some kind of market-type mechanisms and competition within public services; and focus on reducing costs, improving efficiency and injecting rigorous managerial practices.

For the civil service this meant a drive to reduce costs and improve efficiency (the Rayner scrutinies and FMI), to forcibly reduce numbers through closures, to privatize (including some of the executive agencies), reduce staff costs, contract outservices, and so on.

The experience of these reforms was mixed. Costs were cut, but often it was difficult to distinguish between cuts to actual programmes and cuts to the overhead costs (referred to as running or administrative costs) of the civil service (Flynn, 2002; Talbot, 2004). Overall Civil Service numbers were drastically reduced – by a third or more (but overall public service employment stayed more or less stable – see (Talbot, 2001b)). Most interestingly, despite the very high-profile backing of a powerful prime minister some reforms just did not seem to happen.

The lineage of the United Kingdom's massive executive agency programme is usually seen as Rayner Scrutinies to FMI to Agencies. According to Peter Hennessy's account, by 1986 Thatcher had recognized that neither the Rayner scrutinies (which only realized about a third of the proposed savings) nor the FMI had made any fundamental impact on Whitehall. A review, conducted along Rayner scrutiny lines, produced what was eventually published as the *Improving Management in Government: The Next Steps* report (Jenkins *et al.*, 1988). It concluded the previous initiatives simply could not succeed without much larger, structural and cultural, changes to back them up. According to Hennessy the original version of the report was so critical it was delayed until after the 1987 General Election for fear of embarrassment (Hennessy, 1990), which also gave time for the opposition of the Treasury to the proposed reforms to be overcome.

The net result was the Next Steps programme, announced to Parliament in a short statement by Mrs Thatcher in 1988.

Agencies in the United Kingdom

The size and scope of the UK agencies programme is well known and does not need repeating in detail here: suffice it to say that over a 10-year period around 80 per cent of UK Civil Servants were transferred into around 120 agencies or bodies said to be working on agency-lines (e.g. Customs and Excise and Inland Revenue). For general accounts of Next Steps see, for example: (Goldsworthy, 1991; Greer, 1994; James, 2003; Kemp, 1993; O'Toole, 1995).

The original Next Steps report suggested that 'agencies', used as a generic term, might take several forms: agencies within departments; whole departments (as in so-called non-ministerial departments); non-departmental public bodies outside departments (quangos); and even public corporations. However, by the time Thatcher made her statement to Parliament this had already been reduced to only one option: executive agencies within government departments. Thus, in our terminology, agencies were less than 'more autonomous bodies' (MABs) but more than simply departments within a ministry (e.g the status still held by the Immigration and Nationality Department within the Home Office). With their framework documents; Chief Executives on term contracts and accountable directly to ministers (in most but not all cases); and their annual reports, separate budgets and Key Performance Indicators (KPIs) these were clearly something novel in the Whitehall Village. Some current aspects of agencies have evolved since their inception as a programme, while others originally present have mutated. We will examine these through the lens of our 'Tripod' model covering dissagregation or separation; autonomization; and performance.

Separation

To what degree have UK agencies been separated out from their parent ministries? The answer to this question is extremely difficult, even in formal terms. On the one hand, agencies are formally still part of their parent ministry; the Accounting Officer of the ministry (the person who is formally responsible to Parliament and auditors for the stewardship of public money) is also responsible for all the agencies in their ministry whose accounts are included in the overall ministry accounts; agency staff are still civil servants; and the like.

On the other hand, each agency produces its own Annual Report; holds its own budget; its Chief Executive is also an Accounting Officer for the agency (meaning each agency has two Accounting Officers); it reports its own performance; and so on.

The ambiguity of agency status is also affected by the history of each function re-organized into an agency. Most UK ministries were, prior to agency creation, multifunctional organizations. Some were organized internally along these functional lines – for example, the Home Office had separate internal structures organizing prisons, forensic science, fire service training, passports and immigration and nationality. Others, like the Department of Social Security, were organized primarily on a geographical basis, with multifunctional district organizations delivering most of the department's services to the public through a single local structure (although at the actual service delivery level they were divided into separate offices).

When agencies were formed the Home Office simply drew lines around the existing internal structures – one branch of their internal organizational chart for each service delivery function – and designated it as an agency (except Immigration and Nationality). In Social Security, however, a much greater upheaval took place, with the internal structure completely recomposed from geographical to functional: creating single-function national agencies covering Benefits, Contributions, War Pensions, and so on (Greer, 1994).

In fact, most agencies were pre-existing structures (Talbot, 2004) often with a strong identity despite the pledge of the Next Steps Project Manager that the programme would not indulge in what he called 'badge engineering' – that is, simply re-naming a pre-existing structure as an agency (Treasury and Civil Service Committee, 1988).

Many agencies also already had a unique identity in their personnel systems. Around half of all UK Civil Servants worked on grades unique to their organization or functions and half on 'generalist' grades prior to Next Steps, and many personnel matters had already been devolved (Talbot, 1997).

This somewhat ambiguous position is compounded by the informal and cultural issues surrounding agencies. The fact that many already existed as organizational identities within their ministries, reinforced by separate personnel systems, meant that the creation of agencies had less impact than might have been expected at the cultural level.

On the other hand the 'technology of agencies', as one former Next Steps Project Manager has described it (Jeremy Cowper, personal discussion), completely contradicted prevailing Whitehall customs. The whole system of Framework Documents, Quinquennial Reviews of agency status, separate Budgets and Business Plans, Annual Reports, Key Performance Indicators and crucially, Agency Chief Executives reporting directly to Ministers is counter-cultural to Whitehall's ethos of informality, collegiality and clannish behaviour. Indeed the principal architect of implementing the agency programme claims that his forced early retirement was due to reaction within Whitehall against the revolutionary nature of these changes (Kemp, 1993). So the change to agency status of specific organizations, whatever the formal position and history of individual functions and the ambiguity of their position, is seen as significant. They are not truly separate, but neither are they any more simply a part of their parent ministry.

Perhaps the most symbolic aspect of this change has been the public identification of agency Chief Executives and their willingness to speak in public about their agency's work and sometimes even contradict government policy. Prior to Next Steps it was rare for any senior civil servant to appear in public and almost unheard of for them to say anything controversial. However several agency CEs became regular speakers at conferences and even raised specific issues through the media. For example, Mike Fogden, then CE of the Employment Service and Michael Bichard, CE of Benefits, both spoke out on problems being created by the Government's 'market testing regime' in the early 1990s; successive Prison Service Director Generals have spoken out on issues such as escalating prison numbers, overcrowding and under-funding, and so on. While this should not be exaggerated, there has been a clear trend towards greater public identification of agency CEs and a growing expectation that they will answer publicly for 'their' agencies, which reinforces the view that agencies are independent bodies, even when formally they are far from Laving such a status.

Autonomization

As we have seen (Chapters 1 and 2) having even formally separate agencies (which UK agencies are not) does not necessarily guarantee managerial autonomy. US agencies, for example, are subject to a host of externally imposed restrictions and regulations on what agency managers can and cannot do (Graham and Roberts, 2004).

The case of UK agencies could probably be best described as 'creeping autonomization'. At the inception of the Next Steps programme the Treasury was extremely concerned that it would lose control of the carefully crafted set of controls which it had built-up to constrain ministries' spending and personnel policies (Hennessy, 1990; Kemp, 1993; Thain and Wright, 1996). In the opening stages of Next Steps there was therefore very limited delegation to agencies of any real power over financial or personnel issues.

During the 1980s the Treasury had however been developing a new approach to controlling ministries spending and this proved to be applicable to agencies. This approach involved setting very clear boundaries on what a ministry could spend overall, as well as strict controls on 'running costs': that is, the non-programme overheads. This new approach was allowing the Treasury to gradually relax other controls (e.g. on staffing numbers and pay and grading issues) and allow ministries more freedom to choose how to spend their money within the overall spending 'envelope' (Thain and Wright, 1996).

This approach proved transferable to agencies so that the Treasury (and the particular parent ministry) could set and police strong controls on how much each agency could spend on both its programmes and, most importantly from the point of view of driving up efficiency, its overheads. It also began to allow for space for greater managerial autonomy over how to allocate the overhead budget within each agency.

These freedoms on finance issues were further enhanced by several other innovations. First, some agencies were placed on slightly different funding regimes. While most remained funded directly for all their expenditure, some were moved, over a period, on to one of two new regimes. The first and largest was to become a 'net funded' agency. These were agencies which accrued income from various charges and fees (e.g. fees for passports or driving licences). They were allowed, under the new set of rules, to retain some of this income and offset it against their overhead costs. This created incentives for them to increase their income and enabled them to cover additional costs from the increases.

The second innovation was Trading Fund Agencies, which moved onto a completely self-financing basis in which their revenues were to cover not only their running costs and the costs of the services they provided, but also to provide a notional return on capital employed (i.e. their asset base) to the Treasury (usually set at around 5 per cent).

The third innovation consisted of changes to the accounting systems themselves, including the introduction of what is called 'end year flexibility' (allowing managers to carry-over some budget from one year to the next or spend some of next year's budget this year) and of resource accounting and budgeting (accruals and capital accounting). Both of these changes allowed managers greater control over how their (strictly limited) resources were to be deployed.

Alongside these increases in managerial autonomy over finances came changes to personnel practices. The degree of centralization and uniformity of personnel practices in the civil service has often been exaggerated but there was undoubtedly still a fair degree of Treasury control. While ministries had taken responsibility for managing their own personnel in terms of recruitment policies and the grading allocated to individuals, the overall pay and grading structures were still subject to tight control from the Treasury, together with controls on staffing totals.

From Treasury's point of view, this system however was weak: while they controlled the overall system and the total numbers of staff, ministries utilized their freedom to designate individuals and/or jobs at higher grades as a way of rewarding staff. This produced what was called 'grade drift' and meant Treasury did not effectively control total expenditure which, on staffing at least, had a relentless tendency to creep upwards. The introduction of running cost totals for ministries was seen as the solution to this problem: ministries could play around with grading of individuals as much as they liked but they had to stay within overall spending totals. It also meant Treasury could relax its controls on grading and pay systems, secure in the knowledge that this would not result in a massive increase in spending (Thain and Wright, 1996).

During the mid-1990s the Treasury began delegating responsibility for setting pay and grading systems to agencies – first the larger ones and then all agencies. However this was not a straightforward process. Agencies were forced, whether they wanted to or not, to conduct reviews of their pay and grading structures and to adopt new, more diverse, systems. Moreover the process of reforming these systems was closely supervized by Treasury and parent ministries, with agencies having to gain authorization at several points in the process (Talbot, 1997).

Thus this was, somewhat paradoxically, a centrally imposed devolved and dissimilar grading and pay system.

We have so far concentrated mostly on the relationship between agencies and Treasury, which is perhaps understandable given the enormous power exercised by the latter in the UK system. But the principal day-to-day relationship is between ministers and parent ministries and agencies, so in understanding real agency managerial autonomy both sets of central actors need to be considered.

The degree of genuine autonomy for agency managers has therefore been somewhat gradual and substantially circumscribed by continuing Treasury controls and direction and the power relationship with their parent ministry. This is true for all agencies but the impact has been highly differentiated, partly based simply on size but also on political sensitivity of the agency concerned.

The larger agencies have been able to exercise greater autonomy, partly due to information asymmetries between themselves and Treasury and their parent ministries. They have often had more direct access to Treasury – for example, during the various crises in prison numbers the Director General of Prisons was frequently involved in direct negotiations with Treasury over funding to meet the crises. This situation has evolved to the point where the recent review of the agency policy concluded that ministries were losing effective control over some of their agencies (Alexander and Agency Policy Review Team, 2002). On the other hand, some of these large agencies have also been highly politically sensitive and as a result ministers have been apt to intervene directly in operational as well as policy decisions – the Prison Service crisis in 1996 being the most obvious example (Learmont, 1995; Lewis, 1997; Talbot, 1996).

For smaller agencies the reality of managerial autonomy has been much more heavily circumscribed in practice by the inequality in the power relationship between very small agencies and large ministries (Talbot, 1996, 2004). Where these smaller agencies have also been the subject of political controversy – for example, in the case of the Child Support Agency – their managerial autonomy has been heavily constrained.

Performance contracting

One of the most prominent features of the Next Steps reforms was the introduction of publicly reported KPIs for every agency, specified by ministers. From 1990 onwards these KPIs were collected together and published centrally in the 'Next Steps Review' (later Report) with, in later editions of this central reporting, detailed comparative analysis of agencies' results.

KPIs are formally set by ministers and were originally envisaged to form part of a quasi-contractual annual agreement covering resources, policy and performance between ministers and their agencies (see Kemp in evidence to Treasury and Civil Service Committee, 1988). The reality however evolved somewhat differently. First, the policy framework was separated out into a three-year (later five) Framework Document which covered policy, aims, financial status and governance arrangements – more of a quasi-constitution than a quasi-contract. It said nothing about specific resources, which continued to be dealt with through normal ministry – Treasury spending processes nor about specific performance targets, which were set separately and annually through the KPI process.

The rationale for this emerging system, which emanated as a standard set of techniques from the Treasury and the Cabinet Office, seems to have been as follows: there were already strong mechanisms for controlling expenditure (inputs) then all that was needed were strong controls over outputs to effectively steer agencies towards the desired areas, level and efficiency of performance. A small set of output oriented KPIs would therefore be sufficient to drive agencies in the required direction.

KPIs themselves were however extremely variable in quantity, quality and focus. While most Agencies had KPIs numbering close to the average of 7 to 10 KPIs per Agency (there was gradual increase in numbers), there were some wide variations. The Royal Mint had only one, while Customs and Excise usually had almost forty KPIs. The quality of the KPIs themselves and the data used to report them was also highly variable and external audits highlighted some major problems (Comptroller and Auditor General, 1995, 1998, 2000). Although KPIs were supposed to focus on outputs, this took a long time to evolve and initially there was much greater emphasis on inputs and processes. The central reporting of KPIs was highly innovative and had some impact, but this was abandoned in 1999 making comparisons across the 120 or so annual reports for individual agencies much more difficult.

KPIs were not the only form of performance steering or reporting. One problem which emerged was that a plethora of different systems (KPIs, business plans, corporate plans, Citizen's Charter statements, market-testing plans, training plans, etc.) imposed centrally from either Cabinet Office or Treasury and mediated through parent ministries created a host of usually poorly aligned performance steering systems (Hyndman, 2002; Hyndman and Anderson, 1998; Talbot, 1996, 2004).

So, could UK agencies be said to be working within a performance contracting regime? They have certainly been required to report, sometimes extensively, on their performance, but this is not the same as performance contracting. In a performance contract the link between resources given by the principal (the Minister/Ministry) to their agent (the agency) would have a direct and explicit link to performance targets and rewards and/or penalties for good/poor performance set out. Moreover such a contract could be expected to be a two-way affair in which changes to requirements by the Principal would have to be (re)negotiated with the Agent and lead to changed performance targets or changed resources or both.

As has already been outlined, the UK system has separated out performance target setting (KPIs) from the budgetary process and there is no discernable link between the two for most agencies. Moreover ministers have felt free to impose new requirements on agencies regardless of the contents of the budget or the KPIs. There is also little or no evidence of poor or good performance affecting decisions about what resources an agency gets. So from all these criteria the UK system is clearly not performance contracting in any hard sense, and indeed there is little or nothing contractual about it.

One key test of such systems is how much they feature in a crisis. If the performance regime for an individual agency was important, then, if there is some crisis in performance, one would expect the KPIs to feature heavily in the ensuing discussions. There have been several examples of such crises (Prisons over escapes, Passports over delays in issuing, Child Support over failures to collect, etc.). What is remarkable about all of these crises has been the almost complete absence of discussion of formal performance. In the case of Prisons, for example, the agency was actually succeeding against its targets for escapes set by the Home Secretary when their Director General was sacked over two high-profile escapes (Lewis, 1997). One performance-related system was brought into play in the recent crisis in the Passport Agency but this was the Charter Mark system rather than the KPIs (the Agency had its Charter Mark, which is awarded on customer service criteria, removed).

What can be seen in the UK agencies' performance systems is broadly a highly formalized system for setting and reporting some relatively high-level targets for ministers, but one which has had more limited impact on the actual steering and management of agencies. Rather than a move from 'conformance to performance' it is more a move from conformance to process rules to a new kind of conformance – to performance rules. This new system has taken on a somewhat symbolic and formulaic character. Agencies certainly have not been free to perform in the sense of performing as best they think they can.

Conclusions

The whole Next Steps initiative and the 'technology of agencies' are clearly counter-cultural to previous norms of the Whitehall Village. The basic notion of establishing agencies on even a semi-formal basis (Framework Documents) and the associated paraphernalia of KPIs, accountable Chief Executives, public reporting, and so on, have been contrary to the usual informality, centralism, and collegialism dominant in Whitehall. Many of these innovations are now being applied (since 1997) to ministries themselves but when they were introduced for agencies from 1988 onwards they were very radical.

Formally, the whole initiative has also been clearly constrained to a fairly limited form of quasi-separation, quasi-autonomy and a somewhat formalized performance system at the official level. The actuality of evolving relationships between agencies, ministers, ministries, and central organizations (Cabinet Office and Treasury) is rather more complex and messy than some of the official accounts would suggest. In some cases agencies have achieved greater autonomy than their formal status would imply, while in others there has clearly been a degree of 'badge engineering' and agencies have been less affected than the official position would suggest. It is interesting that the Next Steps programme has become so famous internationally, and that it is frequently portrayed as having created the epitomy of the modern, autonomous, performance-oriented executive body. The reality, compared to some of the agency initiatives internationally which have been purportedly based on the Next Steps programmes, is less dramatic (Pollitt and Talbot, 2004). Close up, the UK programme appears rather less radical than on first inspection.

Part III
Comparing Tasks

7
Prisons

> There are prisons, into which whoever looks will, at first sight of the people confined, be convinced, that there is some great error in the management of them: their sallow meagre countenances declare, without words, that they are very miserable. Many who went in healthy, are in a few months changed to emaciated dejected objects. Some are seen pining under diseases 'sick, and in prison'; expiring on the floors, in loathsome cells, of pestilential fevers, and the confluent smallpox; victims, I must not say to the cruelty, but I will say to the inattention, of sheriffs, and gentlemen in the commission of the peace.
>
> John Howard, *The State of Prisons and an Account of the Principal Lazarettos in Europe*, 1777.
> (Muncie and Sparks, 1991)

Introduction

It is time for our account to move in for a closer focus and a more intensive comparison. Having given a general account of the development of agencies at national levels, we now put four specific functions under the comparative microscope, beginning with prisons.

This chapter therefore looks at the institutional, management and performance arrangements for prisons in our countries: Finland, the Netherlands, Sweden and the United Kingdom. The specific organizations covered are:

- Finland: *Rikosseuraamusvirasto* – the Criminal Sanctions Agency (CSA) which includes the prison service;

- Netherlands: *Dienst Justitiële Inrichtingen* – National Agency for Correctional Institutions (DJI);
- Sweden: *Kriminalvården* – Swedish Prison and Probation Service (KVV);
- The United Kingdom: HM Prison Service (HMPS).

(For brevity we will use the labels CSA(F), DJI(N), KVV(S) and HMPS(UK)).

Prisons in democratic countries have always represented something of a paradox. On the one hand, prisons are institutionally very inward looking, focussed on the job of providing secure incarceration of those detained, looking after their welfare and at least to some degree of rehabilitation. On the other hand, prisons are frequently in the public eye – they are 'home' to some of the most extreme and notorious individuals in our societies, and an easy focus for 'moral panics', helped along by the mass media.

There are enormous difficulties associated with depriving large groups of people of their liberty. Above all, this involves a degree of physical force and certainly construction of elaborate physical obstacles to their escape from custody. It also means prisons are '24/7' institutions, responsible not just for keeping inmates in, but for their food, health, hygiene, welfare, education, and so on. Prisons are one type of what the sociologist Erving Goffman memorably called 'total institutions' (Goffman, 1961). While there are, in European prisons, varying degrees of licence granted to prisoners to be outside of prison for shorter or longer periods (which creates its own managerial problems) it remains the case that for most prisoners total incarceration is the norm and they are indeed 'total institutions'.

In most democracies prisons are only manageable on the basis of an ongoing process of compromise and accommodation between prison authorities and their charges – prisons do not function on pure physical restraint but require a delicate balancing act between physical restraint and negotiated order. These mutual adjustments sometimes fail and when they do, they can lead to prison riots or individual or mass escapes. These disturbances show that purely physical means are not enough, in a normal situation, to restrain prisoners, maintain order and prevent escapes.

These factors inevitably make prisons very inward looking institutions, literally and metaphorically operating behind closed doors, sealed off from society at large. This is what we might call 'managing outside-in'.

The other side of the paradox is that at the same time as being so sealed-off, prisons are also very visible. Prison systems exercise the greatest power that modern democratic states wield over their citizens – that is, locking them up. [We leave aside the issue of the death penalty, which no longer exists in any of our four countries.] It is precisely because of this highly charged, value-laden and politically sensitive power that prisons are often subject to intense scrutiny. This is reflected in popular culture in the success of the many TV series and films set inside prisons – the citizenry seem fascinated by the inner workings of prisons, probably in part because it is so far removed from the day-to-day experiences of the vast majority.

Issues of prison security and prison regimes feature regularly and often loudly in debates about penal policy, alongside wider issues of sentencing policies, rehabilitation versus punishment, and the like. High profile prison escapes or prison riots frequently generate major political crises – in terms of riots these include the Tidaholm riots in Sweden (1994), disturbances and riots in over 40 prisons in the United Kingdom (1986) and the major Strangeways riot (1990) and the Groningen revolt in the Netherlands (1971). It should be noted here that whereas the UK prison system has had regular riots or major disturbances over many decades the Dutch system has had no major disturbances since Groningen (1971) and there have been only relatively few similar episodes in Sweden and virtually none in Finland.

Controversial escapes include examples like the break-out from the high security prisons in den Haag (1986) in the Netherlands and the escape of IRA prisoners from Whitemoor maximum security prison in the United Kingdom (1994).

Where large disturbances or controversial escapes have occurred they have nearly always been followed by some sort of formal investigation and attempts at reform (for discussions of these see de Frisching *et al.*, 1997; Vagg, 1994).

Even minor changes to prison regimes (e.g. allowing television in prisoners' cells) have created major controversies (e.g. in the United Kingdom and the Netherlands – see Lewis, 1997; Vagg, 1994).

It must sometimes feel to prison managers and staff that their institutions are sealed off with walls of glass rather than stone and prison managers have to 'manage inside-out' – in other words, they always have to take into account the possible external repercussions of decisions about how prisons are run internally. As one UK review by prison managers puts it:

> Prison services across the world tend to have a negative public image and this plays back into the standing and self-image of the staff. At one level, this is intrinsic to the work that they do – literally as well

as metaphorically 'behind the walls'. Unlike the police, for example, prison staff are not in day to day contact with the public, who therefore have little appreciation of what they actually do. What is newsworthy about prisons is when things go wrong – at one end of the spectrum, failures in security or good order and control, lapses in judgement over release decisions, or regimes which are seen as too lax; at the other end of the spectrum, allegations or instances of poor or ill-treatment. It is not easy therefore to convey to the public the positive work that is done with prisoners and the success of some of the rehabilitative work. (de Frisching *et al.*, 1997, p. 129)

Prisons – some basic facts

Some apparent basic divergences in broad penal policies and/or institutional contexts appear immediately when the four countries are compared. The first and most obvious is size. Our four countries are themselves of very different sizes so we should expect some major differences in prison populations, as indeed there are. But these absolute size differences are not just due to disparities in the size of country cases – there are also big *relative* differences in prison populations.

First, *absolute* size: while Finland holds under 4000 prisoners and Sweden around 6500, the Netherlands has nearly 15 000. Meanwhile, at around 73 000, the United Kingdom has nearly 5 times as many as the Netherlands, 12 times as many as Sweden and 18 times as many prisoners as Finland. The sheer magnitude of the size differences do make for divergence – indeed at one point a Director General of the UK Prison Service declared it was probably 'simply too big to be managed as a single unit and it should be broken-up' (this opinion was expressed to one of us privately).

Next, let us look at *relative* size (see Figure 7.1): the two Scandinavian countries exhibit low levels of relative imprisonment (as measured by prisoners per 100 000 of population) with Finland at 65 and Sweden at 63 in 1992. Both have remained fairly stable over the past decade, although there is a small but significant increase in both (to 70 and 73 respectively).

The United Kingdom, at the other extreme, shows a much higher relative prison population at 90, around 43 per cent higher than the two Scandinavian countries, a decade ago. Within ten years this had climbed to nearly double Scandinavian relative rates, now standing at 139 per hundred thousand. The Netherlands lies somewhere in between these two extremes – it mirrors the United Kingdom's rapid increase, nearly

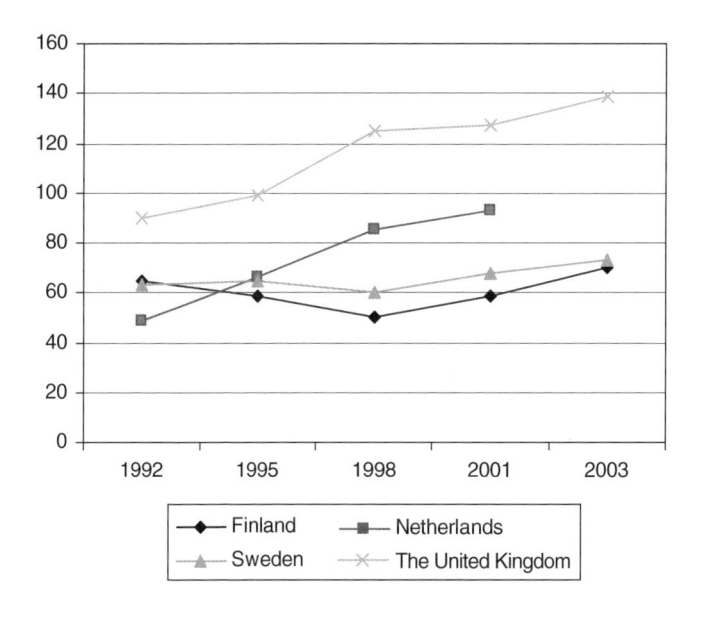

	Finland	Netherlands	Sweden	The United Kingdom
1992	65	49	63	90
1995	59	66	65	99
1998	50	85	60	125
2001	59	93	68	127
2003	70		73	139

Figure 7.1 Prisoner numbers per 100 000 population

doubling its relative incarceration rate to 93 per hundred thousand in 2001. But because it started from a lower base than any of the other countries at only 49 in 1992, it ends only mid-way between the United Kingdom and Scandinavian overall rates.

Pre-trial and remand detainees represent very different percentages in our four countries as is seen in Figure 7.2: the Netherlands has a staggering 37 per cent of its inmate population in this category, compared to only 14 per cent in Finland. Overcrowding also presents a very mixed picture with a variation from 11 per cent overcrowding in the United Kingdom to 10 per cent below capacity in Finland. Two categories show relatively small variation: women and juveniles.

Figure 7.2 Diversity in prison populations

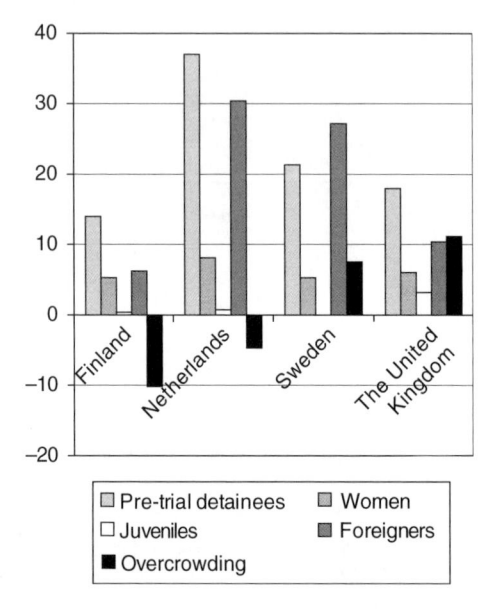

	Finland	Netherland	Sweden	The United Kingdom
Pre-trial detainees	14	36.9	21.4	17.9
Women	5.3	8.2	5.3	6.1
Juveniles	0.4	0.8	0	3.3
Foreigners	6.2	30.3	27.2	10.4
Overcrowding	210.2	24.7	7.5	11.2

The number of non-nationals inside prison varies widely, with 30 per cent in the Netherlands and 27 per cent in Sweden compared to 10 per cent in the United Kingdom and only 6 per cent in Finland. However, this clearly does not reflect the real ethnic diversity within prison systems. The United Kingdom and Holland have much greater ethnic diversity in their citizen populations, because of their long-term former-migrant populations mostly from ex-colonies, compared to either of the two Scandinavian countries. This amplifies their issues about managing diverse populations within prisons.

These wide variations also suggest either very different criminal justice policies (e.g. on pre- and post-trial remand, sentencing policies, etc.) or contexts (different crime rates) or a mixture of both across our sample countries.

Changing policy contexts

In all four countries there have been shifts in penal policy over the past two or three decades, sometimes quite dramatic policy reversals. As suggested at the start of this chapter, prisons objectives can be broken down into three areas: carrying out the sentences by securing prisoners for their full sentences; providing a humane regime for prisoners while they are inside prison; rehabilitating them for re-entry into society as persons who are less likely to re-offend.

As the Swedish Kriminalvarden's website puts it: 'there is an unavoidable, built-in contradiction between society's motives in locking away a person and the desire to, at the same time, rehabilitate him to a normal life.' We would add that to the contradiction between punishment (locking away) and rehabilitation there is also the tensions with what sort of prison regime (style of living) should be provided.

So policy which advocates greater emphasis on punishment tends to imply greater emphasis on security and a tougher prison regime and less effort at rehabilitation, while a more liberal approach suggests a more trusting, open, security regime, more comfortable living arrangements and much greater emphasis on addressing offending behaviour, providing education and training opportunities, and the like.

In each of our four countries there have been distinctive swings in public policy on these issues.

Sweden was – until the 1990s – renowned for a very liberal penal policy with short prison sentences, liberal and fairly open prison regimes. The election of the first non-socialist government in four decades in 1991, however, brought about a sharp shift in policy. One of the new right of centre government's slogans had been 'Keep them locked in so that we can go out' and the incoming Minister of Justice produced a report with the title 'To restore a degenerated criminal policy' (Leander, 1995). However this policy shift can be exaggerated in two ways. First, the shift in sentencing policy which saw a rise in the proportion of prison sentences to other types of sentence (e.g. fine or probation) actually began in the 1980s. Second, the change in sentencing patterns had limited impact due to a fall in total convictions in the early 1990s and it was not until the latter part of the decade (after the Social Democrats had returned to power) that prison numbers started to increase. So in Sweden the start of a change in penal policy affected mostly the internal workings of the prison system, with a distinctive shift towards a more managerialist, less liberal, prison regime from about the mid-1990s onwards (Leander, 1995).

In the Netherlands a rather similar, though perhaps more complex, set of changes in prison policies are evident. As the Netherlands has had prolonged periods of coalition government then it could be expected that shifts in policy would be less dramatic. The Dutch system up until the 1990s has been described as one of relatively short prison sentences, automatic parole after two-thirds of the sentence regardless of behaviour, well-appointed prisons but with strict timetables for prisoners of work, education, and recreation (van Swaaningen and de Jonge, 1995). The Dutch system also included a lot of preventative social-welfare intervention aimed at avoiding prison sentences and the Dutch level of incarceration at the start of the 1990s was the lowest of our four countries.

It has been suggested that four White Papers (1982, 1985, 1990 and 1994) constituted a marked shift in Dutch penal policy from 'humanitarian paternalism' to 'penal business management' (van Swaaningen and de Jonge, 1995). These changes were accompanied by changes to non-prison social-welfare preventative policies and sentencing to produce the rapid rise in prison population (about double in ten years) and changes to the internal management of prisons.

In the United Kingdom penal policy has gone through sharp changes in direction over the past 30 years but curiously this has not been related to changes in government. The United Kingdom has usually had a far more punitive approach to prisons and downplayed the rehabilitation, and to some extent even the humanitarian, aspects of imprisonment (especially when compared to the other countries under study).

Following the extensive riots of 1986 and especially the Strangeways riot of 1990 which lasted for 25 days and was televized nightly, there was a distinct shift in policy. The commission of enquiry established after Strangeways, chaired by Lord Justice Woolf, produced a 600-page report which received widespread political endorsement. Woolf emphasized the necessity of providing humane conditions in prisons, the need for much greater emphasis on rehabilitation and that prisons 'often made bad people worse'. The Conservative government responded with a very liberal White Paper *Custody, Care and Justice* which received wide political support, even from the right wing. Within five years, however, the same government had completely reversed course and the then Home Secretary, Michael Howard, memorably declared that 'prison works'. Prison regimes were tightened, more custodial and longer sentences were encouraged and prison numbers began to escalate in a dramatic way.

Finland's history on penal policy has to be viewed on a slightly longer timescale than the other countries in the sample. Because of its history,

Finland's penal traditions reflected the Russian rather than Scandinavian traditions. In the 1950s, Finland's incarceration rate was 200 prisoners per 100 000 people – a normal rate for East Bloc countries such as Poland and Czechoslovakia where justice systems had been Sovietized, but four times the rate in Sweden, Norway and Denmark. In the late 1960s and early 1970s Finland began comparing itself with its Scandinavian neighbours and embarked on a twenty-year period of consistent reform aimed at reducing imprisonment and offending. By the 1990s its profile was much closer to the Scandinavian norm, if not indeed more liberal. Incarceration rates were down to around 50 per 100 000 (compared to 600 in the former Soviet Union). A snap-shot of 1996 shows that of 64 000 convictions, only 6000, less than 10 per cent, resulted in actual prison sentences. The regime within prisons is well captured in the following excerpt from a newspaper article:

> Look in on Finland's penal institutions, whether those the system categorizes as 'open' or 'closed,' and it is hard to tell when you've entered the world of custody. 'This is a closed prison,' Esko Aaltonen, warden of the Hameenlinna penitentiary, said in welcoming a visitor. 'But you may have noticed you just drove in, and there was no gate blocking you.'
>
> New York Times, 1 February 2003

One may compare this with the description of the state of European prisons in John Howard's account from 1777 at the start of this chapter.

As early as 1983 a Council of Europe report expressed concern about rising, and more difficult prison populations, increasing demands by prison trade unions on the one hand and for more humane treatment of inmates on the other, all in the context of 'the critical economic situation in many countries' (Council of Europe, 1983). Overall in the four sample countries we can see there has been a differential swing in the 1990s towards more and longer custodial sentences, tighter and more managed prison regimes and an emphasis on efficiency and cost cutting.

In the United Kingdom the Woolf interregnum (early 1990s) was a very short-lived period of attempted liberal reform of an otherwise quite illiberal penal policy which became even more so towards the end of the 1990s and subsequently. In Sweden and the Netherlands there were distinctive shifts from previous liberal approaches towards more restrictive, or at any rate managed, regimes – more so in the Netherlands than in

Sweden. Finland has a different history – having moved from a fairly brutal Slavic prison and criminal policy up to the 1950s it has become arguably the most liberal of the regimes in our sample and seems to be remaining so – though under new pressures. Together with the resultant differences in absolute and relative size of prison populations, this provides a very different context for the organization, management and performance of prisons in each of the four countries.

Patterns of institutions

Level of government

The first issue here is at what level of government prisons are managed. In all four cases the answer is at the national level (as opposed to local government) with the partial exception of the United Kingdom. In Sweden, Finland and the Netherlands prisons are all organized and managed within a national framework, but in the United Kingdom there are three organizationally separate prison services. What is usually known as, and discussed as, 'the' prison service is HM Prison Service but this actually only covers England and Wales.

Scotland – for reasons to do with the Act of Union with England in the eighteenth century – always retained its own legal system and along with it a separate prison service. Northern Ireland retained, along with most other institutions, a separate identity when it was partitioned from the rest of Ireland in 1920. As a quasi-colony it retained a colonial-style separate administration, including prisons, as was the tradition in the British Empire.

This is reflected in HM Prison Services' 'parent' department – the Home Office. The Home Office is responsible for a range of criminal justice and law functions – for some of which it only covers England and Wales (e.g. police, prisons, probation) and for others of which covers the whole of the United Kingdom (e.g. immigration and nationality). Given the very small relative sizes of the Scottish prison administration and the rather unique character of the Northern Ireland service (because of its role in holding large numbers of terrorist prisoners) we have concentrated our comparative analysis on just HM Prison Service.

Setting aside these quirks of the UK system, prisons are essentially a facet of national public administration of all of our four countries, as opposed to, say, Australia where prisons are managed at state level or Canada and the United States where prisons are managed at both state and federal levels (and even locally in the United States).

Function – carrying out the sentence of the courts – the prison and probation connection

In all four countries prisons exist to 'carry out the sentences of the courts' but in all four countries these sentences may include both incarceration and/or periods of non-custodial supervision. These may be either simple 'oversight', sometimes after a period of imprisonment or sometimes instead of prison, or programmes of community service or other forms of punishment/rehabilitation in the community. In English translation these are invariably referred to as 'probation' functions.

Given the close functional proximity of prison and probation, the issue of whether these should form part of the same organization or be separate is an obvious one. Here we have a clear cleavage in our sample countries: in Finland and Sweden prisons and probation are organized together, in the Netherlands and the United Kingdom they are not.

Finland and Sweden are clearly part of an emergent 'Scandinavian' model of prison and probation organization: in both of them as well as Denmark and Norway prison and probation form part of a common structure but interestingly these emerged at different times: Sweden in the 1940s; Finland and Denmark in the 1970s and Norway in 1980 (Home Office, 1998).

In the United Kingdom and Holland the position is different. In the United Kingdom the prisons are part of national public administration but probation was, until very recently, a local quasi-independent but public service. The probation service grew out of a court function separately from prisons and was seen, and saw itself, as primarily not about punishment but about rehabilitation. Its slogan was to 'advise and befriend', by which of course they meant offenders, not victims. In the Netherlands probation is also organized separately through a publicly funded but 'private' probation institution (70 per cent), the Salvation Army (10 per cent) and a national organization dealing with addicted people including 16 affiliated organizations (the remaining 20 per cent).

Although there is a close functional proximity between prison and probation there is one vital policy cleavage which seems to affect, albeit imperfectly, institutional design choice. This is the tension between rehabilitation and punishment. As already mentioned above, one of the fundamental debates in prison policy is how much prison is for punishment and how much for rehabilitation. This links to the wider debate about whether non-custodial sentences or imprisonment is the best way of dealing with offenders.

Broadly speaking, in countries where policy has focussed very much on trying to avoid imprisonment except in serious cases and instead to rely on varieties of probation there has been a stronger tendency towards combined prison–probation organization (e.g. Sweden, Finland, Denmark, Norway, federal Canadian and some Australian states), whereas where there has been a stronger emphasis on punishment they have remained separate (Home Office, 1998). To some degree this can be seen as the punishment/rehabilitation dilemma being resolved on the one hand by an institutionalization of the two into separate structures, thus providing 'punishment' in prisons and 'rehabilitation' through probation or on the other by tilting in the rehabilitation direction and creating a single structure where the emphasis is mainly on rehabilitation except in a small minority of very serious cases.

Localization of prison establishments

There appears to be another, albeit secondary, factor influencing institutional arrangements and related to this punishment/rehabilitation debate: that is the issue of localization. In those countries with a stronger emphasis on rehabilitation there has also been a tendency to try to develop, as far as possible, local prisons close to communities with integrated probation services. Thus Sweden, for example, which has only a relatively small prison population has almost as many prison facilities as HM Prison Service which has over ten times as many prisoners. Moreover even the relatively larger UK prisons are not evenly distributed according to population but have historically been un-related to prisoners' communities (de Frisching *et al.*, 1997). Thus even the distribution and relative size of the prison estate is linked to some degree to policy considerations.

This however also has managerial consequences – even a relatively small service like Sweden's with only 7500 staff (for prison and probation) when scattered over 140 organizational units (recently regrouped into 37 management units but still geographically spread out) is a very different management challenge than a more spatially centralized service would be. HMPS has around the same number of institutions, even slightly less, yet has more than five times the staff.

Status of prison organizations

The next institutional question is the status of the prison organizations. Here the picture is rather more diverse.

If we were to describe a continuum with at the one end prison organizations being completely integrated into a Ministry and at the other being completely separate, then the Netherlands and Finland (until recently) would probably lie somewhere close to the former and Sweden very much at the latter end, with the United Kingdom somewhere in between.

In the Netherlands, the DJI is part of the Ministry of Justice and it is formally, since 1995, described as an 'agency'. However it is unclear how this differs from a department within the Ministry, as for example the UK prisons department was prior to agency status, or the Finnish prison administration was until a few years ago. It is certainly not a ZBO, the more independent and formalized type of 'agency' (see Chapter 4) – indeed one of our interviewees argued strongly for the DJI to be moved to ZBO status to gain the types of freedom enjoyed by such organizations. He said 'the Minister tends to get the impression he personally controls all the prisons in the country.'

This ambiguity was captured in a comment from one interviewee:

> If a member of parliament is not completely satisfied [with the answer to question to the Minister] then the Minister can take two possible responses (1) he can say that he is responsible for prisons (2) he can say the operations are the responsibility of the agency, so don't ask me for specific information.

DJI actually consists of three divisions – the Prison Service (for adult offenders), the Juvenile Institutions and the Custodial Clinics for those with convictions and mental health problems. (In the United Kingdom the equivalent to Custodial Clinics are the Special Hospitals like Rampton and Broadmoor, which are staffed by prison officers but run by the National Health Service.)

The formal position of the DJI, however, masks the somewhat more complex informal position where the prison system of management has been fairly decentralized and individual prison managers have had a great deal of local autonomy and their national association of prison warders (VDPI) has exercised a great deal of influence in shaping prison policy. (The autonomy of local prisons management is a perennial theme in much correctional management literature – see de Frisching et al., 1997; DiIulio, 1987).

In the UK prisons were, until the 1960s, a separate organization run by the Prison Commissioners, whose Chair reported directly to the Home Secretary (Newsam, 1954). After that the Prison Commissioners were abolished in 1964, prisons became a sub-department within the Home Office and while the Director General still often reported to the

Home Secretary this was under the clear chain of command – that is, through the Permanent Secretary. In 1992 this went almost full circle with the prison service again becoming a quasi-autonomous agency under the Next Steps programme and standard arrangements, with the Director General now formally once more responsible directly to the Home Secretary and enshrined as his principal policy advisor on prison matters. In interviews with two former Director Generals (Derek Lewis who presided over the transfer to agency status, and his successor Richard Tilt) it was clear that agency status, as such, had had only a marginal effect on Prison Service status, although both saw it as an advantage. Lewis pointed out, both in interview and in his subsequent book (Lewis, 1997) that it was the actual working relationship between the Minister (Home Secretary) and the Director General which had the biggest effect (indeed big enough that Lewis was praised by the Home Secretary who appointed him and was later sacked by the next Home Secretary). The ambiguity of these roles and the importance of the working relationship was best captured in a report by the Home Affairs Select Committee:

> It is not possible to lay down a rigid dividing line between the roles of Ministers and of the Director General of the agency. If the arrangements for running the agency are to work properly there has to be a good relationship between the Home Secretary and the Director General. The Home Secretary must leave proper freedom to the Director General to do his or her job. At the same time, there is no point in Ministers, the Director General, or Parliament, harbouring unrealistic expectations of the extent to which Ministers can be excluded from the operational process; the needs of accountability and responsibility to Parliament will require some measure of Ministerial involvement. (Home Affairs Select Committee, 1997)

While probation remained a separate organization in 1997–98 a 'Prisons-Probation' review took place (Home Office, 1998). While this rejected suggestions for a merged service along Nordic or Canadian lines, it did fundamentally change the structure of probation, effectively 'nationalizing' it as a central agency. Here we are concentrating on prisons, and so we will leave that issue aside.

In Sweden the KVV has a much stronger position of independence, determined by the Swedish system of agencies as independent boards guaranteed by the Constitution (see Chapter 5). As an official in the

Ministry of Justice put it to us in interview:

> When the Minister of Justice is asked question by journalists about, for example, the riots in Gothenburg prison, or when an individual sends a letter begging to see a family member the minister is unable to take the matter into his or her hands. They can only say – 'that is a matter for KVV, take it up with them'.

The official went on to point out that this can be a relief to the minister.

Interestingly, the former UK HMPS Director General, Derek Lewis, suggested in both interview and his book that such an arrangement would be much better for ministers in the United Kingdom. The analogy he drew was with the status of UK police chiefs, which is closer to the KVV status (Lewis, 1997).

Our Swedish Justice Ministry interviewee however pointed out that this arrangement also has a downside, as it can make ministers appear powerless and unable to take action when politically important matters (like the early 1990s prison riots in Sweden) happen.

The Prison Administration in Finland was, until 2001, one of four departments of the Ministry of Justice. It then became part of a joint agency with probation service. It is responsible for prisons, probation, after-care and the enforcement of community sanctions. In includes 30 prisons, including 17 closed and 15 open units (some are combined units) and one Mental Hospital.

The old Prisons Department reported through the Secretary General of the Ministry to the Minister and thus it fell very much to the 'department within a Ministry' category, similar to the UK Prison Service (HMPS) prior to 1992. It was not part of the Finnish Board system (see Chapter 3), but rather part of the ministry system. As one of our interviewees stated just prior to agencification in 2001, 'legislative change is coming; we are going to the Swedish model next year'.

From August 1, 2001, the new Criminal Sanctions Agency (CSA), responsible for developing and directing the enforcement of community and prison sentences, came into being as a central administrative board. A Criminal Policy Board has been established in the Ministry of Justice which is 'in charge of the strategic direction in this field of administration' (CSA website, accessed October 2003). The Head of the CSA is also the Director General of the Prison Service but there is a separate Chief Director for the Probation Service. These changes were legislated in the Enforcement of Sentences Administration Act 2001.

Finance

There are few, if any, substantive differences in the financial regimes for prison services in all four countries – all are 'block funded' – that is, they receive their income in the form of a block grant from the government. The exact details may differ slightly: financial distribution mechanisms vary (e.g. the money flow can be through the parent Ministry or direct from the Finance Ministry); the degree of line-item or categories budgets imposed from outside varies (but only in degree).

There seem to be some differences in the way the formal arrangements are worked in practice. In both the United Kingdom and Sweden there seemed to be extensive informal discussions directly between prisons and Finance Ministry staff. In the United Kingdom in particular, the size of the prison system and the rapid changes in size of prison populations from the mid-1990s onwards has meant that HM Treasury and HMPS have evolved systems for negotiating in-year budget variations (sometimes up to two or three times a year) to cope with the changing demands on the system.

We need to look outside of our sample for significant variation in financial arrangements. Prison systems in some federal countries (e.g. the United States, Canada) are funded at central, state and even local levels. In Canada the federal agency (Corrections Canada) also has a budget system which is partially tied to prison numbers, with some automaticity in budget changes based on changing numbers (something which was considered but rejected for HMPS during the 1997 Review).

There is only one really significant difference: privately managed prisons in the United Kingdom. None of our other countries has any private sector involvement whereas the United Kingdom has about 10 per cent of the prison system either managed or owned and managed by private contractors. Some of these are simply managed by external firms, where they have taken over existing prisons. Others are new prisons built under Private Finance Initiative (PFI) deals where the ownership of the property is less clear cut. Privately managed prisons, whether PFI or not, are still fully funded in their running costs by the state.

The purpose of privately managed prisons was clearly to save money through increased efficiency and, in the case of PFIs, to generate capital spending which is supplied by the private sector and therefore off the books for state budgets. A major part of the savings are generated through changed working practices, imposed through the contracting-out process (where existing prisons management is put out to competitive bidding for the contract).

PFI and contracted-out management deals have been subject to some criticisms in general ((Chair of Commission) Taylor, 2001) about whether they do really generate savings and the answers have been very mixed. In the case of HMPS the total contracting-out/PFI estate has been limited to about 10 per cent by ministerial decision and this is intended to act as a stimulus to the rest.

The contracted-out/PFI prisons have had mixed fortunes – there have undoubtedly been improvements in their finances and even in regimes for prisoners in many cases, but there have also been difficulties. This is not the place for a full balance-sheet and in any case the overall effect on the UK system, for international comparative purposes, is relatively small. Contracted-out/PFI prisons remain subject to all the same rules, are fully financed by the state and accountable to HMPS management. As one Director General described it to us, the privately managed prisons had overall proved a success in both financial and regime terms but they had not had the expected impact across the rest of the system, perhaps because of the 10 per cent limit which meant the rest of the service did not feel challenged by the changes.

Performance

Netherlands

The Dutch Prison Service seems to have a history of publishing quite a lot of data about its operations (see e.g. Dutch National Agency for Correctional Institutions, 2001) although this was not 'performance data' in the modern sense. The public reporting of performance information is however subject to some political manipulation. This is illustrated in a remark from one of our interviewees:

> If people ask for information, however, they get it. Recently a member of parliament (Rietveld) raised this question about our performance. We were willing to give him this big report *[interviewee produces report covering a number of aspects of organizations performance]*, but then we thought it just gives him much more opportunity to just ask more questions. The Minister decided to give him more general information about our performance but not about each prison separately.

DJI does now produce quarterly reports to ministers on their performance, much more like formal performance reporting, but this is very much as an integral part of the new, government-wide financial and performance reporting system, the VBTB (see Chapter 4).

The nearest we can find to a statement of objectives for the Dutch Prison Service appears in a brochure posted on their website. In the opening paragraphs it states that:

> The DJI's core task is to ensure safety. Society must be protected from individuals who pose a threat to legal order or the safety of others. Safe working and living conditions for the staff and inmates also have to be maintained within the institutions themselves. The issue of safety extends beyond the sentences served within the protective walls of custodial institutions. After all, once their sentences or orders for detainment have been fully carried out, inmates have to return to society. The DJI strives to prepare inmates to re-enter society such that they will not revert to criminal conduct on their return. (CJI Brochure, from their website, 2003)

The indicators collected and reported quarterly to the ministry regarding each institution type include:

- Capacity requirements (formal capacity, capacity requirements, capacity used, average occupation of institutions)
- waiting time
- daily price per place across different institution types
- balance of accruals
- calculation of actual receipts and expenditure and
- escapes (leaving closed institution, other departures).

According to one of our interviewees measures are effectively set within the agency:

> Formally, the Minister of Justice gives us money and a task. As we receive the money we have to account quarterly for what we have done with it. In practice Headquarters determine the performance measures in negotiation with the prison governors. Just 10 years ago HQ made these decisions without consultation with the field. Previously there was a big distance between the field and headquarters but now this distance is becoming less.

Another confirmed that it was the agency, rather than the ministry that developed the indicators but he stressed that the ministry was formally responsible for setting the measures. It should be stressed that these appear to be just measures or indicators, not targets as in the case of UK Key Performance Indicators (KPIs).

With the exception of escapes, which were seen as extremely politically sensitive, it seemed fairly clear that most of the non-financial indicators were not taken terribly seriously either by the CJI itself or ministers. However there were indications this might be changing:

> I think until recently the indicators were merely used for research purposes, but this is changing. We are asking more managerial questions of our indicators, for example which prisons under perform in the area of drug rehabilitation? Or which prison should receive funds to conduct external programs?

Performance information is not externally audited.

The United Kingdom

Prior to agency status in 1993 the Prison Service (HMPS) had been developing and using performance indicators but these were purely for internal consumption. Through the 1980s HMPS had been developing, with greater or lesser success, systems of setting internal objectives and budgets – such as the SPAR (staff planning and resourcing) accounting system.

Moreover, the new Director General certainly believed (in 1993) that the culture of the organization was very much still about conformance rather than performance:

> The top priority was a change in attitude towards performance. I wanted to see more action and fewer words. Too much attention was paid to whether or not the right procedures had been followed, rather than what had been achieved. It was an attitude born of years of painful political experience. When things went wrong and when inquiries were conducted, the survivors were those who had followed the rule book and created their own alibis. An organization such as the Prison Service, where things are bound to go wrong and inquiries inevitably follow, is particularly prone to this kind of thinking. Many had forgotten what they were really there to do. (Lewis, 1997, p. 73)

A review of HMPS management drew similar conclusions, if in somewhat drier language: 'Although the concept [of SPAR and related business planning systems] was sound, its execution was not entirely satisfactory ... the effectiveness of the system varied widely from prison to prison' (de Frisching *et al.*, 1997).

As an Executive Agency HMPS was required to have a set of KPIs agreed with ministers (see Chapter 6). These are usually relatively few in number (about 8–10) and focus on the key objectives of the organization. Unlike the previous systems developed within HMPS, which had concentrated largely on the management of individual prisons and were for internal consumption, KPIs were national targets for the whole of HMPS and were to be publicly reported. Internal and more localized targets are supposed to flow from these national objectives.

The process of setting these KPIs (and objectives, which are more long term and embedded in the five-year Framework Document) is formally that they are set by ministers. In practice the setting of KPIs has varied according to relations with, and the preferences of, the current Home Secretary. Since the HMPS became an agency there have been four Home Secretaries (two Conservative 1993–97 and two Labour 1997–2003) and four Director Generals. Accounts from our interviewees and the published account of Derek Lewis suggests that the real setting of targets has swung between the HMPS playing a leading role to the Home Secretary playing a determining role. Moreover an overall interventionist Home Secretary does not necessarily mean that he (they were all 'he') intervenes over KPIs – for example Michael Howard, the Conservative Home Secretary during the Lewis affair seemed to have paid little attention to the formal arrangements such as the Framework Document and KPIs yet intervened on an almost daily basis on operational matters (Learmont, 1995; Lewis, 1997; Talbot, 1996).

HMPS's current objectives are:

> Her Majesty's Prison Service serves the public by keeping in custody those committed by the courts. Our duty is to look after them with humanity and help them lead law-abiding and useful lives in custody and after release. (HMPS website, accessed October 2003).

These objectives reflect the three possible purposes for any prison service discussed earlier in this chapter: holding prisoners securely; providing a humane environment; and rehabilitation. They are fairly similar to the objectives of the Dutch CJI.

The current (2002–03) set of related KPIs are:

Offending behaviour programmes

- To ensure that at least 7100 prisoners complete programmes accredited as being effective in reducing re-offending

- To ensure that at least 950 prisoners complete the Sex Offender Treatment Programme
- To ensure that the number of escapes from contracted out escorts is no more than 1 per 20 000 prisoners handled

Cost per place and cost per prisoner

- To ensure that the average cost of a prison place does not exceed £38 743
- To ensure that the average cost of a prisoner does not exceed £36 539

Staff sickness

- To ensure that the average staff sickness does not exceed 9.0 working days

Race equality

- To have at least 4.5 per cent minority ethnic staff

Education

- To achieve 6000 awards at Basic Skills Entry level
- To achieve 12 000 awards at Basic Skills Level 1
- To achieve 10 800 awards at Basic Skills Level 2
- To achieve 45 000 Key Work Skills awards

Resettlement

- 28 200 total ETE outcomes.

(Source: HMPS website 2003)

A comparison of these objectives and KPIs is instructive. The KPIs do include measures which relate to the objectives, and more as well, but rather imperfectly.

The objective of holding prisoners securely in custody is covered by only one, very partial, KPI about escapes from contracted out escorts. This is very surprising given the 'Lewis affair' in which the Director General was sacked in 1995 was about prison escapes (Talbot, 1996). Previous sets of KPIs included specific targets about overall escapes from 1993 to 1996 and thereafter even more detailed targets about escapes broken down by prisoner category until the latest set of KPIs, where specific targets about prisoner escapes, except for those in transit, have been dropped from the KPIs (website and (HMPS, 2003)).

The objective about looking after prisoners 'with humanity' has completely disappeared from the KPIs. Prior to the 2002–03 set of KPIs, targets about overcrowding and about time in recreational and other activities out of their cells had featured.

In terms of the objectives about rehabilitation there are several KPIs which relate to the processes by which prisoners are rehabilitated – offending behaviour programmes, education and resettlement (placement into jobs or training on release). However noticeably absent is any measurement of actual re-offending (recidivism).

This last omission is very interesting. One of the current authors was a member of the 1997 Steering Committee for the Review of the Prison Service and can report that this latter issue was the subject of heated debate within the Review although it did not feature in the final report (de Frisching *et al.*, 1997). The debate was between those who argued that unless HMPS had targets about the success (outcomes) of rehabilitation it would not be taken seriously. The alternative view, which seemed to be informed by a version of 'principal–agent' thinking, was that re-offending was a 'policy' matter for the Home Office and not one with which the Prison Service should concern itself (which rather begs the question as to why it is in their objectives).

Both our discussions with Home Office and HMPS staff and the many accounts which have appeared of 'critical incidents' like the Derek Lewis affair confirm that the performance targets set for the HMPS have had less than the intended impact. At the time Lewis was dismissed over high profile escapes, HMPS had met and exceeded its target for reducing escapes. The latter were set in broad-brush terms about reductions in overall escapes, though subsequently changed to specify that there should be no 'Category A' (high security) escapes. In none of the accounts of the dispute surrounding Derek Lewis's dismissal does the KPI on escapes feature prominently, if at all.

HMPS performance information is not externally audited.

Sweden

The system for setting performance targets for the KVV seems somewhat complex and ambiguous, partially due to the process of intense dialogue between ministry and agency and partly due to the extra role of the Ministry of Finance which is also involved.

Formally, the system seems to be that the Ministry of Justice, in consultation with the Finance Ministry, sets objectives for the KVV and broad areas on which they expect it to report its performance, but much of the detailed work of formulating specific measures is left to KVV itself. One interviewee put it thus:

> It [KVV performance] is much more focussed on what the government directs us to focus on. Our performance focus really depends on the government objectives. We are very responsive to what government identifies and these targets are sent through to the local organizations. At the moment the conditions of the remand prisons are very important. Also thinking of alternatives to prisons has become important.

But the system seems to be very much one of 'negotiated order' rather than formalization, based on a high degree of trust amongst participants – something which people we talked to in KVV, their Ministry and the Finance Ministry all commented on. One interviewee even told us that other ministries sometimes get involved in discussions about an agency in another ministry where its activities impact on their own policy domain.

There are not the same formalized KPIs as in the United Kingdom, for example, but rather looser objectives. An example, given by one interviewee, was an attachment to the annual letter of instruction that 'all prisoners should receive some education whilst in prison' but the operationalization of this was left up to KVV itself. Another suggested that there were actually two types of performance instructions – one being 'quite general and broad' covering on-going aspects of performance and the other being 'specific commissions' which are usually project or 'milestone' type. The sort of measures included in the annual directions include ones covering:

- Costs per prisoner day by prison (average)
- Costs per day for different types of rehabilitation programmes
- Number of clients participating in rehabilitation programmes.

Escapes and impact of programmes were also widely mentioned, but we could not find specific examples of these. There was apparently a formal study taking place of how to include figures about re-offending, prompted by a visit to KVV by the (Danish) head of Corrections Canada, who make extensive use of recidivism data.

One informant told us that performance information was used extensively by the Director General (DG) of KVV in discussions with the Ministry over budgets. It was less clear that Ministry and Finance Ministry actors saw the performance information as quite so important in relation to budget discussions. On the other hand, there was evidence from people in the Ministry (and one official who had worked in both the Ministry and KVV) that there was degree of 'micro-management' from the Ministry with ministers and officials in the Ministry showing great interest in local prison problems related to specific performance issues (e.g. care of prisoners, escapes, etc.). This was reinforced by at least one other senior official stating that 'what they [the Ministry/ Government] are sending us now are not really steering goals but there are lots of details. People in [KVV] are complaining about the details.'

Interestingly there also seems to be some media interest in performance information. When asked who made the most of performance data one interviewee stated:

> It must be the government because they ask for so much. Perhaps the media also. I know that those who are working in statistics have many inquiries from journalists. We send our statistics reports to them.

Much of the discussion of performance seemed to be internal to KVV between HQ, regional Directors and local prison managers and there does seem to be a degree of emphasis on its internal use. Several actors told us that there was serious and intensive use of performance information at all levels within KVV, but they were not unanimous. One respondent said that 'they [local managers] are not looking at the figures' because 'they can still get their money, the result of the performance doesn't in fact influence the next year's money'.

KVV performance is subjected to annual audit by Swedish National Audit Office (RRV) at least for those elements of performance which appear in KVVs Annual Report. RRV also carries out periodic performance audits and in the period 1990–99 there were several such audits (Swedish National Audit Office, 2000). Despite this one of our interviewees stated that 'internal audit is not too happy with our figures, there has been a lot of falsification in the studies they have conducted'. Evidence from other actors was contradictory, some were sceptical about performance information while others seemed very confident about its relevance and accuracy.

Finland

Finnish prisons have always produced a great deal of information about their activities (see below) but there does not seem to have been any formalized system of what might be called 'performance management' from the Ministry to the prison service. With the change in status of Finnish prisons to 'the Swedish model' has come a much more formalized system of establishing performance objectives and measurement. The similarities (at least in style and to some extent in content) with the UK's system of formalized objectives, values and KPIs is quite striking, as this example of the latest set of statements shows:

GOALS

The goal of Prison Service is

- to contribute to security in society by maintaining a lawful and safe system of enforcement of sanctions
- to assist in reducing recidivism and terminating the development of social maladjustment reproducing crime.

In order to achieve this goal enforcement is carried out so that

- it is safe for society, the convicts and staff
- the chances of the convicts to manage in society and to maintain their health and well-being are promoted
- the capability of the convicts to adopt a way of life without crime is improved.

VALUES

Prison Service and the Probation Service commit themselves to the values of respect for human dignity and justness, highly esteemed in Finnish society. Work is also guided by a notion of the potential of the individual for change and growth. A commitment to these values implies for example:

- safeguarding basic and human rights
- treating convicts appropriately, equally and with humanity
- the lawfulness of all activities and compliance with the principles of justice and reasonableness
- carrying out enforcement in a way that supports the individual growth and development of the convict and his efforts to lead a life without crime.

PRINCIPLES

Enforcement of sentences is based on the principle of normality. Prison Service and the Probation Service moreover adhere to the following principles:

- **Target-Orientation:** Prison Service and the Probation Service are responsible to society for the attainment of the goals set on them. The results, efficiency, effects and economy of their activities are to be regularly and openly assessed. The assessment guides the selection of lines and means of action.
- **Individuality and Responsibility of the Individual:** Enforcement shall pay attention to the situation and the individual needs of the convict. The measures included in enforcement shall enhance the capability of the individual to take responsibility for his own life and for the consequences of his own acts.
- **Professionalism:** Prison Service and Probation Service consist of demanding work with people, work requiring a professional approach. Professionalism comprises, among other things, continuous evaluation and development of the work performed, capacity for cooperation and ability to develop one's own capabilities for interaction and to apply both supportive and controlling methods of work. Professionalism also includes the ability to give priority to professional goals even when they seem to contradict one's own personal feelings.
- **Cooperation:** The staff shall work in constructive interaction and cooperation with each other, with other authorities, the convicts and their relatives, with voluntary organizations, congregations and other interest groups.
- **Sound Administration:** The operations shall be lawful, transparent and predictable, and decision-making as quick as possible. Decisions are to be substantiated and information on the activities shall be efficiently given. The convicts are to be informed about practical matters relating to the serving of the sentence, about their rights and obligations and about the rules and the consequences of breaking them. A convict is entitled to be heard in matters concerning him.

MEANS

Prison Service and the Probation Service are aiming at attaining their common goals

- by supporting and encouraging the convicts in leading a life without crime
- by controlling that convicts observe the limits set on them

- by influencing society as a whole in order to make work with this orientation possible.

The attainment of these goals is promoted by the development of the professional skills and the working conditions of the staff, by extensive use of staff skills and by staff participation in developing activities.

(From CSA website, 2003)

Performance measurement of prisons however has a much longer history and is very extensive. The annual 'Green Book' which reports on prisons' activities runs to some 200 pages (Oikeusministerio, 2000) although much of this volume is because data is broken down by individual prison institutions (something which has only just been introduced in the United Kingdom in 2003, by comparison).

Some of the principal pieces of data in the Green Book cover:

- Average number of prisoners
- Average number of prison places
- Occupancy rates
- Total staff
- Staff per prisoner
- Gross expenditure per prisoner
- Net expenditure per prisoner
- Percentage of prisoners in a rehabilitation activity.

This high level of data production, however, seems to be restricted in its use to discussions between senior managers and planners within CSA, and its predecessor organization, rather than as a management tool between HQ and local prisons. One senior manager (just prior to the change in status) was restricted internally mainly to senior management. Another interviewee, a Ministry of Finance official concerned with management arrangements for the new CSA, was quite unaware even of the existence of the 'green book' data.

Despite the voluminous nature of data about prisons there seemed to be substantial omissions. The most obvious was on recidivism where there was no data, but (like Sweden) a debate was going on about how to develop such measures. This argument had been going on for some time. A Finnish audit office report had suggested recidivism measures in the mid 1990s, but this had been strongly resisted by the prison service who had argued that the scientific evidence indicated that recidivism was heavily influenced by the family circumstances of the newly released prisoners – something well beyond the control of the prison service. Officially we were told at the beginning of our research (2000) that an internal working party was actively looking into recidivism measures, and three years later the message was exactly the same.

The Finnish State Audit Office (VTV) carried out a performance audit in 2001 (prior to the reorganization to agency status and fusion with probation) which was fairly critical (State Audit Office (Finland), 2001). They suggested that prisons had experienced significant reductions in prisoner numbers and reorientation in its objectives without serious changes to staffing, either numerically or in terms of training and organizational culture. However, as so often happens, the circumstances described in this assessment were changing even as it was written. The Finnish prison population started to go up and, perhaps more significantly, the composition of the prison population began to change – in the direction of a considerably more difficult-to-manage mixture. The core of hardened, 'professional' criminals increased, drugs became a serious problem, and more serious crimes were being committed by individuals coming from outside Finland. The new type of prisoner was a phenomenon stressed by several of our interviewees, as it had implications not only for recidivism, but very much for the internal management of prisons. 'The basic problem is that the character of the client has changed completely' (interview 12 August 2002).

Despite the formal differences in CSA's status and organization and the critical analysis of its performance from VTV, some of our interviewees seemed to think that not much was changing, or would change, in the new CSA. On the other hand in 2002 a special project (with Ministry of Finance participation) was underway to strengthen strategic management of the new agency by its parent ministry. Our research was concluded before any sensible estimate of the impact of these changes could be made, but there was clearly a good measure of scepticism both inside and outside CSA. When a senior Ministry of Finance official was asked if sanctions would be applied if a key performance target was significantly missed, the reply was 'that isn't the system, and everyone knows it'.

Conclusions

This is not the place to draw too many conclusions as this will be done more fully at the end of this book. However it is worth highlighting a few important points.

In some respects the basic functions of prisons (security, humanity and rehabilitation) display a clear similarity in the way they are organized at the most basic level – the individual prison. Even here however the policy differences between our countries – and within them over time – have a dramatic impact. In less liberal, less rehabilitative oriented regimes (e.g. the United Kingdom, except in the early 1990s, and Finland until the 1970s) the emphasis in prisons has been very different from the more liberal regimes (e.g. Sweden, Finland after the 1970s, the Netherlands up to the 1990s, and very briefly the United Kingdom).

The differences extend beyond penal policy however. The political/administrative cultures of our different countries clearly have a big impact. In those countries with consensual style politics (Finland, Holland, Sweden) the way in which the higher level institutional arrangements for organizing prison services are formalized and operated is clearly different from the United Kingdom.

The 'performance regimes' pick up these differences. In the United Kingdom we now have a highly formalized, contract-style, performance regime between the minister and the agency and a relatively strong implementation of performance management internally. In Finland we have had almost the exact opposite – with publication of large amounts of performance type data but (until very recently) little by way of formalized performance contracting or performance management. Sweden and Holland lie somewhere in between. Sweden has a highly developed system of dealing with performance issues between ministry and agency but this is much more in the form of what we might call a 'performance partnership' than a performance contract. Furthermore, Sweden is a special case to the extent that 'steering' is handicapped by the small size of the ministry, with the consequences of overload and an inability to develop much specialized expertise (Molander *et al.*, 2002). But in both Nordic states there is a high degree of trust and consequentially less formalization, rather as theories of 'social capital' tend to imply (Fukuyama, 1995). The Netherlands system seems more to be an uneasy amalgam of UK-style managerialism and performance contracting with the more consensual, performance partnership style of Sweden.

The final major point is about 'autonomy'. Whether formally agencies or merely a part of the ministry, prison organizations seem to retain their distinctive cultures and values, as well as many distinctive aspects of their internal management structures, regardless of their status. It seems that the basic functions of prisons – and some organizational consequences such as the inevitable fairly wide geographical dispersal of units, a degree of autonomy for local governors, the 24/7 nature of their business, and so on – lead to a distinctive 'prisons culture' whatever the formal status of the organization. This in itself creates a degree of autonomy in the way they operate. However, another recurring theme in all four countries is the political salience of prisons and in all cases the consequent 'nervousness' of politicians about prison issues, even operational ones. Even in Sweden, with by far the most formally autonomous status, the issue of who is held to account when a riot happens or a prisoner complains is less clear-cut than might be expected. The crises generated in the UK system over such issues are all too obvious. So prisons are, as we suggested at the start of this chapter, in the somewhat paradoxical position of being simultaneously very introverted, relatively autonomous, organizations and at the same time highly exposed to external gaze.

8
Meteorology

> If at morning the sky be red, it bids the traveller stay in bed.
> (Kingsbury *et al.*, 1996, p. 330)

> Mist is the residue of the condensation of air into water, and is therefore a sign of fine weather rather than of rain; for mist as it were is unproductive cloud.
> (Aristotle, 1962, p. 71)

Introduction

Observing and making predictions about the weather is an ancient practice. It is also a relatively established function in the public sector, with many National Meteorological Institutes (NMIs), including those examined in this chapter, being created in the mid- to late-1800s. Already at this time, the function of meteorology had an international character and international commissions were active in designing standard forms for how meteorological data should be recorded (Nebeker, 1995). This, along with other task features such as its 'scientific' professionalism (sceptics of forecasting science are asked to refrain their scoffs), infrastructure demands, commercial potential, and light policy load, could be expected to promote similarities in the way these NMIs are managed. For instance, some of the performance indicators being collected in our meteorological cases would suggest convergence.

National differences can also be observed in the way that meteorology is being conducted and managed in the Netherlands, Finland, Sweden and the United Kingdom. Local weather conditions and culture have left their mark on the kinds of forecasting models used, forecast presentation and research specialities. Also, with regard to the institutional patterns characterizing these NMIs, we find important distinctions regarding their legal status, their organizational status, their board types and their capacity to conduct commercial activities. The United Kingdom and Dutch Met Offices for instance present us with two poles on the commercial/non-commercial divide. The Swedish Institute would appear to be unique in its explicit expression of democratic ideals within the performance measurement framework it has developed, and continues to develop.

The presentation of our findings will begin with a background discussion of the meteorological scene, its recent international controversies and agreements, followed by a discussion of the specific features of the meteorological function. Each of our Meteorological Institutes will then be presented and their institutional patterns described. Finally, we will discuss our findings about the performance management frameworks in each national institute and present our conclusions regarding the role of functional and national influences upon these frameworks.

Background

At a most rudimentary level meteorology in the public sector has involved the collection, maintenance and exchange of observational weather data, the production of weather predictions and warnings, and research into the atmosphere (see Freebairn and Zillman, 2002a,b). Today, these tasks revolve around the collection of numerous daily weather observations from a network of national weather stations. In order to make even the most basic short term weather prediction possible, a small country like The Netherlands has some 30 stations (while Sweden has approximately 140) that collect a range of observations about the weather throughout the day. To get some insight into the wealth of information being produced at these weather stations, commentators have calculated that the Australian Meteorological Institute (hardly the biggest operator) collects on average two weather observations every minute (Curran and Gunasekera, 2003, p. 25).

Aside from national networks of data collection, there is also a global system of data exchange between NMIs. These international exchange arrangements codified in international agreements have been made possible through long standing (in excess of 100 years) co-operation within the World Meteorological Organization (WMO), and its predecessor, the International Meteorological Organisation (Curran and Gunasekera, 2003; www.wmo.org). National membership of these organizations was inspired by the desire to improve understanding of the atmosphere as well as the recognition that 'weather forecasts for any country depend upon the meteorological data collected over other countries and international waters round the globe' (Curran and Gunasekera, 2003, p. 25). Add to this the kinds of financial partnerships that have been forged between nations in order to finance meteorological satellites such as the European Meteosat, and you have some insight into the kinds of international collaborations that the weather has generated. However, with technological advances and the creation of new economic markets, the increasing commercial potential of the weather has been argued to present numerous threats to this international collaboration (White, 2001).

Meteorological knowledge has become a very profitable and desired product in recent years, with more possibilities to package forecasts to particular customer groups and in *more fora*, as well as the identification of more strategic uses for meteorological knowledge. The marketability of meteorological data has perhaps its most profound examples on financial markets, where 'weather derivatives and other financial instruments are now being offered by energy and commodities traders to offset risks posed by weather or climate conditions' (White, 2001, p. 1433). Aside from these more extreme examples of rampant capitalism, otherwise referred to as the 'weather risk industry', meteorology has also attained a more significant role in such growing markets as media communications and tourism. With the rise of internet and mobile telephones there are now many more mediums through which weather forecasts can be presented, just as there are many more aeroplane companies and leisure activities to which the weather can be marketed. These commercial opportunities have promoted the growth of private sector meteorological services, as well as heightening the thirsts of budget-stretched NMIs.

At the same time as commercial opportunities in the meteorological field have increased, many NMIs, like much of the public sector, have undergone substantial cuts in their budgets. This has not only led to cuts in staff but also in their ability to maintain and upgrade their infrastructure. One of the solutions available to (European) Institutes, and encouraged by New Public Management (NPM) philosophies, has been a policy of cost recovery, whereby the costs of running these institutes are partly recovered by the introduction of user fees, and where profits are also pursued on commercial markets. It should be noted that profit making itself was not a particularly novel activity for meteorological institutes, since they have long had commercial contracts with radio and television networks. Rather it is the extensive potential for commerce, the rise in competition for commercial contracts, and the increasing dependency of NMIs on non-government sources of funding that make their present circumstances unique. Interestingly, it is often former staff of NMIs that are responsible for setting up private sector meteorological competitors. All of these developments would suggest that the stakes around commercial activity in meteorology have risen substantially for both public and private actors.

Not only has the public–private divide become a more politically fired divide in meteorology, observers also refer to an American and a European philosophy regarding this divide (Weiss, 2002). America is said to pursue a policy of open and unrestricted access to public sector information, whereby the data collected and exchanged between NMIs (as per international agreements in WMO), is made freely available to commercial companies. The argumentation behind this arrangement would appear to be solely economic with the Americans claiming that their policy actively encourages a robust private sector and will ensure the greatest economic benefits (Weiss, 2002). They seem to be opposed to the government competing with the private sector at all, or providing any meteorological services that the private sector can provide (White, 2001, p. 1434). This principle, particularly in light of the move of some private American companies to get into the weather infrastructure arena (via satellites; purchasing high-powered modelling programs etc. – see White, 2001, p. 1434), has inspired debates about what is left for NMIs to do (see Freebairn and Zillman, 2002a, b). These debates also tend to be conducted primarily within an economic framework; although public safety is also often mentioned.

Alternatively, the more European 'cost recovery' approach has sought to charge for meteorological data in order to cover their infrastructure and running costs, or to invest in other parts of the public sector. This approach does not reject outright the possibility of competition between government and private actors. Indeed, in order to make such competition more viable, ECOMET, an economic interest group representing 20 European Meteorological Institutes, was created in 1995 to 'establish equal competition conditions for the public as well as for the private sector' (see www.ecomet.org). This body has created a number of regulations regarding the data that is available for commercial use, about how competition between NMIs should be conducted, and about the pricing of this data. It also has an objective to ensure the improvement and maintenance of national meteorological infrastructure. In addition, the EU has passed a directive requiring the separation of commercial and non-commercial accounts in order to promote transparency in the public sector's commercial activities. Despite ECOMET (and EU regulations), both it and the commercial activities of NMIs have been the subject of many private sector competitors' discontents, which have sometimes found their way to national competition authorities. Such opposition has led to a much less unified European vision (if there ever really was one), and has certainly made the organizational status of NMIs a much more politicized one than it was at the time of agency reforms in the 1980s or early 1990s. National conceptions of how NMIs should be organized are being increasingly shaped under an American cloud.

Safeguarding the continuing collaboration of NMIs, in the face of increasing competition, has not only inspired agreements within Europe through ECOMET, but also within the WMO. They passed what is widely known as Resolution 40, in 1995 at the Twelfth World Meteorological Congress. This resolution includes a set of guidelines regarding relationships in commercial meteorological activities (WMO, 1996). It recognizes a continued commitment to the principle of free and unrestricted exchange of meteorological and related data and products between NMIs, and thereby identifies a minimum set of 'essential' data and products that 'members shall exchange without charge and with no conditions on use' (WMO, 1996, p. 12). Resolution 40 also identifies 'additional' data that maybe exported with conditions such as a price. While the WMO has publicly applauded the commitment of nations to collaboration in meteorology, as demonstrated by the deliberations over resolution 40, it is clear that the matter is hardly closed. This is evident from recent pleas for increased participation of the private sector in international negotiations, such as that taking place within the WMO (White, 2001). Although this has been a rather compact discussion of the international meteorological scene, it is with consideration of this international background that the following analyses of NMIs and their functions should be read.

Attributes of the meteorology function

Meteorology has a number of attributes that can be expected to influence the kinds of management and performance measurement systems adopted within NMIs. We have already noted that NMIs are primarily responsible for the collection and maintenance of observational data, weather predictions and warnings, and research into the atmosphere. As will be shown, these are tasks governed by scientific norms, requiring considerable and expensive infrastructure, and with few national policy regulations. They are also tasks that do not really attract much political attention, except for isolated incidents or, more recently, with respect to commercial activities. An analysis of seven attributes of the meteorological task is presented in the following paragraphs.

The first functional feature is that it has (to date) and despite all the commotion around its commercial potential, established itself as an *essential* public service. This is primarily because the most basic tasks of NMIs such as weather predictions and warnings, have come to be closely associated with national security. During warfare for instance, meteorology often had an important strategic role and has been 'a standard element in military organisation' (Nebeker, 1995, pp. 83–4). Meteorological information was used to time bombardments and military attacks in both the First and Second World Wars, as well as more recently in the coalition attacks on Iraq and Afghanistan (UK MET Office, 2003). Indeed, many authors subscribe technical advances in the meteorological field to the conditions of war, not least because it led to much greater financial investment in meteorology.

The prospect and event of natural catastrophes such as flood, drought and more recently, global warming, also give gravity to the idea that meteorology should be a public good. Here its role in defending the nation is not just about protecting human lives but also protecting important national markets like agriculture. It is with these crises in mind, and their argumentative power in debates about public sector tasks, that NMIs can defend their public character as being of similar calibre to those other musts like the secret services and the armed forces. In interviews, for example, one director explained:

> there are some things that should remain part of the public infrastructure simply because of the safety that they provide to the community. (Director, KNMI)

With regard to performance management systems, we would expect emphasis upon indicators that seek to demonstrate and monitor how well NMIs are protecting the national interest, and that these particular kinds of indicators attract a more than passing interest from responsible ministers and ministries.

A second functional feature of meteorology is that it requires considerable and expensive infrastructure. This feature also relates to the public character of NMIs, since until quite recently it has only been governments that have been willing to invest in the technical instruments required. The operations of NMIs depend upon networks of weather observation stations across land and at sea, weather radar, radiosondes, super computers, specialized computer models and programmes, as well as satellites (see WMO, 1999). To get some insight into the kind of expense involved, the UK MET is reported to have recently purchased a new supercomputer at the cost of £25.5 million (www.vnunet.com), while the US Government finances its own weather satellites for some $USD 600 million per year (White, 2001). While weather hobbyists might still be using the old Stevenson's box, those days are long gone for the professionals. This means that observing and predicting the weather, while claimed to have become much more accurate, has also become in total more expensive than from say 50 years ago, although it is becoming cheaper with many observing stations now being automated.

At the same time, the yearly budgetary expenses of meteorology hardly compare to social security and its yearly programme costs, or to other defence costs. In this respect, meteorology has seemingly avoided the kind of political attention that social security has attracted. Nevertheless, the expense of infrastructure has become more important for NMIs as they have explicitly related it to their ability to perform well (UK MET Office, 2000). Also with the rise of competition, investing in technological advances may become more important as a point of differentiation from, and keeping up with, one's competitors. Performance measures to illuminate the gains from technological advancement might be expected to be an important management tool in this task.

Third, the meteorological task has a highly international character. This is also evident with respect to the previous feature infrastructure, where some nations have collaborated to finance weather satellites. The international character of meteorology is related to the character of its main object. It has long been understood that in order to make reliable predictions about the weather in any one nation or region, one must also have access to observations in other regions, indeed from around the globe. This has fostered collaboration between NMIs, as well as an extraordinary open exchange of meteorological knowledge. Contrary to many economic theories and claims about free markets and competition, the case of meteorology would seem to suggest that exchange between institutes was more open when competition was minimal. At the same time, the international character of meteorology has also promoted a degree of uniformity with respect to both, what should be observed and how. As Nebeker writes,

> the possibility of a meteorologist to use with confidence the data gathered by any other meteorologist ... required international agreements about which instruments to use, about calibration of instruments, about procedures for taking readings, and about the recording

of communication of data. By the end of the 19th century such agreements had been reached. (Nebeker, 1995, p. 12)

Such international agreements continued to be made within the World Meteorological Organisation, where a range of guidelines and standards about the technical character and quality of observational data, the process of obtaining this data, and observational sights, continue to be updated and demanded (see WMO, 1989). To this extent, the performance of NMIs is not only monitored within a national context but also within the international community. Although difficult to substantiate, we might speculate that innovation and openness to better ways of doing things, thus to better performance, is more likely to be stimulated in functions like meteorology, since its international character continually exposes the organization to what is happening in other NMIs.

A fourth feature is that meteorology is predominantly a scientific function. In J.Q. Wilson's terminology (1989), we can fairly safely classify NMIs as *craft organizations*. This is most evident in the scientific ethos that has traditionally characterized these organizations. Many of the current and past directors of Meteorological Institutes are scientists or engineers and have held their positions for long periods of time. They, like many of their personnel, will have most likely begun their career and even finished some of their training within the Institute itself. The representation of university educated staff with predominantly scientific degrees is also very strong. Over 70 per cent of employees in UK MET are described as scientists in their annual report (UK MET Office, 2003), while 53 per cent of employees in the Finnish Meteorological Institute (FMI) hold university degrees – 13.4 per cent of which are doctoral degrees. These conditions, combined with the standards of the international world of meteorology as reinforced through international exchange of data, conferences and international organizations like the WMO, ensure a degree of indoctrination of appropriate professional behaviour and values. The self-regulating effect of these values, at least with respect to scientific issues, is likely to be of great importance in overseeing the performance of NMIs. Peer oversight may be more effective than detailed ministry supervision, since the latter would require specialized meteorological knowledge within the ministry.

A fifth characteristic of meteorology is that it is primarily a delivery or production activity with very little connection to complicated policy guidelines. Unlike social security or even forestry, you would be hard pressed to find any ministry reports regarding the *national weather policy* or even political perspectives on the standards or decision-making priorities of the work being conducted in NMIs. Some exceptions might exist with respect to the timings of warnings, global warming research or with regard to the commercial activities of NMIs – but in this last case it could be argued that we are talking more about the form of meteorological work as opposed to its content. The light policy load that NMIs have to carry can be expected to leave them entirely preoccupied with their operations and research. This space to get on with it, however, also presents such dangers as becoming internally focussed or having to deal with disinterest or lack of understanding in the ministry. It is also a situation that can be advantageous for NMIs in the area of performance measurement and agreements, since ministries become dependent upon NMIs for defining their performance frameworks.

The general lack of a meteorological policy may also be indicative of the predominantly un-political tasks of NMIs. These organizations are rarely in the headlines and when they are this tends to be related to some one-off disaster or dissatisfaction with the weather (not the institution) more generally. The exception remains again with respect to the commercial activities of Meteorological Institutes, which, as was shown in the previous section to this chapter, have inspired a range of political opinions and debates. Even these, however, hardly hit the mass media headlines.

A sixth attribute of meteorology is that it does have commercial potential. This exists irrespective of whether governments choose to allow it to be used or not, and is available at relatively little extra cost. The decision to allow commercial activities would appear to be a national feature, determined by national culture and values. This national dimension is apparent in debates about the *American* and *European* vision of commercial activities in meteorology, and will become even more apparent in our discussion of the institutional patterns of NMIs (next section).

A final and seventh observation to make about NMIs, at least in the developed world, is that they have been around for a long time and have fostered a strong institutional memory regarding their achievements. All the NMIs included within this research have been an institutionalized part of the public sector since the mid or late nineteenth century. They display a wealth of artefacts about their past including depictions of their heroic endeavours during times of national disaster or warfare, old tools of the trade like the barometer, portraits of all past directors, or copies of their announcements regarding scientific or technological advances. On entering one of these organizations it is not uncommon to be confronted with some representation of a significant past or present. They generally have annual reports going back a hundred years and there are various long running historical societies that have made meteorology, and then to a great extent the NMIs, a topic for leisurely discussion among members of the general public. This is far removed from the more negative experiences and identities that public services like prisons or social security have had, and at different times, continue to endure. In interviews, all of our NMIs expressed the good feelings that their work inspired, as is illustrated in the following quotations:

> ... the MET is a bit like the BBC in the UK, well known and well loved – there is a sense of public ownership. (Director, UK MET, 20 November 2002)
>
> ... but as a whole SMHI for me and for most Swedish people has a nice sound. It has a good reputation. (Director, SMHI, 18 September 2000)

NMIs are proud organizations and this pride is reflected in the public record they have kept of themselves. It is also reinforced both by public responses to them (which in turn are related to the pervasive effects of and interest in the weather), their role in crises and their scientific character. As is the case for the well-nourished, attended-to and loved child in the schoolroom, it might be hypothesized that the goal of improving performance may come much easier for well-loved public sector organizations.

Patterns of institutions

The features of meteorology as a task would suggest that there should be many similarities in the way this work is conducted in different countries. Particularly, the international character of meteorology could be expected to promote a way of working that transcends national influences. In this section we will examine our four NMIs and their national patterns of institutions. While broad parallels can be observed with respect to the kinds of basic weather services they provide and their main customers, there are also important distinctions in their legal and organizational status. We also find quite distinctive arrangements regarding the acceptability of commercial activities within the NMIs.

Before proceeding to a discussion of the similarities and differences in the institutional patterns, it is first useful to introduce our four NMIs and some basic figures about them. Our cast is as follows: in The Netherlands the *Koninklijk Nederlands Meteorologisch Instituue* (KNMI), in

Finland *Ilmatieteen Laitos*, commonly referred to in English as the *Finnish Meteorological Institute* (FMI), in Sweden–*Sveriges Meteorologiska och Hydrologiska Institut* (SMHI), and in the United Kingdom, the *UK MET Office*.

With regard to the basic tasks of the NMIs, it should be noted that there is much similarity and that they are all in the business of meteorological observation, prediction and research. Not surprisingly, there are however some differences in the kinds of models they adopt to complete this work, and this is related to the local geography and the different kinds of climates in each country. This difference can also be related to the investment patterns of each country, since as one informant pointed out:

> the technical system that we have is very expensive, you don't just change the model because its combined in a system with other variables and they are dependent on each other...instead of changing your model you just try to make it as good as all the others. (Director, SMHI, 23 April 2001)

All of the models used by NMIs are numerical weather prediction models. In the United Kingdom they have what they refer to as The Numerical Weather Prediction Models, while in Sweden, Finland and The Netherlands they use the High Resolution Limited Area Model (HIRLAM). The United Kingdom is unique in our group of NMIs because in the meteorological world it is what is referred to as a World Meteorological Centre (WMC) and runs global models for short, medium and long-range forecasting. Our other NMIs are National Meteorological Centres (NMCs) and they do not run the globe in their models, but rather have access to this information from the European Centre for Medium Range Forecasting (ECMWF), which is in the UK MET. We should also point out, from the basic figures in Table 8.1, that the UK is also unique with respect to size, being in terms of personnel and receipts some 4 to 5 times bigger than all the other NMIs, which are all of quite similar sizes. Finally, SMHI can also be considered to be unique because its basic tasks include not only meteorology and oceanography but also hydrology.

All of our NMIs also conduct substantial amounts of research, although there are differences in specialities and also the degree of expenditure upon research. None of them are subject to particular national regulations regarding the amount of their total receipts that they must contribute to research, although they all receive some external funding from bodies such as the EU and research institutes and this

Table 8.1 Basic organizational arrangements for Meteorology at time of research (2000–01)

Organization	Status	Ministry	Staff	Government receipts* (million euro)	Commercial receipt (million euro)	Research Expenditure (million euro)
FMI	Agency	Transport and communication	602	29.07	2.82	7.78
KNMI	Agency	Traffic and infrastructure	585	42.2	0	13.5
SMHI	'Uppdrag' agency	Environment	547	33.6	9.5	3.9
Met office	Trading Fund agency	Defence	2229	187**	30.27	30.55

Notes: * These broken down figures are for the year 2000 and were provided by the organizations themselves. They include both direct government receipts (e.g. from the ministry's budget) and from other government authorities. They exclude purely commercial receipts.

** The UK accounts, despite the requests we made, do not distinguish between government and non-government receipts but rather competitive and non-competitive receipts. The bulk of the latter includes direct government receipts and receipts from other government authorities. The figure on competitive receipts for the United Kingdom includes some government receipts and, therefore, exaggerates somewhat their commercial activities relative to the other NMIs. The other organizations agreed to disaggregate their figures for this table.

money is generally defined for a particular research purpose. Both the United Kingdom and Sweden have their own separate meteorological research institutes connected to their NMIs. These are, respectively: the Hadley Centre for Climate Prediction and Research, and the Rossby Centre. In each of our NMIs, climate research and also a number of applied research projects regarding the quality of their observations, models and prediction are being pursued. We also find distinctions in some research activities with Finland being occupied in studies about the arctic, The Netherlands focussing upon seismic activity and Sweden conducting research into the modelling of river run-off. From our basic figures it is evident that the Dutch Institute, KNMI, devotes proportionately more of its total receipts to research. This may in part be related to its shift away from commercial activities, and towards the identity promoted in its annual reports as a 'national knowledge institute'.

A third broad area of similarity concerns the main customers of our NMIs. All of the NMIs identify defence, aviation and road traffic authorities as their main customers. Furthermore, at FMI, SMHI and the UK MET, we also find the media highly ranked among their customers, while in The Netherlands media contracts have been designated as commercial and therefore from a Dutch perspective properly left to the private sector.

The organizational form is a point of some difference among our NMIs. While both FMI and KNMI are considered *agencies* within their national contexts and also internationally, SMHI and the UK MET may be described as being more like state companies, though not quite. SMHI has a special status within the Swedish context and is one of a few *uppdrag myndigheten* that is required to make a profit. Indeed, the Swedish State has been well rewarded by SMHI's commercial activities, since 8 per cent of the organization's turnover is returned each year to the Ministry of Finance. Also, the UK MET has a special kind of agency status as an Agency Trading Fund. It became a Trading Fund in 1996, as part of the then Conservative Government's policy of preparing commercially active executive agencies for potential privatization. Trading Funds are unique in the United Kingdom because they were designed to be entirely self-funded. Officially they do not receive any appropriations from Treasury, although in the case of the MET much of the 'income' that it earns comes directly from other departments, and has its origin in the national budget. Instead of a direct receipt from the Exchequer, with its Trading Fund status all funding for MET services went to its departmental 'customers', who were under no formal obligation to continue to purchase from the MET. Other features of the MET's Trading Fund status is that it is able to retain some of its profits for investment, although it should also repay a dividend to its ministry. The agreements about this dividend would appear to be quite flexible since in the year 2002/03, for example, the MET was not required to pay a dividend at all (UK MET Office, 2003, p. 41).

With respect to the ministries responsible for our NMIs we also see some variation, as is evident in Table 8.1. Again, FMI and KNMI would appear to have some similarities since they are respectively part of the Ministries of Transport and Communication, and Traffic and Infrastructure. FMI was part of the Ministry of Agriculture until the late 1960s and has since that time remained within the Ministry of Transport and Communication. Since 1998 SMHI has been an agency of the Ministry of Environment, while prior to that time it was part of a much bigger ministry: the Ministry of Industry, Employment and Education. The UK MET is a Trading Fund of the Ministry of Defence, and has had a long history with that department during both the First and Second World Wars.

It is interesting to note that each of these NMIs with their different organizational status, also have different kinds of legal status. Since 2001 the 'public' tasks of KNMI have been clarified and recognized in a government statute. This is not a fixed characteristic of being an *agentschap* in The Netherlands, but was decided upon in the particular case of KNMI in order to make the commercial and non-commercial line clear. Not only does the KNMI Statute set out its general tasks, but it also recognizes the establishment of its advisory board. There is also a specific law describing the tasks of FMI, as well as a decree in which the status is regulated. In contrast, SMHI does not have a specific statute regarding its tasks but rather, as a *myndigheten*, is recognized in the Swedish constitution as having administrative independence (see Chapter 5). SMHI also has an advisory board, which is broadly recognized in a government regulation. There is also no specific legislation recognizing the tasks of the UK MET, although it was the application of the Trading Fund Act that gave it its Trading Fund Status. This is a generic piece of legislation that can be applied to any particular organization. The UK MET also has an advisory board in the Ministry of Defence, which must give advice to the minister about UK MET tasks and performance requirements.

The board types in each of our cases also differ to some extent, with the Swedish and Finnish boards having a long tradition of stakeholder representation, including representation of personnel. Annual reports are signed off and presented to their boards and other issues, generally brought to their attention by the Directors of SMHI and FMI, may be decided upon. The KNMI board is not a board of stakeholder representation but rather has the task to advise and report only upon the scientific direction and performance of KNMI. The Minister selects (and can also dismiss) 5–9 members of this board for a period of four years. Finally, the Defence Meteorological Board of the UK MET includes some core customers as board members but primarily consists of representatives from its 'owner', within the Ministry of Defence. The UK MET board would appear to play an important role in giving advice about the performance measurements used to monitor the UK MET's performance. In each of our NMIs the Directors are members of the boards, but they are not chairpersons of the board.

The commercial and non-commercial divide

Among our NMIs we can identify three quite distinct trajectories with respect to commercial activities. At one extreme, the UK MET is extremely active on commercial markets (see Table 8.1) and has even recently become involved in a joint venture with a corporate company on the weather derivatives market. In our interviews, employees displayed a great deal of confidence about their commercial activities and the political acceptability of continuing these. At the other extreme, KNMI in The Netherlands, has since 1999 refrained from all commercial activities, and any such business that was pursued prior to that time was privatized into the company Holland Weather Services (HWS). In the KNMI interviews, we find an organization relieved that political scrutiny about their commercial activities has now been diverted, so that they can get on with the business of being a 'national knowledge centre'. Alternatively, in SMHI and FMI, we find organizations whose status currently hangs in the balance. They continue to conduct commercial activities at this time and, in accordance with both EU and ECOMET regulations, have taken very careful measures to keep their commercial and non-commercial accounts separate. In these interviews, there was some discomfort and uncertainty expressed about their commercial future. This is not unwarranted since in both countries announcements from other government organizations have recommended that their commercial activities be conducted within a separate organization (Statskontoret, 2002).

Our interview findings in each case illustrate further the different national perspectives towards competition. In the United Kingdom for example we find a highly competitive market, at least in the sense of numbers of competitors. Informants advised us that there are approximately ten private sector competitors active in the United Kingdom, including multinational companies such as Weather Services International (WSI, an American company), Oceanroutes of Weather News Incorporated (WNI, a Japanese company) and Nobel Denton. The UK MET has been the subject of at least one complaint within the United Kingdom Competition Commission; however, this was very low key and no evidence of anti-competitive behaviour was found. In our interviews at the UK MET, the issue of a commercial and non-commercial divide did not seem to present too many problems. Rather, there was the view that it was a good thing that there was some flexibility in this divide, and that commercial activities could reduce the costs of public services. As one interviewee stated:

> The commercial department helps reduce the cost of the public Met Service, which is paid for by circa ten government departments. If the CEO was to double the revenue from commercial business but the overall level of profit stayed the same, then nobody would be very impressed. (Director, UK MET, 20 September 2002)

There was no mention of political pressures or controversies regarding the UK MET working more like the private sector and indeed many informants noted their commercial activities as a source of pride both for UK MET and for the parent ministry.

In Finland, at FMI, some commercial activities are also pursued, although this is a much smaller competitive market. FMI has at least one private sector competitor FORECA, which was established by former FMI staff. In addition, SMHI has set up an office in Finland with desires to increase their market share. According to our interviews in SMHI, they have been successful in obtaining commercial contracts with Finnish newspapers. Unlike the UK MET, we find in FMI a much greater emphasis upon the importance of abiding by both EU and Finnish competition regulations. They reminded us that:

> Both EU law and Finnish competition law mean that FMI has to separate commercial activities and that this is directly reflected in the FMI internal structure. (Research Officer, FMI, 20 October 2000)

The commercial activities of FMI include selling forecast messages for mobile phones, lightning alarms and other message/forecast services packaged for specific consumer groups. Their caution about the commercial/non-commercial divide has no doubt been heightened by findings in the Finnish Competition Council (FCC) that FMI has engaged in anti-competitive practices. FORECA complained that FMI had misused its dominant position in the Finnish market by selling degraded radar images to its competitors, while internally selling first grade quality images to its own commercial weather services unit. This was a fascinating case, not least because the images bought by FORECA were sold to it by SMHI, who in turn had purchased these images from FMI. The FCC imposed an infringement fine of EUR 20 000 upon FMI and recommended that 'FMI's commercial service activities are transferred to an independent and separate company' (see www.kilpailuvaristo.fi; accessed October 2003). FORECA has tried to bring another case of unfair pricing against FMI in the FCC but was unsuccessful, since no evidence for these additional allegations were found.

The Swedish SMHI also approaches any discussion about commercial activities with much trepidation and caution. Typical responses are: 'there is a lot of private sector pressure to prevent us from having any unfair advantages' or 'there are organizations that are keeping their eyes on us'. SMHI would appear to have been quite successful in its own commercial activities (Table 8.1) and is active in media communication markets, mobile phone forecasts, energy and agricultural markets. We were advised that there are three main competitors in Sweden, including a Finnish private sector company. These private sector competitors are generally quite small although there are sometimes attempts from American companies to get into the sports and leisure area as well as radio contracts (SMHI, commercial advisor). SMHI has clearly gone to great lengths to arrange both its organization and its accounts in a way that makes some transparency in internal allocations possible. As one director in SMHI explained:

> In our organisation it is quite clear where the line is drawn and that is between what we have called commercial services and government services. I do not know another weather organisation that has paid the same degree of attention to the internal allocation of resources and the contracts that we have between the different units. This helps to ensure that there is no blurring between the financial distribution in the commercial and non-commercial sections. (Director, SMHI, 23 April 2001)

These efforts of SMHI, however, have not protected it from national debates or criticisms regarding its status and commercial activities. Already in 1991, consideration was given to translating SMHI into a state-owned company (Sandebring *et al.*, 2000). Some arguments used for not pursuing this status at the time included the lack of extensive competition in the markets where SMHI was active, and a desire to maintain some homogeneity in organizational structure with other European meteorological offices (Statskontoret, 2002). A distinctive structure such as a state-owned company was thought to impede international cooperation. At the time of interviews, SMHI managers expressed the desire to become (with both commercial and noncommercial activities together) a state owned company since this would advance its abilities to pursue commercial activities, particularly in foreign markets. However, in 2002 a government authority, the Swedish Agency for Administrative Development, published findings from its own investigation recommending that the public tasks of SMHI remain within a government agency form, while the commercial tasks are to be separated into a state owned company (Statskontoret, 2002). Since our interviews, there has been commitment from the Minister of Environment in Sweden to maintain the commercial activities in SMHI.

At the other end of the spectrum, KNMI in The Netherlands does not conduct any commercial activities and is entirely preoccupied with the public tasks set out for it in its KNMI statute. There is, however, a competitive market in The Netherlands with at least three main operators. One of these is the former commercial part of KNMI, now called Holland Weather Services, 75 per cent of which is owned by the Japanese meteorological multinational, Weather News Inc. The other 25 per cent is owned by a Dutch entrepreneur, who is also director of the company. The other two private competitors are Meteoconsult, also established by former KNMI staff, and 'Weather on line'. Some of the kinds of tasks that have been left for these private sector organizations to battle over include media contracts, contracts to the shipping industry, internet services and other packaged forecasts for particular clients, such as farmers. Among the tasks defined as 'non-commercial' are services to the aviation industry, the argumentation behind the definition of this kind of work as 'public' being mainly safety issues. In order to maintain this commercial and non-commercial divide some agreements have had to be made between KNMI and its competitors, in particular with regard to KNMI's warning responsibilities. Since KNMI no longer has contracts with the media, there has been concern that it has less control over the speed with which weather warnings can be provided to the general public. Therefore, in these situations private competitors must ensure that KNMI warnings get to the media in time.

In KNMI there was a great sense of relief about no longer conducting commercial activities. Typically statements from remaining KNMI staff included:

> There used to be a lot of discussions with the ministry at the time when we had a lot of commercial activities in house. People on the market were complaining to the ministry about us and then there were a lot of discussions. But since that time everything is now smooth. (Interview, Director, KNMI, 24 october 2001)

And:

> We ourselves have also better feelings about not having a commercial side. The problem with the commercial department was too much attention ... formally we did not do any cross subsidisation and we tried to prevent it as much as possible, but it's a danger and good that its separated. (Interview Director, Interview KNMI, 24 October 2001).

The embrace of this split between commercial and non-commercial even went so far as one informant envisioning the supply of much of its weather observation information on its internet site for free.

At the beginning of the 1990s there was no expectation or indication that the commercial activities of KNMI would be privatized. Indeed, at the time of its agency creation, there was the belief within KNMI that becoming an agency would correspond with its growing commercial opportunities (interview, former director, KNMI, 18 Febraury 2002). After all, a central feature of becoming an *agentschap* in The Netherlands was the possibility to use 'business like' accounting techniques. Also, the dominant rhetoric around *agentschap* reforms in the early 1990s and the official views of both the Ministry of Finance, and the Ministry of Traffic and Infrastructure (KNMI parent ministry) did appear to promote commercial activities within the public sector. As one interviewee explained:

> commercialisation was something that this department (Traffic and Infrastructure) encouraged but later they did not like it because there were troubles with other commercial parties. (Interview, former director, KNMI, 18 February 2002)

By 1997, after a series of criticisms from a range of parties, including KNMI's private sector competitors Meteoconsult, the Dutch Employers

Council and a parliamentary commission, the enthusiasm for commercial activities in government agencies and more specifically KNMI, was quelled (see Chapter 4). It was within this context that the decision was made to privatize KNMI's commercial activities.

One theme that was consistent throughout the interviews in all four countries, was the lack of any simple objective standard from which the commercial/non-commercial divide could be drawn. All of the NMIs conducting commercial activities cited many contracts with other government authorities as commercial. They were also listed as commercial in their accounting figures. Similarly, in KNMI, we see that tasks completed for the aviation sector are categorized as non-commercial, although clearly we could envision such tasks being conducted by private sector organizations. Some commentators have argued that there are basic meteorological services that are public goods by virtue of their non-exclusability and because of the unlimited marginal benefit that they bring to society as a whole (Freebairne and Zillman, 2002a,b). Aside from this economic rationale, there have also been the arguments about public safety. Perhaps surprisingly in our national context, the United Kingdom has been the least bothered with principles about the commercial and non-commercial divide. Arguments for commercial activities in the public sector because it improves performance and returns money to the public purse have been the most successful in the United Kingdom and least challenged there. As for arguments against competition within NMIs, perhaps the one that was most frequently cited was the tensions it presented for international collaboration between NMIs.

Performance management systems in meteorology

All of the NMIs we visited were collecting and publishing a range of performance measures. They could generally speak quite fluently about the development of their performance measurement systems and how they had been used for planning and decision-making in their respective organizations. They were also no strangers to accreditation systems like ISO 9001 (all but one had their certificates, while the other, FMI, used some parts of this standard in its quality control manual) or to techniques like the balanced scorecard. There were indications that they were quite actively pursuing ways to improve their performance measurement systems whether through consultation with clients or through participation in a variety of forums where performance was a central theme. The following quotation is exemplary of the upbeat way in which many informants described their institute's attitude to performance:

> Oh yes. That's the part I really like about SMHI. I think we are looking outside very much and we made a balanced scorecard for example, talking about performance measures, the market orientation, attendance to conferences etc. (Interview, Director, SMHI, 23 April 2001)

With regard to the performance measurement systems that these organizations had in place, they appeared to be quite sophisticated and embedded in at least two of the cases – Sweden and the United Kingdom. KNMI, the Dutch NMI, would appear to be the biggest exception, or at least, the least well scripted when it came to describing the kinds of links that existed between their performance measures and their management systems. Perhaps due to a less developed performance management system, they could give very few examples as to how their performance measurements were being used aside from in the presentation of their annual report. The following is indicative of the kinds of responses given:

> ... the performance indicators are a subject of discussion, but it is more discussion than reality. We have a lot of problems making good performance indicators. ... At this moment we are trying [to] get new ones but we are still working on this job. But this doesn't influence the organisation at all. (Interview, Director, KNMI, 24 October 2001)

The significance of financial measures and their frequent measurement was strong in all the Institutes, and this similarity held true irrespective of whether the organization was conducting commercial activities or not. The Dutch, for example, spoke of how being an agency presented greater pressures for having your books in order, they said:

> being an agency makes us more in the spotlight, the accounting department and the Rekenkamer (audit office) are checking more on agencies. (Interview, Director, KNMI, 24 October 2001)

There was some indication though that those active commercial activities had financial systems and measures on a whole different plane of sophistication. Consider the following quotation from SMHI:

> We have a structure for SMHI and a business control system called 'The Boss' in which we follow all economic indicators in the same

way, so we talk about key economic ratios throughout the organisation. Every unit is measured in the same way so that we can compare them ... We talk about contributions in different stages, turnover minus costs is the contribution to the fixed costs, and we also talk about contribution margin, the percent of the contribution compared to turnover, that is the margin percent. And we have a target level for SMHI and target levels for different units. (Interview, SMHI, Financial Officer, 18 September 2000)

For the three commercially active NMIs it might be suggested that their highly developed financial systems were not only related to being commercial as such, but also to guard against complaints from competitors that cross-subsidization was taking place. So any internal sales from a government services division to a commercial division could be accounted for. Certainly, in Sweden and in Finland, where complaints from competitors appeared an ever present and politically charged danger, the importance and transparency of such a system was emphasized.

Another common feature among the NMIs was that, although they tended to use more performance measures than they actually published in their yearly reports, there were not enormous numbers of targets (as compared with, say, the forestry function). With the exception of research activities, which were monitored differently, the NMIs in general tended to pride themselves upon designing a limited set of widely used indicators throughout the various units of their organizations. They also tended to pursue the measurement of similar kinds of phenomenon such as accuracy of forecasts, although the way these were measured tended to vary. In Sweden, Finland and the United Kingdom there was a lot of discussion about targets, whereas in The Netherlands the performance measurements were more a record of what the organization had produced. In addition, in Sweden there seemed to be a much greater emphasis upon the uses of the organization to society and the accessibility of its performance measures to the general public. A short overview of the kinds of measures being collected in each organization is presented in the following paragraphs.

In the UK MET office, there were six key measures informants identified as important and were presented in their yearly reports and corporate plans. Most of these measures are actually indexes and made up of a range of indicators thought to contribute to the performance being measured. They are also the measures used by the MET board and its

Minister to assess its performance. These main indicators included:

- Accuracy of forecast
- Quality of service
- Efficiency
- Return on capital employed
- Strategic investment
- Commercial activities contribution
- Staff skills index

Accuracy of forecast is calculated by the Numerical Weather Prediction Index, this is an index designed to measure the overall forecasting skills of the forecasting model (entitled Numerical Weather Prediction) being used by the UK MET office. The *quality of service* indicator is also an index calculated from a range of requirements defined in consultation with customers, not least the core customer group. These requirements include the accuracy of specific kinds of forecasts, for example warnings for the aviation sector, as well as the timeliness of the particular forecast. The *efficiency* indicator measures the change in levels of output in relation to the costs of two core MET tasks (e.g. the accuracy NWP model in Europe and North Atlantic ocean and defence stations). *Return on Capital Employed (ROCE)*, is a profit measure that focuses upon the return on average net assets, while the *commercial activities contribution* is an absolute figure measuring the financial contribution to core services from commercial activities. Finally, the sixth indicator is the *Staff Skills Index* that was still being designed at the time of research. The idea is that this indicator will be made up of a number of core competencies required of employees, that can then be used at the individual level to decide upon performance pay, as well as being used at the organizational level to identify an average staff competence as a whole. The UK MET office has targets for each of these indicators set annually by the Ministry of Defence.

The SMHI used a range of performance measures that were both demanded from the government and set internally. Generally speaking, many of the indicators required by the government were focussed upon the basic services of the organization with some economic indicators, while those set internally were more orientated towards the commercial services and the customers of the organization. The main performance measures required by the government annually included:

- Accuracy of forecast (should be at least 85 per cent accurate)
- Accuracy of warning services (should be at least 78 per cent accurate)

- The practical use of observations collected (at least 95 per cent applicable for prediction)
- The practical use of research and development for society (written reports)
- The level of co-operation with other authorities.

Aside from the monthly, quarterly and yearly financial figures that all agencies in Sweden are required to report, SMHI also presents the government with figures on their turnover and marginal turnover. Among the indicators that SMHI collects for its internal management, there are indicators and targets for production costs, turnover and profit. Except for the government services division (which only has targets for production costs) all of these targets are collected for the different divisions of the organization. These figures are compiled and revised regularly in their business management system, and can be accessed on the internet by management staff wishing to check up on whether the organization or division is working to target.

As in the UK MET, in SMHI too, there was a strong emphasis upon customer focus and this was also monitored throughout the organization, despite not being requested by government. Rather than a uniform set of figures, customer focus tended to be gauged by tailoring specific indicators for specific clients and projects. As one interviewee described:

> Some of our important customers have asked us to produce quality indicators, for example the Civil Aviation Authority is our most important customer, so every year we produce a report with the different types of quality measures of the services which we give them. (Interview, Director, SMHI, 18 September 2000)

Similarly, another informant explains:

> we are all working for our customers and we measure most of the time processes that we use in different projects, so we can see how much we work directly for a customer ... we are making a deal with customers, where we develop a system to take 100 hours to finish a task and then we measure if that was also the case. (Interview, Director, SMHI, 18 September 2000)

In order to maintain a strict separation between the commercial and non-commercial activities of SMHI, performance measurements and targets played a role in a number of internal agreements between different units in the organization. These internal agreements not only included specification regarding the unit cost of a particular service and thus the charge that would be made to another division, but also demands regarding the timing of its provision. This can be illustrated by the following citations:

> We also buy and trade internally, these agreements are not only labelled with a certain amount of money but also performance, for example if it should be a 24 hour service or a back up. (Interview, Director, SMHI, 18 September 2000)

Or as another informant explained:

> There is between the IT services and other units, a discussion every year about what they are expecting from each other. (Interview, Director, SMHI, 18 September 2000)

These internal contracts which were developed in the planning processes of the organization each year, were designed to encourage the whole organization to be performance orientated.

At FMI we also found a number of similar indicators, such as accuracy of forecast and weather warnings. Here too, there was an emphasis upon cost prices and the internal transactions throughout the organization. They also distinguished between financial performance indicators, indicators regarding performance for customers and society, indicators regarding their operations, staff and also their research activities. Some of their main performance indicators included:

- Accuracy of forecast
- Accuracy and timing of warnings
- Turnover (a target of a 3 per cent increase was set)
- Degree of automated observations
- Externally funded research (at least 40 per cent)
- Increased job satisfaction.

FMI used a balanced scorecard throughout their organization, the design and implementation of which had been promoted by the Ministry of Finance. While informants expressed satisfaction with the use of this scorecard in their internal management system, they were less satisfied about its ability to say anything about the impact of FMI's work in the wider society.

In the Dutch Institute, KNMI, the performance measures collected were organized around a number of 'product' groups that they have distinguished. These product groups include, among others, general weather forecasts, climate research and advice, warnings, warnings and forecasts for aviation, and research. For each product group, levels of output and cost prices were being collected and published. In addition, the organization was using some measures of the quality of forecasts – for example, in the case of forecasts about rain and for ship warnings – further measures of forecast quality were still being developed. Although KNMI does not really seem to use the term 'accuracy of forecast', its measures of quality of forecast include the average difference between a forecast (of their model) and the actual weather, as well as the timeliness of the forecast. In the area of research, KNMI uses an independent review council to assess the quality of research products, the number of scientific publications and presentations and the average number of externally funded projects.

Accuracy of forecast

Of all the indicators that our NMIs are collecting, accuracy of forecast presented us with some of the most interesting discussions and responses. Even though this measure was collected by all of the NMIs, it became apparent that each of the institutes had their own way of measuring this, thus limiting the possibilities for international comparison of performance. There was also some difference of opinion regarding the extent to which such comparisons would be useful. The UK MET advised us that their Numerical Weather Prediction Index (NWPI) was

> *the* measure by which accuracy is determined. When comparing the accuracy of the UK MET with other MET offices then this is the absolute measure that is used, and it can be used as a benchmark on a number of different benchmarks. (Interview, Director, UK MET, 20 November 2000)

However, it soon became evident that the scientists did not agree that there was 'one best way':

> No we do not use this [NWPI]. The meteorological service in England is bigger and they conduct forecasts for the entire world – this may have something to do with why they use the model they do. However, it does not mean that it is the most appropriate for Sweden. (Interview, Director, SMHI, 23 April 2001)

In addition, we were confronted with quite complicated responses regarding what counted as an accurate forecast: for example, respondents pointed to a number of different perspectives upon which the weather could be assessed:

> It is still a very technical issue but we are trying to identify a number of parameters that will make the presentation of our forecast more sensible and reflect the issues around what makes a performance good. Also we want to show how accurate the forecasts are from a number of perspectives – it is not just the weather forecast is good or bad. We can say that it is going to rain today in Norrkjoping but if it does not rain all over the town, that does not make the forecast wrong. Place and the perspective of the user are also connected with how accurate a prediction is. (Interview, Director, SMHI, 23 April 2001)

and:

> I mean when they are asking if how good we are at predicting the weather, and how do they measure that, it can be that the wind is a bit less than we predicted but that all aspects of the prediction were good. (Interview, Operations Manager, SMHI, 18 September 2001)

A third dimension of controversy concerned friction between attaining scientifically accredited measures of accuracy and meeting other performance requirements. This friction had clearly been exacerbated by the rise of commercial activities in NMIs, unleashing competing value systems of science and markets:

> For most of the meteorologists they are most concerned with the accuracy of their forecasts. Of course, for people working in marketing and selling, the revenue is the most important indicator ... also it can be different between what the customer wants and the meteorologist wants, the customer can be most concerned with the delivery time but for the meteorologist it is whether the quality of the forecast is good. (Business Director, SMHI, 18 September 2000).

> The MET have made measures more about customers and less about other things – it is no good producing the most accurate forecasts if the price is prohibitive. This view would not have entered the equation of the office during its first 135 years of operation, and many staff would rather it still did not, we must not forget they are scientists. (Director, UK MET, 20 November 2000)

It becomes apparent that commercial activities have not only raised questions about the public nature of meteorological tasks, but it has also presented some challenges to its scientific character.

The interview questions

Aside from comparing the kinds of performance measurements that were being used in the different NMIs, it is also useful to contrast their responses to our questions regarding

- What are the most important performance indicators?
- Has there been, or is there foreseen in the near future, significant change in the framework of the performance measures used?
- How are performance measures set?

What are the most important performance indicators?

If we look at the way our respondents replied to questions about the most important indicators of good performance, there is no ultimate measure that stands out. We find instead that different respondents in the same organization identified different measures of performance as important, or that they tended to refer to some general idea of performance as opposed to a particular existing indicator. The UK MET was perhaps an exception in this variation, with all of their respondents always providing a recital of their key performance indicators in one order or another. The Dutch KNMI was also quite consistent in its responses in the sense that research and quality of production was continually cited, although no particular indicators were held up as 'the' one or two. This KNMI response clearly eschews from emphasis upon commerce. The Swedish respondents tended to cite performance indicators least frequently (although they did on one or two occasions) when discussing what counted as 'good performance'. This was despite the fact that the organization does indeed have quite a systematic list of indicators. Instead, one tended to obtain a number of replies referring to the possibility for employees to develop, about being professional or scientific or about flexibility in the work place.

Has there been, or is there foreseen in the near future, significant change in the framework of performance measures used?

All of the NMIs – including KNMI when respondents reflected on its past – made some reference to the effect of commercialization upon the performance of the organization. They related commercialization both to a greater customer focus in the organization and to being able to recover costs. In addition, cost consciousness as a result of both downsizing and the collection of extensive financial measures, were common themes in discussions about how thinking about conceptualizations of performance had changed in the last ten years.

The UK and Swedish Institutes both offered the most explicit examples of important organizational changes that had contributed to thinking about performance and to the way their performance framework had become more customer focussed. In the UK for example, informants pointed to the shift to a Trading Fund Agency and the requirement that they were to operate completely on a cost recovery basis. This arrangement meant that the UK MET no longer received direct appropriations from the budget but instead was to entice their public sector customers to continue choosing to maintain their services from the MET. It also presented incentives for the MET to increase their commercial activities, since their Trading Fund status would allow them to keep some of their profits for investment in their organization:

> The 1996 change must be made clear because it made a difference to the way performance was thought about. It related performance to the market place. So measures of performance have become much more customer focused. (Interview, Director, UK MET, 20 November 2000)

> The most important impact on staff is the need for someone else to want their services. The biggest change in culture is the fact that there is a customer focus. This has happened gradually over time... since becoming a Trading Fund. (Interview, Director, UK MET, 20 November 2000)

In SMHI, a shift towards greater customer focus was also associated with change in the organization, although this time it was not a change in status but rather a change in organizational structure. The structural changes were proposed by SMHI in the early 1990s against the background of reductions in government appropriations and opportunities for commercial work (Sandebring *et al.*, 2000). Separate divisions correlating with SMHI's different types of customers, and the kinds of fees they were expected to pay, were created. Instead of a production orientated organization based upon meteorology, hydrology and oceanography, the divisions were split into government services (financed by direct appropriations), commissioned work (financed by contracts with other government authorities at cost price, e.g. the aviation sector) and commercial services (purely commercial character e.g. contracts with media). In addition to a division that served all of the other units, for example, with IT services, this structure provided the framework from which contracts within the organization could be developed, such as, a contract between government services, which collects observations, and a commercial division. A director at SMHI describes the significance of the new organizational arrangements as follows:

> We found that we had very problematic organisational relations with the customer because some were paying on a commercial basis and some were paying another tariff and what we did was we analysed what we are doing, under what conditions and to whom. From there we have developed the different divisions in our organization, so we organized ourselves to meet those customer requirements. (Interview, Director, SMHI, 18 September 2000).

In interviews it was stated that since the structural changes in SMHI (completed in 1992) very few changes had been made to its performance measurement system. Investigations to develop new measures for accuracy of forecast were, however, underway. The assignment to develop these new accuracy measures was less a management requirement, but rather, a request from the parent ministry to construct measures that would be more accessible to the general public. The motivation behind the new measurements of accuracy was expressed as follows:

> It is more a communication problem, our measures have been too scientific and the person on the street doesn't understand it. It is not that it was wrong but just in the respect that people may not be able to understand it, that has become a problem. (Interview, Communications Manager, SMHI, 18 September 2000)

In our analysis of the meteorological function, the Swedish SMHI was the only organization which voluntarily expressed some concern with the informative nature of their performance measures from a democratic perspective.

Except for SMHI's investigation into accuracy of forecast, they, the UK, and the Finnish bodies generally expressed satisfaction with their performance measurement framework and did not foresee any significant future changes. At the other end of the spectrum, however, KNMI was far less confident about its measures, and indeed, seemed to be still in the process of developing a performance framework:

> We have the feeling that we do not have good performance indicators, they are difficult to develop. Our production is based so much on time orientation rather than question orientation. We have a plan to internally review our indicators. (Interview, Director, KNMI, 16 January 2000)

How are performance targets set?

If one had to identify an issue of greatest similarity among our NMIs, it must surely be with regard to the matter of determining performance measures. In each country, and in many interviews, reference was made to their own role in proposing and developing the indicators and targets to be reported to their ministries. Yes, the ministry could theoretically insist upon the collection of particular measures, and this did happen in Sweden with regard to accuracy of forecast, but in general ministries did not get too involved in defining the indicators. Even in the Swedish case it was SMHI itself which was given the task of constructing an indicator that was easier for the public, and no doubt the ministry, to understand. Also, it was clear there were some distinctions in the way performance reporting relationships were institutionalized. For example, in Sweden, targets were formalized in the budget letter presented yearly to parliament; while in The Netherlands, KNMI's indicators were presented in the year plan that they were required to deliver each year to their ministry. It should be noted that only in the United Kingdom did there appear to be a consistent point of contact about performance reporting through the 'Fraser figure'; no such figure seemed to exist in the other countries, and there were many complaints about changes in their point of contact:

> the contact people are changing a lot, since we have been in the Ministry of Environment we have had two different contact people, so it's more that we have to explain again what we need. (Interview, Manager, SMHI, 23 April 2001)

Despite the institutional differences in reporting systems, the observation remains that all of our NMIs gave a similar response that they themselves were quite influential in deciding upon the performance measures that they should report.

The Netherlands: Formally the ministry decides. We report to the assistant SG, but we suggest the measures that she should use. Sometimes she may ask for changes in these figures but these requests are part of a very light discussion. She is not in a position to argue with us about what indicators are possible (KNMI, 16 January 2001).

Finland: We suggest measures and the Ministry approves them. They don't usually ask for more than minor adjustments. Within the FMI, the DG and the Board take the final decisions about what the indicators should be (FMI, 20 October 2000).

Sweden: Every year we are discussing next year's budget with the Ministry. We are discussing what targets they will give us, but we have a lot of influence on what targets will be chosen (SMHI, 18 September 2000).

The UK: Formally, the Secretary of State for Defence as the owner determines the performance measures and targets. In practice, the MET Office proposes measures, which are then bedded (e.g. a proposal is tested for one year and accounts of measures are taken). The Secretary of State can either agree or modify these proposals. The Defence Meteorological Board (which is not the same as the management board) acts as an advisory body on measurements and targets. It is the case that the Secretary of State generally always accepts the recommendations of the Defence MET Board (Interview, UK MET, 20 November 2000).

The limited role ministries appear to play in the determination of performance seems primarily related to the task characteristics of meteorology. Its scientific character, particularly with respect to indicators like accuracy of forecast, leave ministries very much dependent upon the knowledge of their NMIs. However, the passivity of ministries did not hold when it came to financial indicators, since these were most clearly set by governments and their finance ministries.

What happens if targets are not achieved?

As with determining performance measures, there were also some common responses regarding the consequences of not meeting a target. On some occasions, such as in interviews with the UK respondents identified the likeliness of not meeting a particular target, but then did not connect this with any kind of repercussion from their 'owners'. With the continental European countries we even got responses that suggested outright disinterest from the ministry – even where a target had not been met:

> At the ministry hardly any attention is paid to these indicators. Even if performance was bad I suspect they would not react unless we pointed their attention to this. (Interview, Director, KNMI, 16 January 2001)

> Even when we do not meet our targets, well its no big deal. Of course we have to explain why, if it was the same kind of weather every year then they could compare very easily one year's performance to another, but this is not the case. (Interview, Director, SMHI, 23 April 2001)

To be fair, some respondents did suggest that where the safety of the population was at risk, by example in the event of a natural disaster, failure to provide adequate warning would be expected to unleash discussion and discontent from the ministers and parliament.

> Of course if we weren't ready for a big storm I would expect that that would become an issue for the parliament. (Interview, Director, SMHI, 18 September 2000)

This apprehension was borne out, in the UK case, by the famous, but rare, failure of the MET TV weather forecaster, Michael Fish, to warn viewers of the huge storm of October 1987 (which stranded at least one of the authors of this book for a day in a train on a tree-strewn track with all telephone wires down). Media questioning of 'what went wrong' was intense.

The finding that the consequences of poor performance are (usually) pretty limited is not so difficult to explain. Ministries are in a situation of acute information asymmetry. It is hard for them to judge which errors are culpable and which are not. Making the connection between poor performance and a failure to predict certain weather conditions is, from a scientific perspective, by no means always obvious. This is because, for all the technological advances, the weather itself is not at all a controllable or an entirely predictable phenomenon. A forecasting model might be working perfectly well and still not predict some unusual weather conditions.

> Some types of weather are much more difficult to predict – so there also needs to be some inclusion of the degree of difficulty in the assessment of accuracy of forecasts. (Interview, Director, SMHI, 18 September 2000)

One can imagine that these kinds of explanations are not as readily available to a social security manager, who is requested to account for how ineligible recipients are receiving a social security payment. Again the scientific aspect of the meteorological function may leave it less subject to aggressive scrutiny.

Who makes the most use of performance indicators?

The use of performance indicators also seemed to point to some shared characteristics among our NMIs. Standard responses included managers and employees, the National Audit Office and to a lesser extent ministries – although there was some suspicion among respondents that this last group did not really use the indicators but were more concerned about the mere receipt of them. As one respondent exclaimed, 'well I hope somebody in the Ministry is reading our annual report'.

Beyond this standard role call of performance indicator users, there was also consistent identification of important customers, competitors and fellow NMIs as users and receivers of performance measurements. The interest of these groups in the performance measures, while for different purposes, can be attributed to the features of the NMI's task. As has been discussed, it has become a highly competitive and commercial activity, promoting a customer focus and, therefore, also customer interest in the kind of product that is being delivered. Our research suggested that it had become quite important that NMIs invest in their relationship with their customers, including tailoring performance measures to important customers as a method of ensuring their loyalty. This was most evident in the arrangements that had been made in the United Kingdom and in Sweden. The NMIs engaging in commercial activities also pointed to their competitors as likely users of performance measures, but then primarily for the purpose of uncovering evidence of cross-subsidization or anti-competitive behaviour. This fear had its greatest expression in Sweden.

Alternatively, the interest of fellow NMIs in one another's performance measures may be attributed to the extensive international co-operation and exchange that characterizes the meteorology function. These users of performance measures were primarily interested in information regarding the quality of data being collected and exchanged.

Conclusion

In this chapter we have discussed the function of meteorology and the way that it is institutionalized in different national contexts. We have observed that there are a number of task characteristics that have an effect upon the performance management systems of our different NMIs. This was most apparent with respect to the kinds of indicators collected, the emphasis upon accuracy of forecast and warnings, and the lack of detailed ministry scrutiny or understanding of the measured performance. These similarities in our findings may be ascribed to the task requirements of the operational focus of NMIs, their role in ensuring national security from natural disaster, and the scientific character of their work. In addition, the quite un-political work of NMIs and their relatively small yearly budgetary demands, at least compared to social security, are also likely to contribute to the passive role of ministries.

There were also significant differences in the NMIs' performance management systems and these would suggest that the task features of meteorology were not the only influence shaping management practices. In particular, the lack of any universal system of measuring and comparing accuracy of forecast seems contrary to the international character of meteorology. We might speculate that increasing competition presents a disincentive for such comparisons, although the different local weather conditions and modelling system are also likely to be influential. We are not in a position to give very conclusive explanations as to why such a significant indicator is subject to such diverse operationalizations. It does, however, point to the more general impression that meteorology is not such a transparent function as its positive public image may lead one to suppose.

Clearly, there are also important national distinctions in the institutional patterns and performance management systems of our NMIs. This was evident in their different organizational and legal arrangements. There were also different kinds of national personalities when it came to their performance management systems and ideas of performance more generally. The Dutch KNMI for example clearly had a much less developed performance management system and ideas of a customer focus were scarcely mentioned in our interviews. Alternatively, the other NMIs were more satisfied with their performance management systems and seemed to have a more sophisticated approach to promoting performance, including collecting special indicators for target customers. The influence of commercialization upon these differences between KNMI and our other NMIs cannot be ignored as one possible explanation for this national difference.

We can also see a continuum emerging with regard to national perspectives and experiences of commercialization in our NMIs. The UK MET at one end of the pole seems to have embraced commercialization whole-heartedly and with little interruption from national or political critics. At a kind of mid-way point we then find SMHI and FMI also dabbling in some commercial work, but with the continuation of this regularly under political fire and still hanging in the balance. At the other end of the spectrum there is KNMI, which now expresses relief at being without commercial activities. From these observations it might be posited that the social democratic states of northern continental Europe tend to be far more pure and principled in their approach to the issue of commercialization than the more pragmatic British.

A final personality difference relates to the less tangible issue of perspectives on performance. Here we see a much greater emphasis in Sweden, and to a lesser extent in Finland, upon the use to society of NMIs and broader performance issues of flexibility and equality in the workplace, as well as upon the accessibility of their performance information to the general public. This is in stark contrast to rather rigid and tightly focussed replies about performance that were elicited in the United Kingdom.

9
Forestry

> We be the yeomen of this Forest
> Under the Greenwood Tree
> We live by the King's decree
> Other shift have not wee
> And ye have churches and rents and full good plenty
> Give us some of your spending
> for Saint Charitie
> (*The Greenwood Tree*, England, circa 1600 – one of the texts from which the modern legend of Robin Hood was 'translated' – see Schama, 1996, p. 151)

'It takes less than an hour to fell a tree. It can take a lifetime to replace it. If we are serious about sustainable development, we must show we are serious about sustainable forestry management.' (Tony Blair, speaking at a special session of the General Assembly of the United Nations, June 1997 – quoted in Reunala *et al.*, 1999, p. 263. One might add that if it took any of the organizations where we conducted research anything approaching an hour to fell a tree, then they would be in serious trouble. This speech was probably not written by a forestry expert.)

Introduction

The aim of this chapter is to compare the same sector – forestry – in four countries. We will be looking for both similarities and differences. *Similarities* may (subject to further analysis) indicate distinctive features of forestry as an activity, features which in some sense require or encourage particular institutional solutions or management techniques. They may point towards the value of a task or functional perspective, whereby 'task' is meant the idea that management, instead of being a homogenous, generic activity, is in practice substantially shaped by the particular characteristics of the activity which is being managed (see Pollitt, 2003, chapter 7, or Whitley, 1988 and 1989, for more philosophical expositions of this idea). Note, however, that what we are envisaging or hypothesizing here is a limited kind of influence. There is certainly no suggestion that every feature of management is the way it is because of some functional imperative – we propose no 'one best way' or 'rational actor' who is driven by considerations of pure efficiency to adopt similar or identical procedures and arrangements. This would be a pointless claim anyway, since it is abundantly clear (as we shall see) that procedures and arrangements do differ somewhat from country to country. No – the kind of task/functional influences which are suggested here are milder and less deterministic, together constituting only one set of variables – though an important one – in the total mix.

Differences between the four countries can be read in various ways. If the differences are typical of the national administrative cultures (e.g. if forestry management in Sweden turns out to be very collective and corporatist, while forestry in the United Kingdom is very commercial and individualistic) then this finding might be taken as evidence that national cultures were of great importance, over-riding the distinctive task characteristics of particular sectors. Legal differences may also play a part. The three continental countries all partake, to some degree, of the continental tradition of a highly developed system of administrative law. The United Kingdom, by contrast, has tended to be a 'law light' state, with a foundation in common law and ministerial secondary legislation and rule-making, rather than in a Napoleonic or other legal code. Such 'national characteristics' were extensively discussed in Chapters 3–6.

Alternatively, differences may derive from concrete environmental or economic differences. Finland is a large country with extensive forests and a cold climate. The Netherlands is a small country with very limited forests and a much warmer climate. One would not be surprised to find that these environmental differences had some impact on the way the forestry function was administered.

Similarities and differences will be explored under a number of headings. To begin with, we will glance at the background to the forestry organizations in the various countries – at the forests themselves, and their place in each national economy and culture. Then we will focus directly on the institutions concerned – how the forestry function has been organized in Finland, the Netherlands, Sweden and the United Kingdom. Third, we will consider, in turn, three rather fundamental issues in forestry policy:

- What is, or should be 'commercial', and what not
- Balancing production, recreation and environmental protection
- The relationship between doing forestry, giving advice about it, and regulating it.

In each case the aim will not be to offer some definitive analysis of the issue itself, but to show how it connects with the management and performance of our 'target' organizations. Subsequently, in the light of the foregoing discussion of the above three issues, we turn our attention directly to performance management systems *per se*. Here, our main concern is how the systems of measures and targets figure in the relationships between agencies, ministries and legislatures. Finally, we will review all of the above, returning to the theme of similarities and differences. Are there patterns, and how far does the nature of the forestry function itself seem to account for them?

Background

Forestry used to be a crucial strategic industry, and among the European powers worries about shortages of timber suitable for warship construction played an important part in forestry policy from at least the sixteenth until the nineteenth century. This led to many local and national attempts to regulate forestry, and to an international trade in timber (Scharma, 1996). In the electronic age, forestry is no longer crucial for defence, but it can still be an important economic sector, providing the raw material for the paper, furniture and construction industries and, increasingly, offering touristic facilities and satisfying 'nature values' (Reuala *et al.*, 1999). Forestry occupies a very different place in the economies and societies of our four countries. In Finland and Sweden it is very important, in the United Kingdom it is of moderate importance (although, interestingly enough, mainly in Wales and Scotland rather than England) and in the Netherlands the afforested area is miniscule.

Economically, the differences are vast. In Finland the forest industry is responsible for 30 per cent of total exports (1997 figure – see Ministry of Agriculture and Forestry, 1999, p. 13). It has 16 times more forest per capita than the EU average and, thanks partly to the summerhouse tradition, one Finnish family in every six owns some forest (Reuala *et al.*, 1999). In Sweden, too, forestry is a major sector. More than half of Sweden's net income from exports comes from forestry products – for example, Sweden is responsible for about one quarter of all EU newsprint. By contrast, forestry products are an almost invisibly small part of Dutch exports.

The geographical differences go hand in hand with the economic. The northerly positions and relatively bleak terrains and climates of both Sweden and Finland both encourage forestry (the northerly parts of these two countries are hospitable neither to farming nor to large urban settlements) and at the same time reduce the rate of tree growth. There is a considerable difference even within single countries – for example, when comparing the productivity of the Finnish state forestry enterprise with large private forest owners it is important to allow for the fact that the state enterprise has most of its holdings in the northern and eastern parts of the country, where poor climates and soils mean slower-growing forests. Even the chill and wet of UK Forest Enterprise's most northerly Scottish plantations fail to rival the rigors of Nordic forestry on the Arctic Circle.

Socially, there are equally profound differences (see Table 9.1). The Dutch and the Finns probably occupy the two extreme positions in our group of four countries. In the Netherlands forests are seen as unusual: small and special areas to be preserved for communal recreation and biodiversity. The forestry agency itself declares that:

> Staatsbosbeheer has a lot more to offer than just woodland. Only 90 000 ha of the 230 000 ha which Staatsbosbeheer owns and/or manages is woodland. Furthermore we also manage heathlands, dunes, poor grasslands, fenlands and culturally-historically valuable elements such as forts, country houses and dikes. (Staatsbosbeheer, 2001a, p. 7).

Table 9.1 Basic background on four forestry agencies (all figures from 1998–2000 period)

Agency	Hectares managed	Of which Forest/woodland	Annual income (euros)
Metsähallitus	12 000 000	3 340 000	212 m.
Staatsbosbeheer	230 000	90 000	102 m. (65% from ministry, 35% from own earnings)
Skogsvårdsstyrelsen (SVS)	4 000	4 000	82 m.
Forest Enterprise	1 057 316	830 820	161 m.

The Netherlands is a crowded and very carefully partitioned landscape. One can drive all around the central area between Amsterdam, Den Haag, Rotterdam and Utrecht and see only a few small and isolated stands of trees. Significantly, perhaps, the cover of the annual report of the Dutch Staatsbosbeheer features rather few trees. In the edition we examined there was a picture of rushes and a lily pond, and smaller pictures of a silver-haired man in a deck chair looking through binoculars, a charming young fox and a stately home (Staatsbosbeheer, 2000).

By contrast:

> Forests are, for the Finns, a part of their national identity and for many artists their source of inspiration. In art, forests are often depicted as comforting arms offering shelter from danger and grief.
> (Ministry of Agriculture and Forestry, 1999, p. 24)

Almost 75 per cent of the Finnish land surface is afforested, and by EU standards Finland is a large country. The forest presses in to the outskirts of even the biggest cities. One fifth of it is directly managed by Metsähallitus, and the private owners who manage most of the other four-fifths are advised and monitored by the Ministry of Agriculture and Forestry.

Finally, it should be mentioned that, as in so many other sectors, forestry policy is becoming increasingly internationalized. The EU does not have a forestry policy to sit alongside its famous Common Agricultural Policy, but many international organizations, from the United Nations down, have statements or guidelines or conventions to do with forestry (Granholm, 1999). For example, principles for the management and protection of forests were accepted at the 1992 UN Conference on Environment and Development (Rio), and the first European ministerial conference on the protection of forests was held in Strasbourg in 1990. One of our countries provides the home for the European Forest Institute (EFI – based at Joensuu, Finland) which carries out research.

Forestry is also international not only in the obvious commercial sense that timber and timber products are traded between countries but also because there is a growing international traffic in consultancy and advice, aimed at both commercial and environmental aspects of the activity. Finland, for example, has been active in providing advice on forestry policy and operations to both Estonia and Russia.

Non Government Organization (NGO) environmental groups such as the World Wildlife Fund, Greenpeace and Friends of the Earth themselves operate on an international basis. During the 1980s and 1990s their campaigns and activities in the forest sector seemed to grow and develop as the general environmental movement flourished. These groups took more or less critical, more or less radical stances with respect to state forestry authorities – for example, Greenpeace tended to be openly critical and distrustful of such authorities, while WWF tended to act more 'moderately'. In all four countries the forestry authorities nowadays stress their efforts to work in partnership with environmental and heritage groups.

The possible influence of the nature of the task on arrangements for management

In the introduction we mentioned the possibility that part of the explanation for 'the way forestry is' (managerially and organizationally) may lie in the nature of the primary task itself. But what, exactly, might such task influences be? Several can be mentioned here. First, forestry is a highly *tangible*, concrete (or perhaps one should say wooden) business. Unlike social security, where what is managed is principally a set of abstract rules, or even prisons, where an important part of the task is psychological and educational (to change the attitudes and skills of the prisoners), forestry is about *things:* physical and biological entities that can not be manipulated simply by changing administrative rules or offering training. There is a certain stubbornness to a forest – it is literally part of the landscape and (short of an environmental catastrophe) cannot easily be redefined or 'rebranded'. When Spruce Bark Beetle ran riot and killed more than a million cubic metres of Swedish spruce forest in 1997 this event had a definite 'facticity' to it, and debates about fancy management techniques or the optimal degree of organizational autonomy took second place to the simple question of what to do to stop it. (Interestingly, some commentators attributed the beetle epidemic to the pursuit of pro-environmental policies, especially the practice of leaving more deadwood on the forest floor.)

To take one further small example, consider what we were told in Sweden about the problems of comparing the costs of offering advice to forest owners in different parts of Sweden. The SVS compares the costs of advice-giving by its different regional boards: this is part of their effort to encourage a more performance-oriented, analytical approach by those boards. But the validity of such comparisons is undermined by some rather inescapable physicalities:

> But there are many different factors you can put into this: the travel distance, the size of the forest owner properties, the cost of the rent

of offices in different regions, snow conditions. Sometimes, in the northern part of Sweden, you can't be in the field between November and April. (Interview with senior SVS planning official, 29 April 2001)

Second, forestry is a long term business. In Finland, for example, 'forests are allowed to grow between 60 and 120 years, depending on the tree species and the composition of the site' (Ministry of Agriculture and Forestry, 1999, p. 7). The 'product' cannot be changed or even redesigned overnight. Forest Enterprise (UK) may decide to plant more than the minimum UK Forestry Standard of 5 per cent of broadleaved species, but the fruits (both aesthetic and economic) of that policy will not ripen for many years – long after the government that approved it, and the management team that took it on, have entered the history books (Forest Enterprise, 1999, pp. 19–20).

Third, forestry is also primarily a commercial business, although everywhere with increasingly important tourism/recreation functions (which may themselves be managed in a more or a less commercial manner) and environmental protection goals. There are physical products, and these are traded on an international market. Market trends cannot be reversed, or ignored, by ministers in any country.

In most years timber sales account for about 75% of our total income and our overall financial performance is therefore very much affected by the cyclical movements in round timber price, driven by factors such as currency exchange rates and international trading conditions beyond our control. (The Chief Executive of Forest Enterprise UK, explaining why his organization achieved a cash surplus of only £25.8M against a 1998/99 target of £29.8M: Forest Enterprise, 1999, p. 3)

Patterns of institutions

None of our four countries runs forestry as a unit within a central government ministry (although some used to). Equally, none treats it as primarily a local government function. So to that extent there is institutional similarity. Beyond that, however, there are considerable differences between the four countries. The basics are set out in Table 9.2.

The Finns have two bodies – one for research (Metla) and one for forest management and conservation (Metsähallitus). The research body is an agency, the forest management body a state enterprise (with a management board) – in the terms of Chapter 1, a 'More Autonomous Body' or MAB. Both are responsible to the Ministry of Agriculture and Forestry

Table 9.2 Organizational arrangements for forestry (at the time of our research, 1999–2002 – for recent changes see text)

Name of institution	Status	Relationship with ministry	Significant other bodies
Metsähallitus	State enterprise	Ministry of Agriculture and Forestry. Also Ministry of Environment for Natural Heritage Issues.	METLA (state forest research agency) 13 regional forest centres (regulation of the forest, both state and private)
Staatsbosbeheer	ZBO (a type of quango – more independent than a UK executive agency)	Ministry of Agriculture, Nature Management and Fisheries (LNV)	
Skogsvårdsstyrelsen (SVS)	Agency	Ministry of Industry, Transport and Commerce	Sveaskog AB, a state-owned company, manages 3.5 m. hectares of state forest and reports to the same Ministry (see text for more details)
Forest Enterprise	Executive agency	Forestry Commission (a government department) which is itself responsible to three 'forestry ministers' (one each for England, Scotland and Wales)	Forest Research (another Executive agency, also responsible to the Forestry Commission)

(and, for 'protection' functions, to the Ministry of the Environment). But Metsähallitus does not exercise regulatory powers. The Ministry of Agriculture and Forestry performs most of its supervision and regulation of private forest owners not through Metla or Metsähallitus, but by means of a network of 13 regional forestry centres. So there is a kind of production/regulation split here which does not exist in quite the same way in, say, Sweden. Private ownership is widely spread, with about one in six Finnish families (440 000) owning at least a bit of forest. In addition to the bodies mentioned above, the prominence of forestry in Finland has given rise to a bewildering range of institutes and associations, including the influential Federation of Finnish Forest Industries (representing the wood processing industries – see Hänninen, 1999).

The Swedes have an agency, Skogsvårdsstyrelsen (SVS – the National Board of Forestry). A national board was created in 1941. Prior to that regional boards were responsible for their respective areas (ten regional boards still exist, and play an important role mediating between the central SVS and the 100-or-so districts). SVS is headed by a Director General and has a supervisory board which includes employee representatives and private forest owners. In 2000 the Swedish state claimed that it directly owned only 3 per cent of the productive forests so, unlike Metsähallitus in Finland or Forest Enterprise in the United Kingdom, direct management of wood production does not loom large in SVS's responsibilities. In 1993 most government-owned forests were transferred to AssiDomän, a partly privatized corporation in which, by 2001, the government only retained a 35 per cent holding. However, in October 2001 the government launched a new policy of buying out the holders of the other 65 per cent of shares. AssiDomän then became a part of Sveaskog AB, a state enterprise that bills itself as 'Sweden's largest forest owner' (www.sveaskog.com). Sveaskog is a giant organization, managing 3.5 m. hectares of forest, running a large industrial operation and boasting an annual turnover of roughly 800 m. euros. Sveaskog is wholly owned by the Ministry of Industry, Employment and Communications. So the Swedish assertion that the state owns only a small part of the forest must now be taken with a large pinch of salt. In fact the state wholly owns a company that owns and manages almost a fifth of a huge total area of forest. Another state company, Skogindustrins tekniska forkningsinstitut (the Swedish Pulp and Paper Research Institute) conducts research into forest products and, as in Finland, there are powerful forestry trade associations.

Nor is this all. There is also a National Property Board (Fastighetsverket) which is responsible for public buildings, common land and forests which are climatically difficult. In total this Board manages a huge 6 m. hectares of land, within which there is 300 000 hectares of commercially viable forest (well over three times as much as the Dutch ZBO, Staatsbosbeheer, and much more than UK Forest Enterprise manages in England alone).

In the Netherlands Staatsbosbeheer is a ZBO (a MAB – 'further out' than an agency) within the jurisdictional sphere of the Ministry of Agriculture, Nature Management and Fisheries. In 2001 it employed approximately 100 staff. Staatsbosbeheer has existed (in various forms) for 100 years, and became a ZBO on 1 January 1998. As is fairly common in the Netherlands, it has both a supervisory board (appointed by the minister) and an advisory board. Its pamphlet lists three objectives, of which the production of raw materials is only the last. The first is 'maintaining, restoring and developing woodland, semi-natural sites, landscape and cultural-historical values' at its sites, and the second is 'promoting public access' (Staatsbosbeheer, 2001a, p. 5).

The United Kingdom has two agencies working for the Forestry Commission, which describes itself as a government 'department', although it does not have its own minister (but reports to the Ministry of Agriculture, Fisheries and Food in England and to the Secretaries of State for Wales and Scotland). The two agencies are Forest Enterprise (created 1996) and Forest Research (1997). Forest Enterprise actually manages the forests, and is our main focus of interest.

In every country commercial, touristic and environmental functions are combined within a single organization, although (also in every case) these are somewhat separated out between internal units within the organization. Even if we take the most fully commercial of the various bodies discussed above – the Swedish state-owned company Sveaskog – we find their website proudly proclaiming that its business activities must be conducted in such a way as to,

- ensure the productive capacity of the forest is maintained in the long term work to preserve its biodiversity
- restrict the number of negative influences imposed on the external environment, e.g. the water environment
- protect valuable cultural environments
- develop accessibility and enrich people's experience of the natural environment. (http://www.sveaskog.se, accessed 22 August 2002)

In every case there have been movements of function or boundary during the last ten years, so, despite the long term nature of the basic business, forest organizations have not been particularly stable. For example:

Finland: Metsähallitus was given nature protection functions in 1973, and had its powers of regulating private owners transferred away from it (to the Regional Forest Centres) in 1989. Having been a central agency or board between 1859 and 1992 it then became an enterprise within the state budget for a period of two years, after which (from 1994) it was an independent state enterprise (i.e. off the state budget, though still

part of the overall public sector financial system). In 2002 it gained responsibility for managing the forest lands previously run by the Ministry of Defence and the state forest research agency (METLA).
The Netherlands: Until 1 January 1998 Staatsbosbeheer was part of the Ministry of Agriculture, Nature Management and Fisheries (LNV). It then became a zelfstandig bestuursorgaan (ZBO – self-standing management body).
Sweden: SVS used to report to the Ministry of Agriculture until the mid-1990s, when it was moved to the Ministry of Industry. In 1999 its seed-selling operation was removed and made into a separate state enterprise. In 1993, as part of a major 'liberalization' of forestry policy, most of the state's productive forests were transferred to a commercial enterprise, AssiDomän, in which the government continued to have a (minority) holding. In 2001 this was 'de-privatized' when the non-state shares were bought by Sveaskog AB, a wholly government-owned company which henceforth managed 3.5 m. hectares of productive forest (18 per cent of the total forested area of Sweden).
The United Kingdom: Prior to 1992 the functions of Forest Enterprise were simply part of the Forestry Commission (originally set up in 1919). From time to time new functions were added,for example the 1985 Wildlife and Countryside Act added a duty on the Commissioners to balance 'between the interests of productive forestry and the environment'. Between 1992 and 1 April 1996 Forest Enterprise was managed as an internal department of the Forestry Commission. It then became a 'Next Steps' executive agency, as did Forest Research. In 2002 a quinquennnial review of the organization recommended that Forest Enterprise be split into three agencies, one each for England, Scotland and Wales; this was in response to the devolution of political authority to the Scottish and Welsh assemblies in 1999. One can discern, therefore, some broad similarities here. In all four countries there has been a movement 'outwards' – further away from direct ministerial control – especially, but not only, for the basic commercial task of growing and selling wood. In all four countries environmental and touristic responsibilities have, during the past two or three decades, been added to the basic forestry functions. And in all four countries the pace of institutional change seems to have quickened since about 1990. Re-structuring remains a popular international political sport. Whether it makes much difference to the way in which activities are managed remains to be seen.

On the other hand, the differences between countries are quite significant too. The United Kingdom has agencies for production and for research. Sweden has an agency for regulation and advice giving and planning, plus a state-owned company for managing most of the state's holdings. The Netherlands have a MAB for management and the small amount of production which that country can sustain. Finland has a state enterprise for production, an agency for research and regional boards reporting to the same ministry for regulation. It is interesting how differently regulatory powers are distributed in the four countries. In Finland they are mainly carried out by the regional forestry centres, which are quite separate from the state forestry enterprise, although reporting to the same ministry. In Sweden regulation is the main business of the SVS agency (whereas timber production on former state lands has passed elsewhere). In the United Kingdom regulation falls mainly to the government department itself (the Forestry Commission), not to Forest Enterprise (the agency). In the Netherlands regulation is the responsibility of the LNV.

Managing the commercial/non-commercial frontier

In every country (but to varying degrees) there is discomfort over the commercial/non-commercial boundary. It isn't hard to see why. A forest is not a very pure type of 'public good'. Commercial companies grow and sell timber, manufacture timber-based products, provide advice on forest management, offer forest planning services, provide touristic services and conduct scientific investigations. There are also voluntary associations of forest owners and environmentalists (in effect, NGOs) which can perform some of these activities. So almost everything the state forest organizations do could, at least in principle, be carried out by commercial companies and/or voluntary associations. Even nature conservancy could be contracted out, once the goals have been defined.

The way the boundary is treated varies from country to country (and from one time period to the next). Consider first the Swedes. In their agency,

> We have to keep commercial and authority work separate economically. The work we are doing must always have a nil result, we can't spend more money on a product than it costs for us to make it ... We have four different results areas, each one of these should have a nil result, and you can't move money between these areas ... if a private company sees that we have made a big profit, they would be very quick to say that it is because we have done something wrong, like

putting money from the state into our products. (Interview with senior planning official, SVS, 29 April 2001)

Some functions, like planting and selling seeds, have been taken away from SVS and made into a free-standing state enterprise, Svenska Skogsplantor. Meanwhile, in neighbouring Finland, seeds have been made a profitable subsidiary company of the state enterprise, Metsähallitus. So now, when a forest plan is being sold to a private owner, SVS cannot sell seeds as well. Even in selling plans, it feels obliged to take a fairly low profile.

But we are not putting advertisements in the newspapers or so on. If we were a private company, we would go out commercially and say our product is the best and the others are rubbish, but as an authority we have a much lower profile. We have to be modest ... . (Interview with senior planning official, SVS, 29 April 2001)

In short, the agency has commercial functions but believes that it is not allowed – either in terms of finance or in terms of HRM – to behave as a commercial company would. And the main commercial function – productively managing state forests – was partly privatized in 1993, and then taken back into state ownership (but not SVS's) in 2001.

The Dutch are generally (i.e. not just with respect to forestry) very concerned that commercial functions should not be performed by agencies. Staatsbosbeheer, as an MAB rather than an agency, definitely performs commercial functions, including the manufacture and marketing of wooden garden furniture and fences and boards. However, their annual report betrays very little of the inherent profitability of these enterprises and, in general, in this respect, it appears a more opaque organization than its equivalents in any of the other three countries (compare Staatsbosbeheer, 2000 with Forest Enterprise, 1999, or Metsähallitus, 2000). It was the only organization in any of the four countries which initially rejected our request for research access, telling us, rather gratuitously we thought, that previous encounters with social scientists had not been very useful. Later, they changed their minds. At any event, the English language pamphlet on Staatsbosbeheer makes no reference whatsoever to commercial functions, and concentrates entirely on its 'friendly' conservation and recreational functions. This is indeed the 'image' that Staatsbosbeheer seems to have managed to cultivate among the general Dutch population (Staatsbosbeheer, 2001a).

The annual report does, of course, give basic financial details, but not in a way that would permit the reader to see what the profitability (or otherwise) of individual activities had been. However, as one might expect, in its annual negotiations with the LNV ministry Staatsbosbeheer discusses specific revenues in much more detail. The planning system works on the basis of quite a large number of objectives, each one of which is priced. The price is arrived at by subtracting from the gross cost of achieving that particular objective any revenues that Staatsbosbeheer believes it can earn from that activity. Individual services which Staatsbosbeheer provides can be priced to make a profit, but must not be priced at a loss, to prevent cross-subsidization (interview with Staatsbosbeheer managers, 30 January 2002, see also Staatsbosbeheer, 2001b).

In UK Forest Enterprise the level of 'commercial consciousness' in most of our interviews seemed high. The agency contains overtly commercial units, such as Forest Holidays. However, management believes that the Treasury financial regime is unsuitable for their business operations. Unlike a real commercial business, they are not allowed to borrow capital, and this limits their ability to ride the fluctuations of the world timber market. They would like to have 'trading fund' status to help with these problems, but there are also cogent reasons why this is unlikely to be granted. Trading fund status includes a Treasury requirement of making a 6 per cent return on assets. But the main asset – land – is unlikely ever to make that kind of return, and government rules prevent more than a small amount of it being sold. 'There is no way, with a balance sheet of £1.4 billion, that we are going to be able to show a return on assets ... Forests are not just there for timber. Conservation, recreation are not tradeable goods' (Director General, UK Forestry Commission, interview, 3 May 2002). Management at Forest Enterprise also believe that the recreational and environmental functions need to be further separated out from the timber business and given their own, more secure lines of funding. 'The politicians are not the problem, it is the Treasury' (Chief Executive, interview, 11 December 2000).

One might think that forest research organizations (Forest Research in the United Kingdom, METLA in Finland) would be more 'pure' and free of the worry of constantly thinking about the commercial borderline. But this is not so:

> The Ministry just keeps giving us higher and higher targets for our commercial work. (METLA interview, 19 October 2000)

The Corporate Plan is taken seriously. We have a requirement to make a 6% return on our investment and we strive to make this. We have weighted chargeable days. My costs, for example, are charged out to the branches. In other words we have an internal market of cost centres. The scientists hate it but we know the true cost of science this way. (Interview with Head of Personnel and Administration, Forest Research, 30 November 2000)

Actually, 90 per cent of Forest Research's work is done for the Forestry Commission (FC) (their parent body) but the FC uses competitive tendering, so Forest Research has to be on its toes. Our general impression was that METLA was much less 'pinned down' by measurement systems than Forest Research. METLA does have target areas, but their staff did not work to 'weighted chargeable days', and much of their work seemed to be multi-year research projects approved by the parent ministry without competitive tendering.

One interesting exception to the general continental nervousness/reluctance about state agencies performing commercial functions is the international market place. There the morality seems to be quite different – one of rampant capitalism! For SVS, for example, it is only in the international arena that their units are allowed to show a profit (interview with Planning Director and Planning Officer, 15 September 2000).

Furthermore, it must not be overlooked that the category of 'state enterprise' remains very important in the two Nordic countries (whereas, since Mrs Thatcher's privatization onslaught, it has largely disappeared from the United Kingdom). So in Finland Metsähallitus, as a state enterprise, and in Sweden Sveaskog AB as a state-owned company, are both highly commercial operations. One might say that, in the case of UK Forest Enterprise, the agency form was being stretched to encompass the kind of large-scale commercial functions that in Sweden or Finland would be regarded as suitable for a state enterprise, but not for a state agency.

Balancing production, recreation and the environment

In all four countries we have been told that environmental and conservation objectives have become more important over the past decade. So has the use of forested and wilderness areas for a variety of touristic purposes. To some extent the three basic purposes (commercial forestry, environmental protection, tourism) can coexist. But to some extent they are also in competition with each other, and in each country the balance to be struck between these three is a political issue which is reflected in a variety of institutional, financial and 'public relations' arrangements. This state of affairs has obvious and important consequences for performance management. The set of performance targets one would design to encourage an environmentally prudent approach to forestry, giving priority to preserving traditional habitats and maintaining biodiversity, would look rather different from the set one would need if commercial profitability and efficiency were to be maximized.

By way of example, one may consider the ongoing argument between some environmental groups and the Finnish government over the designation of additional national park areas. Greenpeace (and some others) are pressing for 400 000 ha of new parks to be created in southern Finland. That is where most of the Finnish population is, but it is also where the most profitable commercial forests are. Metsähallitus would lose a considerable amount of revenue if such a wide designation were to go ahead. Metsähallitus already has its own set of environmental goals, carefully worked out with its parent ministry for natural heritage purposes, the Ministry of the Environment. But Greenpeace rejects these goals as insufficient, and criticizes the state enterprise as giving too much emphasis to short-term commercial goals.

There is no way of balancing these interests that will leave everybody completely happy but there are certainly ways of minimizing dissatisfaction and of making the process of balancing a tolerably responsive and transparent one. The appropriate balance is by no means necessarily the same in all four countries: the Finns, for example, simply have much more forest to play with than the Dutch, and public attitudes may differ, not only from country to country but from one locality to another.

The balance that has to be struck is not simply a trade off between making money out of timber and preserving particular habitats and species (biodiversity). There is also the third variable, namely tourism. Touristic activities can sometimes be fitted well with the other two aspects of the forest, but sometimes not. Open and unsupervised public access to an area where there are rare and delicate species may endanger those species. Tourists are sometimes the cause of forest fires which destroy many valuable hectares. Touristic activities may even interfere with each other: giving mountain bikes access to public footpaths can lead to altercations, and certainly no sensible person wants to permit the general public to wander through parts of the forest where hunting may be going on.

How do our four agencies handle these difficult balances? There are strong similarities. All support policies of 'multi-use': none sees its mission as solely commercial or, for that matter, solely environmental. Essentially, all four perform the balancing act within themselves, and thereby save ministers from fighting over it more publicly. They develop detailed technical plans and put them to their supervising ministries (both forestry and environmental). Of course, in principle, ministers could throw these plans out and insist on quite a different balance, but in practice this is unlikely, and the ministries themselves are in a weak position (in terms of available expertise) to substitute an alternative plan for the one that the forestry agencies put to them. Adjustments at the margin, yes; a fundamentally different balance, no. Asked how the balance was struck between business concerns and environmental concerns, a senior manager at Metsähallitus put it to us most clearly:

> There is no ministerial conflict between how these things are handled – they are managed within the organization. (Interview, 5 September 2001)

And within that organization, the Natural Heritage directorate retained considerable independence. More than half its funding came from the Ministry of the Environment (rather than the Ministry of Agriculture and Forestry) and it regarded itself as an authoritative and useful commentator on the plans of the business side:

> We don't feel like bureaucrats – we feel like some sort of a service company. (Interview, Director of Natural Heritage Services, 5 September 2001)

What is more, far from being just a carping critic, the environmental directorate brings benefits for the business side. The latter get

> a softer, greener profile. We have millions of customers, the forestry business has about three (same interview).

In Sweden the Director General of SVS told us that 'we now have equal goals as regarding both the protection of the environment and production' (Interview, 15 September 2000).

In the United Kingdom the annual report of Forest Enterprise contains an interesting reference to the issue of balance. After listing the agency's objectives, which include profitable production, environmental and recreational goals, the report remarks that:

> Where these objectives appear to conflict a balance is achieved through a corporate planning process in line with *The UK Forestry Standard: the Government's Approach to Sustainable Forestry*, (January 1998) and available resources (Forest Enterprise, 1998, p. 5).

In other words here, too, the trade-off is done mainly within the forest agency itself, not through public debate or through inter-ministerial struggles at departmental level.

In the Netherlands the planning system distinguishes between different categories of woodland:

> While in woodland that belongs to the first class (approximately 1/3 of the total acreage) the nature conservation function is primary, in the multifunctional woodlands the production, recreational and nature conservation functions are equally important. The most far-reaching form of integration between the core tasks is therefore achieved in multi-functional woodland. (Staatsbosbeheer, 2001b, p. 7)

Below this top level of classification more detailed objectives are developed for each site.

One interesting issue which illustrates the complexity of the production/environment/ tourism balance is that of forest certification. Forest certification 'refers to a procedure whereby an impartial third party performs an inspection to determine whether the management and use of a specified area of forest comply with previously determined ecological, economic and social standards and the principles of sustainability' (Juslin and Kärnä, 1999, p. 288). It is thus one approach to measuring 'performance'. A good idea, one might think. In practice, however, certification has proven a complex and contentious issue. Certification can serve a number of different purposes. It can be used as a guarantee that sustainable management practices are being used – as a kind of reassurance to environmental groups, legislators and the public. On the other hand it can be regarded principally as a marketing tool. It can be directed principally towards procedural issues (*how* things are done) or towards outcome issues (what is the *actual state* of the forest) or some mixture of the two. The ISO 9000 and ISO 14 000 systems are procedurally-oriented examples. By contrast the Forest Stewardship Council certification (FSC), which is quite widely used in both Sweden and Finland, defines a set of indicators of the state of the forest. [The FSC is an international NGO with national branches]. Certification can be very detailed, or very general. If it is too detailed, however, it may not be applicable to different forests in different locations:

> A uniform system of forest certification must not impose unreasonable expenses on any one country, to the extent of being impossible to carry out. Were this to happen, it could be seen as being discriminatory. (Juslin and Kärnä, 1999, p. 288)

Certification systems have been developed as voluntary initiatives. If they were applied to every forest holding this could easily grow bureaucratic and burdensome for smallholders. On the other hand, as soon as a system is selectively applied – only to certain forest lands but not to others – it becomes necessary to have an audit trail which permits independent assessors to trace a wood product back through transportation and manufacture to ensure that it does indeed come from the certificated location. This can be an expensive and document-heavy process.

Attempts have been made to develop a European certification system, but these have not been entirely successful. Metsähallitus and various private forest owners (in Finland and elsewhere) have produced a 'Pan European Forest Certification' (PEFC), which sounds very official, but which, according to our interviews, has 'been developed in a voluntary, independent way', is 'a marketing tool' and is 'not related to governments' (interview with senior manager, Metsähallitus, 5 September 2001). The PEFC attempts to incorporate pre-existing national systems, such as that of the Forest Stewardship Council, and is linked to the ISO approach. However, it is not liked by all. 'There is a bit of a power struggle between the Pan-European system and the FSC' (interview with senior official, Finnish Ministry of Agriculture and Forestry, 17 June 2002). There have also been disagreements between environmental groups, favouring one kind of system, and forest agencies, preferring another. In Sweden at the end of 2000 FSC certification covered nearly 12 m. hectares, while PEFC certification covered only 1.8 m. hectares. The PEFC is not used by UK Forest Enterprise, but they, too, have been caught up in the certification game. Forest Enterprise observes the UK Forestry Standard, applied to itself and to private forest companies alike. However, this standard is promulgated by the Forestry Commission, and so the search is on for something more visibly 'independent'. The Forest Enterprise annual report refers to 'a lively debate within the forest industry' and announces that, despite the virtues of the UK Forestry Standard,

> we also recognise that many of our timber customers and, more particularly, their own customers, see a marketing advantage in being able to produce evidence of independent assurance through an auditing process. The establishment of the UK Woodland Assurance scheme provides a route whereby independent certification against agreed standards can be achieved in the United Kingdom, and it is our intention to seek independent certification of the Forestry Commission forest estate during 1999–2000. (Forest Enterprise, 1999, p. 42)

In the Netherlands the Staatsbosbeheer was 'rolling out' FSC certification at the time of our research (Staatsbosbeheer, 1999, p. 21).

In short, certification is spreading, and can certainly be considered as one aspect of performance management. However, there is no commonly accepted global or European system (not for want of trying) and quite strong arguments have taken place both within the forest sector and between the forest sector and environmental groups about which systems should be adopted.

Doing, advising, controlling

Somewhat submerged in the printed and interview material we gathered, one may discern an uneasy balance between three different kinds of activity that are part of the responsibility of forestry authorities in all four countries ('authorities' here meaning the whole assemblage of state organizations do with the forest, from the ministry down – not just our four forest agencies). First, they must actually manage their own state lands – the 'doing' part of their remit. They plant trees, chop them down and sell timber and timber products. Second, they must provide advice to the private sector (both to small private owners and to big commercial companies). This advice may be highly scientific and research-based, or it may be more on how to manage a particular piece of land (like the Forest Plans which the Swedes are so keen on selling to owners, but which many owners seem rather reluctant to pay for). Third, although the rhetoric of the annual reports and brochures do their best to disguise and downplay it, state forest authorities also have a monitoring and regulating role. Both the private owners and the state forest organizations themselves have to be 'policed'. In Finland most of this policing is carried out by 13 regional forestry centres, which fall within the jurisdiction of the Ministry of Agriculture and Forestry (Ministry of Agriculture and

Forestry, 1999, p. 17). They apply the same rules to Metsähallitus as to the private owners. In Sweden, however, SVS is in the uncomfortable position of being the regulator and at the same time the purveyor of priced advice services. In the United Kingdom regulation lies mainly with the Forestry Commission (a government department) and in the Netherlands, too, regulatory aspects are handled by the Ministry.

The different functions present different challenges to the designers of performance indicator systems. *'Doing'* is easiest to measure. How many trees have we planted? How many cubic meters of timber have we produced? What profit/loss did we make? These things – within one's own organization – are relatively straightforward. For the *advice* function it is easy to measure inputs and processes – how many staff hours do we spend on advising, how many courses have we run, how many forest owners have attended, and so on. Advisee satisfaction can also be measured (and is). But the big problem is measuring outcomes – how far does this advice affect behaviour?

> But what is really important is if they have changed their behaviour through what they have learned, that is much harder to measure. Indirectly we can see whether this has happened because we could look at how successful a forest owner has been with their regeneration efforts. And we also have records about which owners have been on our courses and those that have not been, so it is possible to compare these forest owners. We are not doing this yet, but we are trying to do it, but there are no indicators that are followed every year.
> (Interview with senior manager, SVS, 29 April 2001)

Finally, there is the *regulatory* function. This is again difficult to measure – a bit like crime statistics:

> It is very hard for us to know for example if we are doing a good job at legal supervision, in fact its almost impossible. We know how many legal actions we have taken but not if we are discovering all the illegal activities that the forest owners may be doing with regard to the forest. Apart from this idea about satellite photos we are also visiting the forests and making sure that forest owners understand what they should be doing. We have no possibility to go out on every forest and checking, so we need to find a more efficient way to find out the difficult ones. (Interview with senior manager, SVS, 29 April 2001)

Thus 'doing', production-type activities are much easier to measure than either advising or regulating. But there is another important difference between the three functions, and that is their political and organizational legitimacy. In political terms production is OK, advice is good but regulation seems almost something to be ashamed of. Most of our interviewees either didn't mention regulatory aspects or they bent over backwards to emphasize that what they wanted was a 'co-operative' relationship with private owners. Indeed, when asked what the staff thought was the most important measure or indicator, the Director General of the SVS surprised us by replying that 'for our field personnel it is important that they have equal relation with forest owners, that they are not seen as an authority' (interview, SVS, 15 September 2000). One possible interpretation of this shyness about regulation and enthusiasm for co-operation runs as follows. First, in the three continental countries, there is an ideology of consensual democracy and/or corporatism – everything is talked about in a co-operative way between associations and groups, and there is a strong ideological bias against punishment and explicit public sanctions. Private owners are part of the community, part of the network, and discussion and information should be the tools for getting them to behave responsibly, not the heavy hand of state regulation. A Swedish manager put it like this:

> There are times when we can hit things on the head with the law book but to really fulfil the policy there is a lot of voluntary work from the forest owner needed. That's where we come in, we give him a lot of knowledge from seminars, we go to them with messages about what they need to learn and how they work with the forests. And then they go back to manage the forests hopefully in the way we want them to do, but it is a voluntary way. (interview, SVS, 15 September 2000)

Second, perhaps, we are hearing echoes of the general loss of confidence of western governments about giving orders. Somehow giving an order, enforcing a law or regulation is slightly shameful – a confession of failure by the authorities, an admission that 'partnership' doesn't work. On the other side, however, the still-growing environmental group may well be pushing for *more*, not less, regulation.

Performance management systems in forestry

The NPM has certainly had an international effect (Pollitt, 2003, chapter 2). Everyone now has performance indicators for their organizations, and almost everyone we interviewed, in all four countries was comfortable in using the language of performance. All claimed that the indicators were disaggregated down to the level of local work units (at least those indicators where it was practicable to do this) so that the whole organization was 'working to target', not just the head office. Some (especially the Swedes and the Finns) suggested that this process could go further – that is, that district level local operations were not yet as closely tied in to the overall planning and targeting system as they might be.

Many of the indicators themselves are more-or-less common between the four countries (with some technical variations in how things are defined and measured). Also, in interviews, we gained the impression that another common feature – certainly in Finland, Sweden and the United Kingdom – was that the financial targets were the most precise and most tightly enforced by government. The other targets – for protective and recreational/touristic aspects – tended to be less rigid, more negotiable – or, at least, that was the perspective of a number of our interviewees:

> When we were set up as an agency we were given four financial targets so those are the primary ones. But, having said that, I also know that there are an awful lot of secondary ones which are also allied to that .... (Interview, senior official, Forest Enterprise, 11 December 2000)

> [Question: who determines what the current set of performance indicators should be?] Well, that is of course the government ... they give us the money and tell us to report what we have done. Lately we have had more pressure on us to show what results we have used this money for ... On the other hand, when it comes to non-monetary indicators, we tend to choose them ourselves, we do this in co-operation with universities. (Interview, senior official in contractual services, SVS, 29 April 2001)

A further common feature is that every forestry agency has a large number of targets – dozens, or even hundreds. Not all feature in the exchanges between ministries and agencies, and certainly not all appear in annual reports and the like, but internally there are lots and lots. Each autumn, the Natural Heritage division of Metsähallitus holds a detailed discussion with the Ministry of the Environment, on the basis of a large technical document and utilizing a set of more than 100 indicators – and that concerns the heritage aspects only (e.g. a target number for nesting pairs of golden eagles), excluding the forestry business side. SVS operates with a similarly detailed set of 'key numbers'. For example, if we look at the advice, education and information side of their responsibilities we can see that they collect data on:

- Percentage of forest owners contacted (broken down by size or type of ownership)
- Costs of advice in the field per participant
- Costs of education per participant

and on their main tasks they measure:

- percentage of commissioned tasks (amount of working days on commissioned tasks/total amount of working days)
- Area of private forest covered by SVS forestry plans/total area of private forest
- Median size of forestry plans
- Economic results for forestry task
- Economic result for nature reserve management
- Economic results for international work
- Amount of measures concerning the rural labour market.

Staatsbosbeheer has an elaborate planning system in which it negotiates with its ministry over about 30 top objectives and 90 sub-objectives. For each one it explains how much it is capable of doing and what it will cost. Each objective is defined in some considerable technical details, and then priced (e.g. the price per hectare for preserving heatherlands, and the total area of heatherlands that are to be preserved). Prices are net – that is gross minus any revenues that Staatsbosbeheer can raise from that activity (e.g. by selling hunting rights on heatherland). Each year there is a 'performance justification' exercise in which a sample of about ten per cent of the estate is inspected to see how far the defined objectives have been achieved (interview, Staatsbosbeheer, 30 January 2002, see also Staatsbosbeheer, 2001b).

The Forestry Commission shows 13 main targets in its annual report, but also has many more management-set internal targets – we could fill this whole book by just listing all the internal and external measures used by the managements of our selected agencies in the four countries.

Furthermore, these complex measurement systems are – in every country – steadily evolving. Individual measures are constantly refined, and new measures are sometimes added, and links between measures and activities are strengthened. One brief example may suffice to illustrate the point. During the 1990s the Natural Heritage Directorate of Metsähallitus wished to promote the breeding of golden eagles – an endangered species – in northern Finland. These birds were not, however, well regarded by local reindeer owners, whose animals regularly served as eagle prey. A system was therefore set up whereby reindeer owners were given compensation payments if they produced concrete evidence (e.g. dead young reindeer) of their losses. Unfortunately, this system didn't work terribly well. Owners sometimes thought the damage caused by the eagles was more costly than the available compensation and, anyway, it was sometimes impossible or inconvenient for them to find and produce the necessary physical evidence. Thus this system 'maintained predator hate among the reindeer owners' and there were incidents where nests were destroyed and fledglings were shot (Metsähallitus, 2002). In 1998, however, a new compensation system was launched, backed by a new measurement system. Now the eagle nests are counted, and owners are compensated according to the number of nests in a certain condition in their area. For example, in the northern forest areas a 'decorated' (inhabited) nest counts for one point and a nest with chicks counts for three points, where each point translates into compensation of 549 euros. Concrete evidence of each eagle attack no longer needs to be produced. The reindeer owners are happier (no more vandalism or shooting) and the reproductive success of the golden eagle is highly satisfactory (146 ringed fledglings in 2002). The total costs of the compensation scheme are roughly the same as under the old system.

It is therefore true to say that all four forest agencies have well-developed sets of measures, that performance against some of these are regularly published, and that a process of constant, incremental refinement seems to be proceeding. What varies, however, is how the indicator sets are regarded, and the part they play in the relationships between the forest organizations, their parent ministries and the national legislatures. To investigate these aspects we may focus more closely on some of the questions we asked during our research interviews. In particular,

- What are the most important performance indicators?
- Has there been, or is there foreseen in the near future, significant change in the framework of performance measures used?
- How are the performance targets set?
- What happens if targets are not achieved?
- Who makes most use of the performance indicators?

What are the most important performance indicators?

We asked this question in two different ways. First we asked interviewees what the 'performance' of their organization meant to them – what did the phrase bring first to mind? Second, we asked: what were the most important indicators, from the point of view of agency staff? The pattern of answers did vary somewhat from country to country. Our first question turned out not to work very well. Several interviewees simply tossed it back to us – what did we mean? Very few gave any sort of specific answer, though the most senior managers often had what sounded like a stock phrase, such as 'to preserve the forest and at the same time make as much profit as possible' (Metsähallitus interview, 5 September 2001). The answers were probably vaguest of all in Sweden, where a common answer to the second question was that the staff liked their work and felt they had 'flexibility' (no one at all there volunteered staying within budgetary targets or any particular environmental target). At the other end of the scale the answers were most precise and concrete in the United Kingdom, where the managers we spoke to could all quickly refer to the key indicators in the framework agreement, and to financial targets. Over all four countries no particular indicator, or group of indicators emerged as most important, with the significant exception already mentioned that, when questions were later asked about sanctions for failure, it became clear that financial targets – good old-fashioned sticking to the budget – were usually cited as being the ones that packed most punch. For example:

> I don't think that there is a key indicator that everyone is looking out for ... But of course we have the economic indicators, that is perhaps the first thing, we can't spend more money than you get. (Senior manager, SVS, 29 April 2001)

Has there been, or is there foreseen in the near future, significant change in the framework of performance measures used?

In none of the four countries had there been a very recent revolution in performance measurement, and nor was one foreseen for the next few years. Typical was a comment from an industry ministry civil servant in Sweden: 'I think that [what] we are collecting now has not really changed for the last ten years and hopefully we have succeeded in developing a good system' (interview, 24 June 2002). In most cases the big change had come in the late 1980s or early 1990s, when performance measurement had become much more prominent and systemized. In both Finland and Sweden that had been part of a government-wide introduction of 'results-oriented management'. In the United Kingdom it had been part of the Next Steps agency programme (also government-wide), with its emphasis on framework agreements incorporating key performance indicators. The most recent changes of real substance had perhaps been those at Staatsbosbeheer, where the achievement of ZBO status in 1998 had been followed by the development of an elaborate new planning system (as briefly described above – and see Staatsbosbeheer, 2001b).

To say that there has not been a revolution is not, of course, to say that everything is static. In all four countries indicators are constantly being refined. Definitions are adjusted, measurement procedures tightened, and so on. There is a continuing effort to get local staff to take (disaggregated) targets seriously, and to structure their activities in ways which reflect organizational priorities. But this is being done within a context in which elaborate, multi-indicator performance measurement is no longer a new thing, but rather a taken-for-granted part of running the business.

How are the performance targets set?

The main targets are always set in dialogue/trialogue with parent ministries and ministries of finance. But the character of these conversations/negotiations seems to vary by type of target, and to some extent by country. In addition detailed targets are often set within the forest agencies themselves.

The most obvious functional difference is between financial and non-financial targets. The financial targets are set – or at least heavily influenced – by ministries of finance. And ministries of finance are generally perceived as less sympathetic/more 'tough' than parent departments:

> The Ministry of Finance do seem to drive the indicator process and encourage us all to ensure that we have relevant indicators. (Interview with Swedish Ministry of Industry staff, 24 June 2002)

> We have a three year funding settlement, but our main income from sales plunged just one year after this settlement. Our parent department is relatively small and therefore we have a junior minister with not much clout. Our problem is with the Treasury. (Interview with senior manager, Forest Enterprise, 11 December 2000)

On the other hand forest agencies usually seem to have the upper hand when it comes to setting non-financial targets. In the Dutch system the Ministry only negotiates the 30 or so 'top targets'. And the Minister is supposed to approve the terms in which each objective is defined. When one looks at these documents, however, it is hard to imagine a minister or his/her civil servants having the time or knowledge to engage in very effective debate on the definitions. They are highly detailed and technical – very much the product of what was described to us as a 'professionally-designed and operated planning system'. (Interview with Staatsbosbeheer managers, 30 January 2002).

In Finland we were told that it was true that the ministry didn't have much expertise in the details, but there was a good level of trust between them and Metsähallitus. On the environmental side 'at the level of preparation [of targets] we are very active ... It is not very difficult to get some acceptance from the Ministry' (interviews with Metsähallitus managers, 5 September 2001). Internally there were about 100 indicators, but only a selection of the more important ones would be included in the discussions with the Ministry.

What happens if targets are not achieved?

The basic answer here seems to be a functional one: it depends on which kind of target you are talking about. Financial targets are usually crucial: to fail to meet these by a significant margin calls down a serious inquest from the parent ministry or, more likely, the Ministry of Finance. In no case did we find that failure to meet an environmental or touristic/recreational target had become a major issue. Then, on top of this functional difference, there seems to be a cultural difference between the United Kingdom and the three continental countries, with 'target failure' being regarded in a somewhat stricter, harsher (or more mechanical) way in the United Kingdom than in Finland, Sweden or the Netherlands. Or, at least, that is the general impression we gained from our interviews – it is, of course possible that what we were picking up was more a style of talking about such events to outsiders than a true reflection of what actually goes on inside the ministry/agency relationship. On the whole, however, we are inclined to believe that a real difference – related to national politico-administrative cultures – does lie behind the words that were uttered by our interviewees.

In Finland we were told that in the last seven years only one major financial target had been seriously undershot (plus or minus five per cent of the main profit target is already allowed for in the system). In 1999 the profit target had been missed by eight per cent. This had become 'a really difficult question' and had gone right up to the highest political level: the Council of State. Eventually it had been decided that most of the loss was because of market movements that had been beyond the control of management, so no censoring action had been taken (interviews with senior managers at Metsähallitus, 5 September 2001). On the other hand, other Finnish interviews revealed that when one of the subsiduary companies had made repeated losses it had taken more than five years before the Ministry had started to put real pressure on. Eventually the relevant director had been moved and finally, in 2001, the company had crept into a small profit (interviews at the Ministry of Agriculture and Forestry, 17 June 2002 and at Metsähallitus, 5 September 2001). And on the environmental side, when we asked what would happen if a target was missed, the manager replied that a common response would be to postpone the date of achievement, or otherwise adjust the target – it sounded a fairly relaxed process (interview, 5 September 2001). Similarly, in the Netherlands we were told that missing a target would probably not call forth much action from the ministry – in law the minister had power to take action to take over the running of the organization, but this kind of thing was not really on the day-to-day agenda (interview with senior managers, Staatsbosbeheer, 30 January 2002).

Who makes the most use of performance indicators?

In a perfectly functioning democracy, parliament and citizen's groups would be deeply and regularly concerned with the published information concerning the performance of public bodies such as forestry agencies. Their reports would be scrutinized and debated. Questions would be asked. Key items would be reported in the mass media. Following debate, if necessary, policies would be adjusted.

In the real world of forestry programmes, little of this happens. In all four countries we were told that MPs seldom asked any questions, while the mass media usually ignore performance reports, although episodically concentrate on some particular aspect which is deemed newsworthy ('attack of the spruce bark beetle!', 'environmental group slams forestry chiefs over "boring" landscapes'). Even parent ministries may be fairly weak monitors and discussants (see later). To some extent it seems that, while performance indicators are increasingly used by managements for internal steering, externally their function is partly decorative – they serve as a kind of symbolic guarantee of 'modern' management rather than actually being used very much. Information about commercial activities is a partial exception to this: in both Sweden and Finland we were told that private forest companies scrutinized state agency data to make sure that they were not offering unfair, cross-subsidized competition.

Some quotations from our interview material may help to illustrate the above generalizations. First, on the lack of interest of parliaments:

Q. Is there much interest from parliament in the reporting from the agency?
A. No, not really ... (interview with Swedish Ministry of Industry civil servants, 24 June 2002).

In Finland a senior official in the Ministry of Agriculture and Forestry said that individual MPs would sometimes ask questions about conservation issues – often spurred on by environmental campaigners – but they didn't actually ask about the target-setting process. Our respondent described the activities of the environmental groups as 'just politics' (interview, 17 June 2002). National audit offices are in principle more assiduous critics, but in practice their attentions are few and far between. Unless it happens to be one of the rare years when there is a performance audit focused on forestry, managers can afford to forget about detailed scrutiny of their PIs from this quarter.

Second, here are some of the comments about the degree of interest shown by parent ministries:

I do not think that many people look at these key indicators, but there are a few people. (Senior manager in SVS, interview, 29 April 2001, when asked how much use the ministry made of the performance data)

We have a small ministry and they are not in a position to judge if our allocation [the system for sharing our resources between the regional boards] is good or bad. (Senior manager, SVS, 29 April 2001)

In Finland, a senior civil servant in the Ministry of Agriculture and Forestry indicated that, while the parliament formally fixed the annual investment limit for the state forestry enterprise, it usually approved the proposals put to it by the ministry. Only occasionally did it want something to be changed. (Interview, 17 June 2002)

In the United Kingdom the situation is rather different, because the parent department is the Forestry Commission, headed by a Director General, not a minister. In the words of its Director General 'there is a strong forestry ethic in the Commission, it is a professional body. We are not a bunch of mandarins here with arts degrees from Oxford and Cambridge' (interview, 3 May 2002). This means that the dialogue over targets can be more technical and that there is ' a sharing and understanding of what forestry is all about'. However, this only means that the usual problems re-appear at the next level up: the Forestry Commission's own relations with the relevant English, Scottish and Welsh ministries, and in relations between the Treasury and the forestry bodies. Asked who made the most use of Forest Enterprise performance data a senior manager replied:

> The Treasury, who are really our bankers, if you want to call them that. They pay most attention to them. They are highly critical about us meeting our targets. (Interview at Forest Enterprise, 11 December 2000)

Concluding discussion: similarities and differences

A first and fundamental point to make is that, despite occasional rhetoric about freedom, autonomy and entrepreneurialism, in none of our four countries is a state forestry agency allowed to behave in the way a private forestry company could. Every one of our researched organizations is hedged about with major restrictions of one kind or another. Metsähallitus and Forest Enterprise are encouraged to make profits, but they don't get to keep most of that money. Since 1995, the Finnish Ministry of Finance has claimed a steadily larger 'dividend' from Metsähallitus' profits. 'We are at the bottom; the Ministry of Agriculture and Forestry is in the middle and the Ministry of Finance is at the top. The Ministry of Finance wants every last mark it can get'. (Interview, senior manager, Metsähallitus, 5 September 2001 – when Finland still had the mark, rather than the euro as its unit of currency.) Meanwhile, in Sweden, SVS is not allowed to show a 'profit' in any of its main activities, and when it developed a commercially viable business selling seeds and planting services, this business was promptly taken away from it and turned into a separate state-owned company (Svenska Skogsplantor AB). Staatsbosbeheer cannot 'loss lead' on one activity in order to subsidize another.

And it isn't only that profits are whisked away by national ministries of finance. Agencies also face major constraints in their use of their two basic assets – trees and land. National governments either prohibit or severely restrict the sale of land, and they also impose strict volume controls on tree-felling. Thus, when timber prices go down, as they did in western Europe in the late 1990s under the impact of cheap imports from Russia and eastern Europe, state agencies can do neither of the obvious things to maintain their income – greatly increase volume (of timber sales) or sell land. In the United Kingdom a senior member of the Forestry Commission put it like this: 'You might say that they [Forest Enterprise] have a strong balance sheet, but all three governments [i.e. of England, Scotland and Wales] have a policy of not selling any government land so we can't even liquidate assets to flow cash balances' (interview, 3 May 2002).

The second fundamental point is that forestry is seldom a politically salient issue at national level. It does not divide major parties along ideological lines. It is not a major burden on the budget (indeed, as we have seen, it is more usually a net contributor to state funds). It is not a sector in which 'human interest' disasters are very common (there are usually no accidents involving multiple fatalities, or heart-rending/ conscious-stirring stories of injustice or inequality or media-grabbing tales of unethical conduct). It may be economically important (as in the Nordic countries) but even in this respect forestry tends to fall into the 'business as usual' category. This means that forestry can work through fairly stable policy networks, with few 'interruptions' caused by headlines in the mass media or surges of interest among significant numbers of politicians. Many of the senior managers we met had been in the forestry sector for many years, or for the whole of their working lives. There are local controversies, of course, and environmental pressure groups are increasingly vocal, but forestry is not usually a priority target for them within their overall portfolio of campaigns and causes – or, at least, not within our four countries, each of which already has in place elaborate legal and procedural arrangements for safeguarding environmental concerns. [The fate of the rain forest and exotic species in Brazil, or Indonesia, is much more likely to attract the attention of environmental 'cause' groups.] So, on the whole, forestry can be 'managed', in a regular, continuing way, without the crises and media blitzes to which, say, prisons and social security organizations are more frequently prone.

A third point is that parent departments struggle to play a very effective role in setting and monitoring environmental targets. Financial targets may be relatively understandable, but setting environmental targets has, in each country, developed as a highly professional and technical matter. Without some relevant scientific and practical background it is hard to enter the debate. The result is that agencies have a large hand in shaping these targets themselves, and that their main interlocutors, if there are any, are environmental groups rather than parent ministries or parliaments.

Thus far we have been describing similarities – features which are present to a greater or lesser degree in all four countries, and which could be said to be 'task-specific'. But our investigation has also suggested some significant differences. It might seem that one of these is in the degree of overt commercialism, where the United Kingdom and Finland seem to come some way ahead of Sweden, and far ahead of the Netherlands.

But to some extent this may be an illusion brought about by our focus on a particular organizational form: the agency. It is more the case that different countries put state commercial activities into different types of organizational category. In the two Nordic countries there continues to exist a substantial population of state enterprises (including the Finnish Metsähallitus) and (even 'further out') state-owned companies (including the big Swedish forest owner, Sveaskog AB). In the United Kingdom, however, 'nationalized industries' and 'public corporations' went seriously out of fashion during the 1980s and 1990s. To have created a new nationalized industry would have been a kind of blasphemy. So, in some cases, commercial activities which, for whatever reason, the government decided it could not privatize, were kept within the organizational form of an agency – Forest Enterprise being a case in point. In the Netherlands the situation is very different from the other three countries, because the potential scale of the income to be gained from selling forest products is so small. To be cruel, one might say that Staatsbosbeheer can afford to be so environmentally and recreationally oriented – and so commercially silent – because in the crowded Netherlands there is so little woodland from which any kind of profit could be made.

A second difference is in the way that the performance indicators are used, where the style appears to be 'softest' in the Netherlands and 'toughest' in the United Kingdom, with Finland and Sweden standing somewhere between these two extremes. The annual reports illustrate this, with the United Kingdom and Swedish ones themselves being written explicitly around the performance target system, while the Dutch one is mainly descriptions of worthy activities accompanied by lavish colour photography. It briefly describes the elaborate planning system (referred to earlier in this chapter) but does not actually give any performance data from that system (Staatsbosbeheer, 2000, p. 27). Our interviews tended to reinforce this rank order. If we are right about these differences, then they are not specific to forestry, but rather exist as broad characteristics of the politico-administrative system and cultures described in the country chapters.

Overall, therefore, we can see that the management of state forestry agencies *is* extensively influenced by the characteristics of the task of forestry itself, and by certain common issues that are specific to forestry, such as the balance between economic, environmental and touristic values. Yet at the same time there is also an overlay of country-specific influences, derived from the national 'ways of doing business' in the public sector.

10
Social Security

Introduction

Unlike meteorology or forestry, social security is a highly politically sensitive field of administration because it touches the everyday lives of millions of citizens. Furthermore, it is typically the largest single item in state budgets. It tends to be heavily legalistic. It is not rocket science, in the sense that, even if the computer systems are complex, the core business of making payments to claimants is understandable to lay people, including ministers and civil servants. In this chapter we explore the consequences of these characteristics for the management of social security, and especially the implications for its management at arm's-length from government. We examine how the responsible agencies in Sweden, Finland, the Netherlands and the United Kingdom have responded to organizational change, and how each of our four social security agencies have interpreted and developed performance management as a means to achieving policy goals.

The reform of welfare services in post-industrial societies has attracted vigorous debate and scholarship in recent times (Considine, 2001; Esping-Anderson, 1996; King, 1999; Levy, 1999; Ploug and Kvist, 1994; Rose, 1997). Fiscal crises and increases in the numbers of elderly and unemployed have forced many governments to search for economies and efficiencies. Against popular resistance to welfare cutbacks, entrenched interests and institutional constraints, political leaders have adopted various reform strategies in their quest for savings and productivity gains within their welfare sectors. Organizational restructuring of operational departments along agency lines has been one such strategy, and a related development has been the introduction of performance measurement to make service deliverers more accountable to their political principals and the public. Thus, in terms of Chapter 2's 'tripod', both disaggregation and a greater emphasis on measured performance have been popular. However, the political sensitivity of the function can make high autonomization hard to sustain – as we shall see.

In the Netherlands, changes in the social security system have been described as 'managed liberalisation' (van der Veen and Trommel, 1999), while in the United Kingdom reform has been characterized as 'enterprise management' (Considine, 2001). The Swedish reforms are described by Premfors (1991) as 'decentralised management'.

In Finland, reform of social security arrangements have been more limited, but there, too, there has been a desire to move towards a more performance-oriented system (Social Insurance Institution, Finland, 2000). Whatever the particular approach – and these have varied widely – reform trends in welfare administration reflect a similar general orientation: that is, towards a more accountable, efficient and businesslike mode of operation, and a strengthening of political steering.

In the United Kingdom, the Benefits Agency (BA), has been marked by a turbulent history, characterized by a series of quite dramatic organizational regroupings and senior management changes following ministerial interventions. These culminated in a large-scale restructure in 2001, which brought together the Employment Service (located within a separate ministry) and the larger part of the Benefits Agency, to create a single super-agency known as Jobcentre Plus. Aged pensions, formerly part of the BA, was separated out to a newly created Pensions Agency.

Political intervention in agencies has been less frequent in the Netherlands and the Nordic countries. In Sweden, ministers are by law prevented from interfering in matters that are the responsibility of agencies (see Chapter 5). In Finland, the Social Security Institute (KELA) is largely beyond ministerial control altogether, reporting directly to Parliament. As one senior official in the Ministry of Social Affairs and Health put it to us: 'there's no formal relationship between KELA and the Ministry' (interview, 18 June 2002). The Dutch Social Insurance Bank (SVB) also has legislative protection from ministerial intervention even though its supervisory body, the Social Security Supervision Board (CTSV), was subject to continuous restructuring following its establishment as an agency.[1] Despite these apparently higher degrees of autonomy, however, the continental agencies have been far from immune from change. Apart from internal reorganizations, there have been external pressures, or even changes of status, in all three countries. The Swedish National Labour Market Board, for example, has experienced some quite major restructuring in recent years. Even in Finland, the agency's high level of autonomy has not prevented the pressure for reform by external stakeholders, expressed, for example, by a recent streamlining of the supervisory board.

The analysis begins with a brief survey of recent reforms in the selected agencies. It then moves to a description of institutional patterns, including functional specializations, structures of governance, and organization. In the third part of the chapter, we examine the agencies' performance measurement systems, and how and to what extent these are linked with the organization's core management systems including financial, planning and human resources management. We also consider problems in these systems and the perceptions of their utility for agency management. Finally, we explore agency relations with central ministries, especially parent departments.

Before proceeding, it is necessary to add two caveats in relation to the data upon which the chapter is based. The first is that, in functional terms, we are not strictly comparing like with like. In Finland and the United Kingdom our cases are social insurance agencies which make benefit payments to clients. Our Swedish agency – the AMS – is an employment and skills training organization, which also regulates unemployment insurance (but is not the service provider). The Dutch SVB (Social Insurance Bank) is responsible only for aged pensions and child benefits. We must confess there was a somewhat opportunistic element in our original research plan, but in fact it would in any case have been impossible to find exactly functionally equivalent organizations in all four countries. We argue that this variety can be instructive: it is itself reflective of the different policy approaches which exist in the various countries. The second caveat relates to our UK case study where a broadening of functions (and name change) of the Benefits Agency mid-stream of the research, forced us to consider how best to present this agency. All our interviews with management staff in the BA were conducted prior to its restructuring and renaming.[2] To preserve the integrity of our data, the agency is referred to here by its original name.

Reform history

Social security agencies were established in the Nordic countries as part of a post-war social compact (Bergmark *et al.*, 2000; Esping-Andersen and Korpi, 1984).[3] They were set up as autonomous, tripartite bodies, independent from government. In Finland, the Social Insurance Institute – or KELA as it is more widely known – was defined by the Pension Insurance Act of 1956, although an ancestor organization existed back to 1937. Sweden's AMS (National Labour Market Board/ *Arbeidsmarknadsstyrelssen*) replaced a wartime Labour Market Commission, and was established as a state agency in 1948. The arm's length nature of social security delivery in the Netherlands and the United Kingdom is of more recent origin. In the Netherlands, the Social Insurance Bank (SVB/*Sociale Verzekeringsbank*) was established in 1992 (through a merger of two departments) as part of the Dutch public sector 'autonomization' reforms (see Chapter 4). The UK Benefits Agency (now Jobcentre Plus) was the largest of the Next Steps agencies established by the Conservatives, separating from the Department of Social Security in 1991.

The Netherlands reform of its social security system began in 1985 following a dramatic rise in social security costs from the early seventies, due largely to the high cost of sickness and disability payments – 'the Dutch disease' as it was known. Old-aged pensions were another important factor, more than doubling in the period to 1996. The Social Insurance Council (SVR) as the responsible body for the implementation and control of social security, was developed as a corporatist style tripartite institution, and the 'social partners' (employer associations and unions) were responsible for the execution of bipartite, sectoral industrial insurance boards. In 1991, a scathing attack on the management of the SVR by the Auditor General prompted a new government to pursue sector-wide reforms. One of these was the institutional redesign of the system through the partial dismantling of corporatist structures. Others included the introduction of financial incentives and the creation of quasi-markets (van der Veen and Trommel, 1999). Organizations charged with supervision, certification or the payment of benefits were transformed into ZBOs (see Chapter 4), giving them greater autonomy than the newly created *agentschappen*, and therefore representing substantial 'autonomization' (Greve *et al.*, 1999). A tightening of rules and regulations and increased monitoring were other features of the reforms.

The United Kingdom's centralized system of government and convention of ministerial responsibility means that its social security system functions as a monopoly under close political scrutiny. In budget terms, the Department of Social Security (now Department of Work and Pensions) has long been one of the largest in Whitehall. As one of the first Next Steps experiments, the separation out of the largest of its operational units – responsible for unemployment and aged pensions – meant some decentralization of authority, but not much by continental standards. The Fowler Reviews of Social Security in 1985 argued the case for reform. Fowler believed the system was too complex, that it failed to give support to those in greatest need and, in true Tory fashion, that the tax-benefit arrangement prevented people from making their own provision and exercising freedom of choice (DHSS, 1985). The government White Paper which followed claimed that reform of the system should be consistent with the Government's overall objectives for the economy, and that the system needed to be better managed. As Bradshaw (1992, p. 82) puts it: 'a belief in privatisation, selectivity, managerialism, incentives and last, but certainly not least, the needs of the economy' indicate the objectives of Thatcherite social policy.

Unlike some departments, which were sceptical of the government's plans to transform operational units into semi-autonomous agencies, the DSS welcomed the reforms (Gains, 1999), although more recent research suggests that senior officials in the department were engaged in 'bureau shaping' (James, 2003). Typical of executive agencies in the United Kindom, the Benefits Agency remained within the civil service, and accountable to the Minister through the Department. Because of the highly legalistic nature of its work and its sheer size (representing 85 per cent of the Department's operations), the relationship and governance arrangements between agency and ministry took on a corporate style. A change of government in 1997 and a new focus on outcome-oriented objectives and co-ordination or 'joined-upness' (James, 2003), changed the nature of this relationship. The corporate structure became more one of 'incorporation' with senior agency management assuming dual roles as both departmental *and* agency officials. Autonomy, then, for the Benefits Agency, is a questionable concept. This was even more apparent when, in 2002, the Agency merged with the Employment Agency and the transformation of benefits as entitlements to benefits as conditional upon 'non-standard' forms of work and training, was achieved (Considine, 2001, p. 38).

Despite their shared commitment to social democratic principles, the social security systems of Finland and Sweden are significantly different. Finland's policy emphasis has been on earnings-related security and it is a late comer to public assistance forms of welfare (Manning and Shaw, 1998). Both Finland and Sweden use local authorities in the delivery of many services, but only in Sweden has there been a legislated decentralization of operations and, albeit limited, policy authority to the County level. The decentralization reforms in Sweden occurred in the mid-1980s and had several objectives, not least to break down the old state monopolies and make the system more responsive to public need.

There are many similarities between these neighbouring countries. Both experienced severe economic recession in the early 1990s and sharp increases in unemployment (around 20 per cent in Finland) following the collapse of the Soviet Union, and also at this time, upheavals caused by their entry into the European Union. Internal factors such as aging populations, changing gender relations and the organization of work, also brought forth pressures for system reform. For Sweden in particular, but also for Finland, the 1990s brought to an end the 'golden era' of the 'Scandinavian welfare states' which was marked by economic prosperity combined with policies aimed at high levels of equality and social justice (Kautto *et al.*, 1999). While not strictly part of the 'Scandinavian model', Finland aligned itself firmly with its western neighbours during the 1970s, especially in its high level of income transfers – although its social expenditure was more on a par with Germany at 26 per cent of GDP, than with Sweden at 35 per cent (Manning and Shaw, 1998).

There was in both countries during the 1990s, a preoccupation with public debt which had implications for public expenditure. A liberalist economic doctrine supporting budget cuts, user charges and 'privatization' via local government, the family and community (the latter especially in Finland) suggested to some commentators that a 'paradigm shift' was occurring (Christensen *et al.*, 2002; Manning and Shaw, 1998). Institutional resistance to change, however, has been much stronger in the Nordic countries than in either the United Kingdom or the Netherlands, due partly to the constitutional autonomy of their social security agencies. Even so, their classic corporatist forms of governance – by boards of 'laymen' – have been considerably paired down. Both systems adopted new public management principles to enhance the efficiency and accountability of their responsible agencies. In Sweden, 'politicisation' of the agencies through government appointed Directors General (typically someone from the ruling party) facilitated internal reforms (Pierre, 1995). And in Finland, where change has been less radical, the current Director General of KELA is a retired politician. Appointments to its supervisory council are seen by some in the ministries as a 'last refuge of jobs for the boys' (interview with senior official, Ministry of Finance, 4 Septemper 2001). In addition, the erosion of independent sources of finance via expanded general budget funded programs and, in Sweden, a redirection of government finance to the local level, enhanced political steering has been observed.

Patterns of institutions

Size, function and finance

Three distinctive features of social security agencies are their size, their functional specialization and their funding base. Size is important not only on its own terms, but in relation to the ministries that agencies have either separated from, and/or are answerable to. The programme budgets of agencies are huge compared to the policy budgets of ministries. For example, the Benefits Agency, which was the largest of all UK executive agencies, had an annual spend of 130 billion Euros. This represented 30 per cent of the total government budget. The agency employed over 70 000 personnel which represents 85 per cent of all DSS staff. In Finland, KELA spends 9 billion Euros which represents a quarter of all state expenditure. The combined operational and programme budgets, and staff size of the four country agencies for 2000 are shown in Table 10.1.

Social security, as a distinct functional activity of government, is important because, as Heidenheimer et al. (1990) remind us, 'almost every citizen at some time in their lives will be a recipient of benefits payments'. Some social security functions are more politically charged than others, however, depending on source of funding and type of benefit paid. There are critical differences, for example, between public assistance ('non-contributory') and insurance-based ('contributory') benefits. If the benefit has a predictable number of clients such as aged pensions, and has dedicated funding (through contributory schemes), then it is less likely to attract negative political attention than are non-contributory benefits paid from the public purse to, for example, the unemployed or single parents. In comparing our cases, we find that differences in the type of functions performed, and their related sources of funding, are reflected in the organization's stability. Where the UK Benefits Agency (which is responsible for a wide range of benefit types, funded from general revenue) has been the subject of much restructuring, the more specialized SVB in the Netherlands, in terms of client numbers and secured budget, has remained stable since its 'autonomization' in

Table 10.1 Financial and staff resources of selected social security agencies (2000)

Country	Total budget (Euros billion)[1]	% of total state budget	Staff
Sweden (AMS)	7.4	8.6	11 248[2]
Finland (KELA)	9	25	5 700
The Netherlands (SVB)	24.2	14.3	3 452
The United Kingdom (BA)	130	30	70 642

Notes:
[1] Administrative + program budget
[2] Includes County level

1990. In Finland, too, greater stability has prevailed, despite KELA's wide functional responsibilities (including social insurance and public assistance programs). Until recent inroads by newly legislated and government supported schemes, KELA was funded largely through earmarked 'employers' contributions'. Sweden's AMS has a long history of relative stability even though there have been some metamorphoses of the agency, particularly as a result of the decentralization reforms. But the AMS has a narrower range of functional responsibilities (various employment schemes) which are publicly funded. Employment insurance is provided by the 39 private funds which the AMS regulates.

An obvious interpretation would be that the corporatist/tripartite features of Sweden and the Netherlands, plus the parliament-based autonomy of the Finnish KELA, have protected these continental institutions from the repeated adjustments to status and borders which were experienced by the UK Benefits Agency. As a senior official in the parent ministry of the BA put it to us:

> It is highly political and decisions are taken in the name of the state. It is also highly litigated, and the idea of 'arms length' is fanciful.
> (Interview, 19 February 2001)

Finland's Social Insurance Institute administers most of the government's social security schemes, including national health. In 1990, the government streamlined service delivery into a 'one stop shop' for which KELA was wholly responsible. Its responsibilities do not, however, extend to employment-based pensions and employment schemes. The Swedish Social Security Agency, AMS (National Labour Market Board) is essentially an employment and training service, but also responsible for unemployment insurance. In the late 1980s, AMS decentralized authority for its local operations to County Labour Boards, which changed the nature of the agency from a service organization to a regulatory body. The insurance division of AMS also acts as a regulator, supervising thirty-nine private funds which are responsible for administering unemployment benefits. Its public–private mix is a distinctive feature of the Swedish agency, which has its origins in the tripartite nature of social security provision and the active role of trade unions and employers. Most of the private funds originated from and are retained by these groups.

The Dutch agency – the SVB – is a pension agency but is not responsible for unemployment payments. Its jurisdiction is child and aged pensions. The UK Benefits Agency, prior to its restructure, was responsible for the bulk of social security benefits, but not for employment and job training schemes, which were part of a separate Ministry. Like the Finnish agency, the BA was also portrayed as a 'one stop shop' for clients. This idea fitted the new client focus of service delivery agencies across governments in the 1990s. It was also a manifestation of the growing complexity of social benefits payments, as the CE of the Benefits Agency explained:

> Whereas in the past, you would have had a single benefit, targeted at a single individual for the circumstances they were in, now there is a portfolio of benefits that actually meet an individual. (Interview, 5 January 2001)

The restructure of the BA in 2001, and separation out of the 'non-working aged' into a new Pension Service agency, mirrors patterns in the Netherlands and in Sweden. The United Kingdom's new 'working aged' agency – Jobcentre Plus – reflects the Swedish 'single window' approach of getting people jobs, as well as arranging their benefits, while the new Pension Service approximates the Dutch SVB, with the exception that the UK Pension Service agency does not include child welfare, which is administered by a separate agency. Although not a central interest of this chapter, it is worth noting that the 'welfare-to-work' policy of Britain's Labour government, which gave rise to the restructure, is consistent with trends in a number of developed countries and is symptomatic of structural unemployment in the West.

Governance arrangements

Governance is not simply about formal structures but implies policy authority, so that while it is useful to distinguish between governing boards, and responsible ministries, it is also helpful to know who has policy authority. According to Mabbett and Bolderson (1999) there are two distinctive patterns of governance in social security agencies: one, where policy authority is highly centralized and it conforms to a principal–agent model; and two, where policy authority is dispersed, and it conforms to a 'multi-level' governance model. From our study, we find that Sweden stands out as the single example of the latter. In Sweden, the County Labour Boards share policy authority (within their jurisdictions) with the AMS and the ministry, while in the United Kingdom, policy authority is centralized in the Ministry alone.

Similarly, we need to look at the membership of supervisory boards to know who governs. Social insurance agencies may include contributors (both workers and employers) on their boards, and thus should be seen as standing alongside central government as principals (Mabbett and Bolderson, 1999). In some cases, even beneficiaries may be represented on, for example, management boards.

The Finnish agency had a supervisory board made up of fourteen commissioners appointed by Parliament and including community and union representatives. Below that, an executive board of directors was responsible for management decisions. In 2001, Parliament reformed its governing body of commissioners, making it smaller, more focused on executive decision processes (by incorporating two directors from the now disbanded executive board), and elevating government input by the inclusion of a ministry representative. Sweden's AMS also has a supervisory board with various stakeholder representation, although in 1992 its classic tripartite governance structure came to an end with the departure of the Swedish Employers Confederation from the Board and the Local Committees. The County Boards have Local Employment Services Committees (established at the time of devolution) with representations from local interests.

Sweden's AMS has a parent ministry – the Department of Industry, Trade and Commerce – while Finland's KELA works with six ministries in the administration of various legislative mandates, but is independent of them. It reports directly to Parliament. This unique constitutional feature has given this agency immunity from ministerial intervention, although the practice of appointing ex-politicians to supervisory boards and even to the position of director general, offers the potential for enhanced political control – though by parliament rather than the ministries. In both Nordic countries, the Ministry of Finance plays an increasingly influential role. In the Finnish case, this has developed by stealth as more of KELA's funds (50 per cent) have come from the General Government Budget through an expansion of legislated responsibilities. Previously, a dedicated source of funding from employers' social insurance payments formed the bulk of the agency's income.

The Benefits Agency, like all UK executive agencies, could only claim 'semi-autonomy' in so far as it had no independent statutory authority, although it was responsible for administering many pieces of legislation. The BA had a formal 'executive' Board and a governing 'Framework Document' (rewritten in 1995) given to it by the minister. The Chief Executive works to a performance contract agreed with the ministry. This agency, in theory at least, functions as a pure example of the principal – agent model. In reality, it is less than pure. A ministerial decision some six years after the BA was established led to the development of a unique management structure and one that ensured the agency's subservience to the ministry. The parent department clawed back most of its core management functions into a Corporate Services Directorate. Senior management within the agency were thus required to carry a wider 'corporate' (as distinct from agency specific) responsibility alongside departmental management.

In the Netherlands, the SVB is classified as a ZBO, giving it considerably more autonomy from ministerial intervention than the *agentschappen*, which are more akin to UK style executive agencies. At the time of our interviews, the SVB was governed by a tripartite board composed of major stakeholders of unions, employers and others appointed by the Crown. However, in 2002, the status of this Board changed to that of an advisory board (reporting directly to the minister) with 50 per cent fewer members.

The SVB was, until recently, supervised by an external body called the Board of Supervision Social Security (CTSV). The CTSV (which had replaced the tri-partite Social Insurance Council when it was dismantled in 1994) had oversight of the legality and efficiency of the organization. In the United Kingdom, the BA also has an external body called the Standards Committee which has a similar function, but in the Netherlands, the CTSV had substantially more authority, rather like a regulator. The SVB reported to the supervisory body rather than the ministry. It was the regulator that reported to the ministry on the performance of the SVB. While the SVB has (at least up until 2002) been relatively unchallenged, the CTSV was subjected to continuous reorganization prior to its reintegration with the ministry in early 2002. Reintegration has inevitably changed the nature of the relationship that the SVB has with its new supervisory body – the Ministry of Social Affairs and Unemployment. A change in the status of the SVB Board to an advisory body will consolidate this new relationship by shifting accountability more directly onto the SVB's senior management, thus ensuring stronger forms of political supervision, a process in common with other social security agencies in the Netherlands (Considine, 2001; van der Veen and Trommel, 1999). The governance characteristics, functions and responsible authorities of the social security agencies in 2000 are shown in Table 10.2.

Regionalization and rationalization

A uniform trend to fewer but larger districts in the delivery of social services reflects a patternacross policy fields and, indeed, across sub-central government in many countries (Caulfield and Larsen, 2002). Our four

Table 10.2 Social security agency governance arrangements (2002)

Country	Ministry	Status	Governance	Function
Sweden (AMS)	Industry and Trade Ministry	Statutory	Supervisory board	Regulatory
Finland (KELA)	Parliament	Statutory	Supervisory council	Distributive
The Netherlands (SVB)	Social Affairs and Unemployment Ministry	Statutory	Supervisory board (now advisory)	Distributive
United Kingdom (BA)	Department of Social Security (now Work and Pensions)	Non-statutory	Advisory board	Distributive

country agencies, which are organized on a regional basis, have not been exempt from the trend, so this would appear to be a sectoral influence that to some extent transcends national boundaries. The AMS works closely with Sweden's County Labour Boards in the delivery of its service. These boards are responsible for the numerous employment offices throughout the country. Since 1996, these offices have been amalgamated into fewer and larger units. KELA also has a contractual/partnership arrangement with Finnish local authorities, but the Agency retains operational responsibility for numerous 'insurance districts'. Rationalizations in the 1990s whittled these down from 188 to 86. The UK Benefits Agency has thirteen area directorates with their own district offices. This agency took a different approach to rationalization by introducing two field operations – North and South – in 1999. In the same year, four central benefits directorates were reduced to three. The BA has a limited partnership with local authorities, notably in the provision of housing benefit. The Dutch SVB is also regionally based, and a rationalization exercise in this country substantially reduced the number of its regions from 23 to 9.

Implementing performance management

In all four countries, the agencies have developed performance frameworks. However, there is considerable variation between them in their approaches to performance measurement, the length of time since first implementing a performance regime, and how performance data is used, and by whom. The integration of performance data with core management systems often remains embryonic. In our research we asked a number of key questions:

- How well developed is performance measurement within the organization?
- How is it perceived by agency management and ministries?
- To what extent is performance measurement integrated with resource allocation decisions and other main management systems?
- What are the perceived problems with its use?

The introduction of performance management into UK executive agencies was a strategy for ensuring not only improved performance in the work of agencies, but was also seen as a means by which principals (ministries) could control agents. Annual performance agreements are negotiated between the Chief Executive and the Permanent Secretary and used as a basis for funding. In Sweden, there is a discernable trend to formalize and centralize performance management. The *regleringsbrevet* (the budget appropriation) for the agency now incorporates not only broad targets but also detailed indicators. In the Netherlands, the first priority of the autonomization reforms was cost control: thus, the initial priority for the newly created ZBOs and agencies was the setting of financial targets (Smullen, 2004; Verhaak, 1997). In later years the focus on efficiency measures broadened to include quality measures. Similarly, in Finland, an initial concern with cost effectiveness and efficiency as key performance measures had, by 1996, also broadened to include quality measures (SII Working Papers 17/2000).

Results-oriented management was a widely adopted reform theme in both Finland and Sweden in the late 1980s, with the main push coming from ministries of finance (Pollitt and Bouckaert, 2000). However, implementation seems to have been more gradual and patchy than in the United Kingdom. Ideas around 'quality management' or 'management by objectives' have also been important in the Nordic countries (Christensen *et al.*, 2002). Indeed, the concept of quality management appears to be the main focus of current reform in both the Swedish and Finnish agencies. In general it might be said that performance measurement, although 'on the agenda', has not been given the same 'bite' or prominence as in many parts of the UK public sector. This may be partly for constitutional reasons – the greater autonomy of Swedish agencies in general (Chapter 5) and the unique status of KELA in Finland (see earlier). However, it is also partly a cultural issue. The consensual and corporatist cultures of these two countries (including strong trade union participation in governance arrangements or through parliamentary lobbying) lead to a 'softer', less punitive use of performance measurement than has sometimes occurred in the United Kingdom. To give some examples from the interviews:

> I should say some of the things that we do are not just to receive good results from the point where you can measure it, it is to attain a society that is human and in some respects guided by the opinion of the people that live here. (Senior Research Analyst, AMS, 3 May 2001)
>
> We are moving to individual performance agreements, but the unions are against it because they see it as foreign, too individualistic instead of our traditional cooperative approach. (Research Director, KELA, 18 October 2000)

In both Sweden and Finland, the commitment to government-wide results measurement and management was strong in the late 1980s. The aim was to save money and increase efficiency. But the implementation, especially in core welfare state services like social security, took a long time to work through. According to some Ministry officials, KELA was the most tenacious of the old agencies or 'bureaucratic power centres' (Senior Official, Ministry of Finance, 18 October 2000). Recent reforms to its governing body, however, suggest some movement towards making this agency more accountable and efficient. Sweden's AMS reformed its organization in 1996 'to extract maximum economization' (Official history). To quote again its Senior Research Analyst:

> ... we have been going through a process over the last 10 years where AMS has lost some of its might compared to the Department.
> (3 May 2001)

Thus, despite their long history of independence, a challenge to the autonomy of social security agencies in both countries, mounted by central ministries, followed the economic crisis of the late 1980s/early 1990s.

In Britain and the Netherlands, strengthening mechanisms of accountability was a key element of the 1980s structural reforms to social service delivery. Devolved management implied accountability for the performance of the new agencies and, in the case of the BA, performance targets were included in its governing framework document. As in the Nordic countries, economic pressures on government were behind the reforms but, unlike the Nordics, the British and Dutch governments also exhibited a strong ideological commitment to market-like efficiency reforms (Pollitt and Bouckaert, 2000; Verhaak, 1997). However, it would be misleading to portray the social security organizations in either the Netherlands or the United Kingdom as gung-ho, trouble-free performance measurement enthusiasts. On the contrary, our interviews revealed, alongside considerable efforts to inculcate a 'performance mentality', extensive evidence of inertia and problems. The top-down pressure for performance indicators was hardly matched by an eagerness from the bottom-up:

> Operational managers are not using the data. A training effort is going on here. We do not have a decent management information reporting tool. There has been no culture of reporting on performance and costing. We are turning up the heat on this a bit. (Senior official, Corporate Services Division of the UK Department of Social Security, 19 February 2001 – notice that this turning up of the heat was taking place a full decade after the BA was created)

> Where we are going is politically driven, and management information is devalued because it is not used. (Senior manager, Benefits Agency, 22 January 2001)

> there is a perception among regional directors that we are very busy with controlling them, but actually we are much more busy with the external accountability processes. So a lot of the information we are getting we use for the external accountability processes and much less for the performance of the regional offices. (Senior official, SVB, 26 February 2002)

Another senior SVB manager explained to us that from the establishment of the SVB in 1990 the focus of performance was narrowly financial, and that a 'balanced scorecard' which also took account of service quality concerns and other factors was only being introduced for the first time in 2001 (interview, 20 November 2000). A third SVB manager told us that with respect to the link between performance reporting and actual improvement programmes in the regional offices, big changes were still needed (interview, 12 February 2002).

Even though performance improvement was a *raison d'etre* for the Agency's creation, the UK BA continued to struggle with a rigid organizational culture and technological backwardness, inherited from the old department. A special Performance Management Unit was set up in 2000, partly in response to negative reports by the National Audit Office on the Agency's performance, but also 'to send a signal' that under pressure of reform plans, the agency should not loose sight of the need to continue performance improvement (Interview with Permanent

Secretary, 19 Febraury 2001). The Unit provides best practice guidelines to the operational areas to ensure common data sets. In the same year, the Agency put in place 'performance' teams in the thirteen regional areas. These teams are drawn from the field, but work closely with senior management to assist regional and area managers. The development of a league table between areas/districts is seen as an important incentive to performance improvement, although the complexities of measuring different geographical areas which are diverse in their demographic and economic characteristics, adds to the burden of measurement accuracy and incentive efficacy.

Overall, the picture that emerges is one where the domain of performance measurement in both the United Kingdom and the Netherlands has been quite limited. In both countries purely financial measures have tended to dominate. In both countries there has been a struggle to persuade rank-and-file staff and local operational managers to actually use performance information as a basis for local decision-making. In both countries a good deal of performance data is produced for external audiences (public accountability), but those audiences don't actually seem to take much interest in it ('the media and parliament do not use this information frequently' – senior SVB official, 21 November 2000; several senior managers in the BA indicated that wider use of performance data beyond the ministry was very limited). Nevertheless, despite these caveats, it is hard to escape the conclusion that the range and depth of non-financial performance data which was routinely furnished by the UK Benefits Agency far outstripped what was on offer from the Finnish KELA, or even the Dutch SVB. These continental bodies certainly published plenty of information, but relatively little of it was organized into a *performance* format.

Measuring performance

The central idea behind performance measurement, according to de Bruijn, is that 'a public organization formulates its envisaged performance and indicates how this performance may be measured by defining performance indicators' (2001, p. 7). Following from which, the organization can show whether it has indeed achieved its performance and at what cost. Measuring performance is not a new concept to social policy institutions, which have traditionally utilized performance oriented research and evaluation (Moores, 2001). However, this has tended to be program specific. Measuring the performance of the organization as a whole, in particular, its efficiency and effectiveness, and developing feedback loops to decision-making processes are relatively recent concepts for social policy managers and staff.

In Finland, performance agreements were first introduced into KELA in 1996. Agreements are concluded annually by the Board of Directors, and by regional directors with the districts. In 1997 the agency launched the Quality Programme and distributed to all staff a list of quality targets. Quality liaisons were appointed in all 99 districts and annual training of staff was undertaken. Based on Finnish Quality Award criteria, self-evaluations of the agency have been conducted annually since 1998. In 2000, KELA introduced the 'balanced scorecard' as a management, planning and monitoring tool. The scorecard, which lists the organization's key targets, performance indicators and evaluation criteria, and plots these across 3 years (immediate past, present and next), is produced by each district under the terms of its performance agreement. In addition, the KELA 'barometer' – an annual survey of client satisfaction with the organization, which has existed since 1996 – is an instrument valued by managers at the unit level. This includes comparative questions where the client rates KELA's performance against certain other organizations.

In Sweden, the public/private nature of the AMS suggests a more ambiguous approach to performance measurement within this organization. While the public 'Employment Service' side has developed a very detailed list of targets and performance indicators, the Unemployment Insurance Division is less heavily engaged with this aspect. To quote its Director,

> We make activity plans and follow up at the end of the year. But the results shown in particular aspects is mainly from the point of view of how should we organize to perform our activities in an efficient way – it is more organizational philosophy than results that decides how we organise. (Interview, 3 May 2001)

As the regulator of the numerous private funds, this rather small, specialized Division's focus is on monitoring the performance of others; that is, the Funds. Within the Employment Service of the AMS, performance targets are set by the *regleringsbrevet*. Target setting was introduced five years ago, but reporting on indicators only emerged as a government requirement for the budget planning process in 2001. That they emerged at all may have been in response to a critical report by the national audit office (RRV) suggesting that performance targets did not go deep enough in their explanation. Benchmarking between providers – in this case, the County Boards – together with client surveys (employers and unemployed) are two recent developments within the Swedish agency.

In line with government policy at the time, the Dutch agency's focus was primarily on financial performance. Planning and control systems were developed to encourage better use of the running cost budget. It is only within the last three years that this focus has broadened to include quality of service, policy and 'production' (efficiency). To this end the SVB, like KELA, developed a 'balanced scorecard', which became operational in 2002, and includes performance indicators for these four areas. In addition, management contracts are made with each of the regional offices, although these are driven by the offices themselves, based on their own annual plans. There does seem to be some evidence here for the international dissemination of generic performance management techniques such as the balanced scorecard and client satisfaction surveys, although detailed implementation of these ideas differs considerably from one organization to another.

As indicated above, social security in the United Kingdom had by far the most developed performance measurement regime among our four countries. Performance targets have shaped the BA's direction from its inception. Performance measures are set for the agency by the Secretary of State and are encapsulated in two, annually revised agreements: the Public Service Agreement (which focuses on outcomes) and the Service Delivery Agreement (with a focus on output). In practice, of course, performance targets are 'worked up' jointly by the agency and the department for approval by the Secretary of State (Interview, Director of Performance Management Unit, 22 January 2002). The BA Board and the Client Directorate Board give their approval, but it is the Treasury that retains final approval for the targets.

Performance targets

Key performance targets are supposed to reflect the primary function of the relevant agency. Those agencies whose prime task is to pay benefits, list 'accuracy of payment' as a key performance target. In the United Kingdom 'accuracy' assumed a priority over the earlier 'claims clearance times' target, reflecting a growing concern with benefits fraud. The BA processes £80 billion worth of benefits each year so fraud becomes a serious matter for governments. Financial management (economy and efficiency) is a key target for all of the agencies. In Sweden's AMS, this is a target mainly for the Insurance Unit which monitors payments made by the private funds. Key targets within the Employment Service include: the filling of vacancies, action plans for the registered unemployed, reduction in long term unemployment, increasing the employment of the disabled, and the containment of wage subsidization (a problem in some of the counties). The latter two targets illustrate the contradictory nature of some performance targets, in this case, the necessity for wage subsidization to guarantee employment for the disabled, especially in rural areas. It also reveals an increasingly proactive stance taken by the Swedish Ministry in recommending certain targets. Despite political pressure to set sometimes conflicting targets, there is evidence that agencies learn over time what works and what doesn't. The premier target for the Swedish Employment Service – the filling of vacancies – replaced an earlier target of 'referrals' which failed to take into account how well matched applicants were to vacancies or, indeed, if appointments resulted. Similarly a strong critique of the formulation of some of the BA's targets by the UK National Audit Office resulted in significant modification of those targets (National Audit Office, 1998).

It would appear that the two country agencies that are required to negotiate with finance departments and central ministries (Sweden and the United Kingdom) have a more tightly defined list of targets and performance measures than those agencies (the Netherlands and Finland) who have dedicated funding and are, therefore, more autonomous of the central ministries. In the Netherlands, the main performance targets are set by the SVB itself and include: accuracy of payments (measured by equality of treatment of all clients and legal correctness of decisions), staff absenteeism, quality of service and financial efficiency. The first is measured by client surveys conducted by an external consultant, while financial efficiency is calculated 'on the basis of total running costs of financial year' (Interview, senior official, 20 November 2000). Performance targets set by the Finnish agency are, in some cases, rather vague. These revolve around the 'balanced scorecard' strategy and include, speed of payment, but also legality and consistency of benefit determinations. Financial targets include: operation costs as a percentage of total expenditures, and the cost-effectiveness of key activities. External evaluations of either KELA or SVB appear to have been rare, although both bodies can be 'stung' by mass media criticisms of their performances, sometimes focusing, fairly or otherwise, on individual cases.

In social security, as elsewhere, performance measurement is becoming more sophisticated. In all four countries quantity measures have been supplemented with measures of quality, and multidimensional measures are beginning to emerge as a better reflection of agency performance than traditional, unidimensional measures. To quote a senior official in the BA, one objective is 'to look at the accuracy of a case in a certain time period or at a certain cost, rather than simply looking at accuracy' (22 January 2001). Performance statistics, however, depend on having adequate technology in place to aid both collection of data and its utility. While information technology underpins the success of better performance measurement, social security agencies are notoriously problematic in this area. The scale and complexity of social security operations, combined with privacy considerations, makes IT projects very challenging. For example, after 15 years of the huge 'Operational Strategy' in UK social security a National Audit Office performance audit commented that:

> it did not achieve planned staff reductions or service quality improvements and was never fully completed. (National Audit Office, 1999, p. 25)

In the Finnish agency, IT capacity is also a major problem:

> Work is more complicated. Staff need more competence. Local offices still have old fashioned IT systems. In 1996 we asked staff what should we do to get better systems? (Senior officers in KELA's R & D Division, 18 October 2000)

In Sweden, the AMS began exploring a computer-based placement system as early as 1972. By 2001, its use of the internet within its County offices had become an invaluable tool save for some local bureaucratic resistance to the implementation of a uniform system.[4] We heard fewer references to computer troubles in Sweden than Finland or the United Kingdom, but given that IT was not our principal focus at the time, this impression may have been misleading.

Performance reporting and auditing

Performance reporting varies among the agencies, largely as a result of differences between them in who sets performance targets. The Swedish and British agencies, whose targets are set by government, work within a clearly defined system of internal and external reporting and audit. In Sweden, the agency's financial performance is audited by the State Revision body. In Britain, the National Audit Office has assumed an important role in monitoring agency performance – and, probably because of the sheer volume of public funds passing through, seems to have taken a special interest in the BA (see, e.g. National Audit Office, 1998). Through its performance audits the NAO extends its scrutiny not just to Agency finances but to its overall, organizational performance. KELA produces a thick annual volume of statistics but, at the time of our research, most of this concerned throughput and trends, and little could be described as measurement of organizational performance (KELA, 1999). It is, of course, Parliament's creature and, in principle, is open to detailed parliamentary scrutiny, but in practice we gained the impression of an organization which had undergone rather a modest amount of rigorous external scrutiny. For the SVB, in addition to the annual report, and as part of the accountability requirements under the Dutch reforms, an annual efficiency report is submitted to the regulator (now within the Ministry), but this appears to be primarily an input–output statement. Regular internal reporting by the regional offices to the centre is standard practice across all four agencies.

Mainstreaming performance measurement

Integration of performance measurement with other main management systems is generally weak in the social security agencies, but varies between countries and management systems. In human resource management and budget allocation, there is little close relation to performance measurement, and even in planning where it could be assumed that a logical link existed, there is little evidence of such. Centrally determined budgets in Sweden and the United Kingdom are linked to agency targets but, as noted above, the Finnish and Dutch agencies have largely avoided government budget controls. In Sweden, the AMS sets its own salaries (negotiated between the unions and the executive), but performance pay is not a part of its HR system. Similarly in Finland: KELA management said it would like to introduce performance related pay schemes but the Union was opposed. Despite staff opposition, the Agency was proceeding with two pilot experiments. The UK Benefits Agency inherited an 'historically poor' HR management information system, but recently it has tried to integrate HR with the other management systems, through the introduction of computer-based programs. The BA experimented with performance-based pay but dropped it as 'it was insulting to staff because PRP only allowed for a difference of £100 between the best and the worst performers' (interview with HRM Manager, 5 February 2001). The BA then moved to pilot an alternative performance related pay system – 'performance in the round' – based on team effort. In the Netherlands, there were no plans for performance pay within the SVB although a bonus for managers who meet their targets was under discussion.

Budgetary linking is also problematic, but for different reasons. Here, institutional factors impede the integration of performance data with budgets. In the Netherlands, while the SVB's balanced scorecard includes an efficiency goal, this does not include a reduction in running costs. On the contrary, the SVB is under no financial threat because its budget has an indexed maximum unrelated to performance goals. Finland's KELA, too, has always been financially secure, in this case because of dedicated funding which comes direct to the Agency via the payroll tax, thereby providing little incentive for performance related budgetary reform. This situation is gradually changing as the government finances more of the Agency's programs from the general budget, bringing it more under Ministry of Finance scrutiny. Recently introduced internal performance agreements do, however, link district performance to devolved budgets. According to the UK Agency Chief Executive, 'performance management is right at the heart of resource allocation'. This rhetoric fits with the wider budgetary process of government allocations in the United Kingdom – that is, through the Public Service Agreements made between departments and the Treasury – but Service Level Agreements, made between the Ministry and its agencies, were found in a recent government survey to be less than satisfactory (Alexander Report). A much less rosy picture of the BA's medium term performance emerges from a recent academic analysis (James, 2003, chapter 5). For example 'agency working, with exception of a period in the mid to late 1990s, was not associated with a consistent improvement in economy' (James, 2003, p. 92). It may be indicative that the Agency itself only linked Area Directors' budgets to their performance for the first time in 2000. In Sweden, decentralization of the Employment Service has led to its own peculiar form of budgetary politics. There is strong resistance from the counties to change the current distribution formula which bears little relation to performance.

Planning systems, one might expect, would be more malleable to performance measurement, but in practice we found very limited evidence of linkages. In the Dutch case, only an appreciation of the potential for linking performance measurement to planning exists:

> I would like to draw in the quality management side, like for example the intensity with which people learn from the information that they receive. I want to know how they analyse these indicators and what they do about them. On the basis of this information I could then develop a picture about the actions they should be taking.
> (Senior SVB official, 12 February 2002)

In the Benefits Agency, the planning process is prescribed by the governing Framework Document which is performance-based. How well performance is measured and the extent to which results are fed back into the planning process for the next cycle is less certain:

> I should perhaps say that a number of our senior managers would not know the difference between information and data and would not recognise a control feedback cycle. (Senior Official, Benefits Agency, 22 January 2001)

In Sweden, it is the *regleringsbrevet* which is the basis of planning. But again, this would suggest a reliance by the AMS on a top-down, quasi-legal or formal link between performance targets and planning. There is little evidence of how operations and their performance results are fed back into the planning cycle. The AMS is, of course, an unusually difficult case in which to integrate performance systems with core management because of its high level of decentralization and multiple institutions.

> Of course there are other considerations that come up throughout the planning process such as the organization of the counties; they are free to organize themselves any way they choose so far. (Senior AMS manager, 3 May 2001)

In Finland, a 'steering by results' process is underway with the introduction of new performance management tools such as the performance agreements, the scorecard method, and annual quality self-assessments (Social Insurance Institution, Finland, 2000).

Tensions and trades-off

Delivering social security is complex. Measuring its effectiveness will inevitably produce tensions and contradictions between the core business of the organization and administrative reform processes. To quote the Chief Executive of the Benefits Agency:

> It is a horrendously complex system, you wouldn't start designing it from here. But we have got fifty years of the welfare state to deal with! Every simplification I have come across so far seems to make it more complex. (Interview, 5 January 2001)

With the possible exception of the Dutch SVB, all our agencies have multiple roles and sometimes conflicting demands. As the Director of Employment Services in the AMS explains:

> One of the problems we have is that we are not a service organization, we are an authority and we have a controlling function when it

comes to the unemployment benefits, that people who get these are looking for a job. We have two roles here that can be conflicting. (Interview, 3 May 2001)

The highly legalistic environment – closely related to the controlling dimension of social security – adds to the complication and tensions and may impede the efficacy of performance measurement:

> Within our supervision activities we find that a fund (private) has taken its own decision and given benefits to someone who was not entitled to it, and that of course could be seen as one indicator (of performance). Then of course, the law has been changed so that it is difficult for us to reclaim the benefit, so it's not a good indicator actually. (Director, Unemployment Insurance Division, AMS)
>
> We have an incredibly tight legal framework within which we operate. All of our systems are actually very much set within a legislative framework of primary and secondary legislation through regulation and such like. We have to apply the law. (CE, Benefits Agency, 5 January 2001)

Confusion and tensions over targets, the requirements of a performance regime and the mission of the organization are not uncommon:

> Clearance time has moved from being a Secretary of State target to a management target and agency measure, and there has been a difference in the message that has gone out to staff in may be the way in which our managers are performing. (CE, Benefits Agency, 5 January 2001)

And, from a director of AMS,

> Performance incentives/sanctions have not been adopted by the AMS. The concern to support under-performing districts takes precedence over ideas of sanction.

The questionable 'morality' of imposing sanctions for under-performance is a general theme we found in all the social security agencies. It can be immensely difficult to separate out the precise effects of those variables which managers can control from those (such as macro-movements in unemployment levels, or demographic increases in the pensioned population) which they cannot. Finally, there are tensions around the allocation of time and resources:

> Accuracy is a very difficult (target) to measure because we have to do it through sampling cases, having real experts going over and scrutinizing cases, checking evidence, making sure everything was done properly. (CE, Benefits Agency, 5 January 2001)

Relations with parent ministries

Constitutional differences across the four countries explain, to some extent, divergent patterns in agency–ministry relations. Nevertheless, one might argue, there is a pattern of some convergence. Our research suggests a trend towards more, not less, ministerial steering. Finland is the single exception, although even in this case parenting is latent rather than nonexistent (in interviews the impatience of some Ministry of Finance officials with KELA's high autonomy was scarcely disguised). While the Finnish Ministry of Social Affairs and Health lacks any formal authority to intervene in KELA's operations, the Ministry of Finance would clearly relish a stronger steering role (see also OECD, 2002b).

Britain is at the other end of the spectrum, where, as we saw earlier, senior officials in the ministry recognize that 'arms length' is a 'fanciful' way of describing the relationship with such a huge spending machine as is the BA. It wasn't always this way, however. The Department of Social Security was one of the first ministries in the late 1980s to embrace the idea of separating out its operations into agencies. A central government policy review of executive agencies, in 2002, identified several problems with parent ministries, two of which have relevance to the DSS (Office of Public Services Reform, 2002). Public Service Agreements, it concluded, rendered departments (perhaps too) dependent on agency performance to get resources. On the other hand, the review found that departments did not always abide by their service level agreements with agencies. In other words, parent ministries expect performance but may not provide adequate support. The social security ministry sees it somewhat differently:

> We are going for a different resourcing approach; one that is built on a partnership rather than a purchaser model .... the Agency has been too opaque. (Interview with Permanent Secretary, DSS, 19 February 2001: this, note, describes probably the most measured and transparent agency covered in this chapter!)

Traditionally, the Swedish parent ministry relied on strategies such as the appointment of Directors General of AMS and the passing of new laws, to exercise influence over the agency. The linking of budgetary controls to objectives in the early 1990s has enhanced the Ministry's role in the work of AMS. The process has, over ten years, grown tighter with broad objectives being replaced by specified targets, to be followed most recently with specified indicators as well as targets. Now the Agency reports on its performance on a quarterly basis which necessitates regular formal and informal contact between the two organizations. Even so, when interviewed, some ministry personnel seemed unaware of procedural detail, for example, that the performance reports of AMS are audited by the National Audit Office.

Conclusions

Study of social security agencies tells us that they are in a constant state of flux. Both organizational restructuring and performance measurement improvements are almost incessant. These agencies are highly political, even where the links to parent ministries are weak (the Dutch case) or latent (Finland). So, on the one hand, we are looking at quite volatile organizations. On the other hand, we are looking at huge operations here – millions of transactions every day – and at immensely complex legal frameworks which are impossible to change overnight. To some extent social security bureaucracies are like the proverbial supertanker: it takes a very long time for them to change course, even after the order has gone out from the bridge. All these features – both flux and inertia – appear to be common to all four countries, and some of these commonalties are rather obviously related to the characteristics of the primary task of paying out social security benefits on a vast scale.

At the same time there are rather glaring differences between the agencies. Institutional factors such as autonomy from central government direction, financial autonomy, functional specialization and client base, distinguish one from another. In this respect Finland and Sweden group together as agencies with high autonomy (for slightly different reasons), whereas the SVB is somewhat more under the active control of its ministry, and the BA is very much so. Approaches to performance measurement display further differences. In all countries there is more of it than in the past, and in all countries the initial thrust seems to have been mainly top-down (with ministries of finance playing at least as important a role as parent departments). Beyond this, however, the differences begin to appear. Performance measurement – and certainly performance *management* – has been pushed harder and further in the United Kingdom than in any of the other three countries. The Dutch, although keen to borrow ideas about agencification from the United Kingdom, seem less interested (or perhaps more cautious) in implementing performance measurement. Indeed, in terms of performance measurement rigour, both the BA and Sweden's AMS seemed more advanced than the SVB. KELA is hard to assess. On paper it has quite a sophisticated 'outcome orientation' (Social Insurance Institution, 2000). But our interviews made us suspect that, in practice, 'indicator pressure' on operational managers was probably fairly mild. So, too, were pressures from above on senior KELA management. While there was certainly strong political (parliamentary) interest in what KELA was doing, that was very different from any sustained political interest in systematically analysing its organizational performance – something we found no evidence for at all.

In sum, despite these variations between the agencies, and their diverse institutional starting positions, social security agencies in the Nordic countries, Britain and the Netherlands have all moved in a similar direction over the last ten years, towards enhanced performance management and measurement and have done so in a climate of eroding institutional autonomy, and tighter fiscal constraints.

Part IV
Conclusions

11
Conclusions

Introduction

The reader who has come this far has already had to absorb a considerable amount of material. The book began in the stratosphere of agencies as a seemingly common international phenomenon, moved through broad academic theories relevant to this phenomenon (Chapter 1), and then looked at practitioner models of how modern agencies should work (Chapter 2). We then flew somewhat lower over the territory, examining programmes of central government agency reform within four European countries (Part II). Finally, in Part III, we got even closer to the ground, reconnoitering four particular functions in some detail (although there is, of course, still a grass-roots layer of day-to-day operational activity which our analysis only occasionally touches upon). The task now is to try to tie these parts together: to construct a synthetic overview of what we have learned.

The obvious findings

Before getting into some of the trickier interpretive and theoretical issues, it may be worth briefly restating some of the more obvious findings to emerge from the research that we, and others, have carried out. At least five points seem to stand out very clearly:

1. The modern executive agency is a highly variable creature, absolutely not a standardized, 'Fordist' solution to the efficient production of public services.
2. In so far as recent reform discourse has developed an ideal type (Chapter 2), this paragon is conspicuous by its absence in all of the

four countries where we have most intensively looked, and seems rare in other countries too (Pollitt and Talbot, 2004). In practice the 'tripod' always seems to have one or more of its legs either very short or entirely missing. Nevertheless, the rhetoric in favour of this model continues, and, if there is a trend – allowing for some counter-examples – it does seem to be in the general direction of more management autonomy and more and more sophisticated performance measurement for disaggregated executive bodies.

3. Both the organizational structure and the management practices of agencies are very frequently influenced by the politico-administrative culture of the country in which they are situated. Our research finds considerable evidence for extensive – though certainly not total – 'path dependency'. A major factor determining where you are now is where you started from in the previous period.

4. Both the organizational structure and the management practices of agencies are frequently influenced by the characteristics of the primary tasks which they undertake. Meteorological offices are not organized and managed in the same way as social security agencies.

5. Performance indicators are 'old hat', at least in the sense that almost all the organizations we researched possess a set of PIs, and these were fairly frequently reconsidered and refined. In most cases the core PIs were reasonably stable – their definitions did not seem to alter much from year to year. Most of the managers we interviewed were perfectly capable of distinguishing conceptually between indicators of inputs, processes, outputs and outcomes. None of this, however, is to say that fully fledged performance management – strategic steering by means of indicators – is common. It is not.

The less obvious findings

We would regard the five 'obvious' conclusions (previous section) as relatively clear and difficult to dispute, at least within the particular domain of our research (i.e. certain types of agency in north western Europe). There are also, however, some less glaring/more debatable findings which deserve attention. These include the following:

1. In all four countries the status and organizational boundaries of many agencies were more or less constantly under scrutiny and tension. Even in Sweden, where the agency form is foundational, long term stability was hard to find. Functions are constantly being added or

removed, and it is not unusual for the basic status or identity of the organization to be under active debate (as was the case with, *inter alia*, UK social security, Swedish forestry and Finnish and Dutch prisons). Considerable quantities of management effort are evidently absorbed in handling these neverending restructuring discussions (even where they temporarily come to nothing). Individual managers, however, appeared to be somewhat more durable than organizational structures – most of the senior managers we interviewed for EUROPAIR had medium or long-term histories with the particular function.

2. Where agencies' primary tasks involved major value trade-offs (as with prisons between punishment and rehabilitation, or forestry between commercial exploitation and environmental protection) performance indicators seemed little used to assist in striking the relevant balance. Usually, the batteries of indicators, however sophisticated they might be in other respects, shed little light on how or where these strategic balancing decisions were made.

3. Among the four countries covered by the EUROPAIR project a degree of UK-exceptionalism was apparent. In the United Kingdom performance measurement was used more intensively, and more extensively than in any of the four continental countries. There was a kind of rude mechanical vigour to the way PIs were often treated by UK ministries and agencies. In the continental states, PIs were regarded less as tests of management's competence and more as one type of evidence, among others, which could inform an on-going discussion between stakeholders about the work of the agency.

4. One significant difference between primary tasks appears to be the degree to which they are embedded in international markets and/or networks. Where this embeddedness was intensive, the dyadic or triadic relationship between ministry, finance ministry and agency became considerably more complex. In these circumstances the agency was constrained (or enabled) not only by the authority of its national government, but also by international agreements, rules and procedures. Of our four functions, meteorology and forestry were clearly intensively engaged with international organizations, whereas prisons and social security were much less so.

Interpreting the findings: paradigms of explanation

Explaining findings requires theories. In Chapter 1 we reviewed a number of theories which had been applied to agencification, and in Chapter 2 we dissected at greater length what seems to be the dominant 'practitioner theory' – the tripod model. Now it is time to return to those theoretical endeavours and relate them to the evidence we have produced in Parts II and III.

We can first situate our own theoretical approach in terms of two fundamental dimensions identified by the doyens of institutionalism, James March and Johan Olsen (1998). They argue that one useful way of categorizing theories about organizations is according to, first, the dominant logics the theorists see 'inhabiting' those organizations and, second, the view of history adopted. In terms of dominant logics, there are two: the logic of consequences and the logic of appropriateness. In the former, rational, or at least boundedly rational actors choose courses of action by calculating their expected consequences. In sophisticated versions of this paradigm the calculation may be distorted by all kinds of bounds and biases, but a calculation it is nonetheless, and the aim of the calculation is to choose the option which brings most benefit/least harm to the decision-maker. In the latter – the logic of appropriateness – decision-makers are more concerned with matching their supposed identities or roles with what they perceive to be the situation they face. They are trying to 'do the appropriate thing', to apply the relevant rule. From this perspective, 'the pursuit of purpose is associated with identities more than with interests, and with the selection of rules more than with individual rational expectations' (March and Olsen, 1998, p. 951). In terms of history there are also two main possibilities: the view that history is 'efficient', in the sense that it tells a story of survival of the fittest (species, organizations, constitutions, etc) and the view that history is 'inefficient', where there is emphasis on 'the slow pace of historical adaptation relative to the rate of environmental change, and thus the low likelihood of reaching an equilibrium' (March and Olsen, 1998, p. 954). All of this gives us a two by two categorization of organizational theories, as portrayed in Table 11.1.

Table 11.1 Categories of organizational theory

	Logic of consequences	Logic of appropriateness
Efficient history	Functional rationality	Functional institutionalism
Inefficient history	History-dependent rationality	History-dependent institutionalism

Source: Adapted from March and Olsen, 1998.

The theories mentioned in Chapter 1 fit fairly readily into this framework. Thus, for example, economic theories are mainly situated within the top left-hand cell of Table 11.1: they fall within a paradigm of functional rationality. Traditional social science theories vary – some are examples of functional rationality, others of functional institutionalism. Social constructivist theories fall within the right hand column – they are either examples of functional institutionalism or, more commonly perhaps, of history-dependent institutionalism. They question the logic of consequences in various ways, not least because they see both 'rationality' and 'consequences' being socially constructed rather than exogenously given.

Our own model – Task-Specific Path Dependency or TSPD – falls squarely in the bottom right hand cell. It is history-dependent in the sense that it finds starting points and 'paths' crucial elements in explaining many aspects of agencification. It is institutionalist in the sense that it sees behaviour being extensively shaped by institutional constraints, and institutions being significantly shaped by the particularities of their primary tasks – whether that be forecasting rain, managing forests, caring for prisoners or delivering cash benefits.

Finally, what can we say of Chapter 2's 'ideal type' – the tripod model of functionally disaggregated, managerially autonomized, performance-oriented agencies? The practitioner rhetoric surrounding this model seems to come from the paradigm of functional rationality associated with the top left-hand cell. The essential argument is that one gives individual managers freedom plus targets plus incentives, and they will then behave rationally to maximize the flow of incentives (and minimize the flow of penalties) by hitting their targets. So far, clear enough. What is noticeable, however, is that some of the practitioner rhetoric mixes functional rationality with functional institutionalism. It argues, for example, that autonomized, specialized agencies will help create a culture of expertise and customer service. Thus, not for the first time, a NPM technology (i.e. agencies) mixes economistic functional rationality with reasoning from the 'culture management' literature, where the latter partakes more of the logic of appropriateness and identity (see Pollitt, 2003, chapter 2).

One of the most interesting, but neglected, aspects of March and Olsen's work is that which concerns the mixing of logics. The differences between the logic of consequences and the logic of appropriateness are sometimes taught and written about as though they constituted an either/or choice. Either you have to believe the world is one way, or the other. This is not our view, and evidently not the view of March and Olsen either (1998, pp. 952–3). They suggest that the logics can be combined in at least four different ways:

1. *When calculation can, calculation will.* That is, when circumstances make the calculation of consequences possible, it will take priority. The logic of appropriateness will survive mainly in those more ambiguous and shifting circumstances where calculation is difficult or impossible.
2. *One logic when the stakes are high, another when they are lower.* This is the view that, while we may use the logic of appropriateness on lesser matters (how we eat, what clothes we wear), when it comes to the really big decisions, then we calculate consequences as far as we possibly can. Alternatively, one could argue that the big decisions are almost always heavily influenced by cultural and legal norms and historical ties (should the United Kingdom have joined European Community; should it have allied itself with the United States in the 2003 invasion of Iraq?) and functional rationality is applied mainly to planning and steering within those broadly determined limits.
3. *The choice of logic is situational or developmental.* For example, 'action becomes more rule-based in a specific situation the greater the accumulated experience in that situation' (March and Olsen, 1998, p. 953). Thus rational, consequential calculation predominates in situations where trust and familiarity are absent ('the law of the jungle'), but as mutual experience of a situation or relationship grows, so do self-reinforcing norms and rules.
4. *Each logic is a special case of the other.* Consequentialists can argue that rules and identities are simply devices for minimizing transaction costs under certain circumstances: they are an efficient form of calculational shorthand. Similarly, those who are wedded to the logic of appropriateness may claim that consequentialist calculations are no more than the rules to be followed in certain, socially defined domains (if you are in a Moroccan market, haggle over the price, because that is the local rule).

Our TSPD model is not entirely wedded to any one of these possible combinations, but we incline more towards the third (situational choice of logic) than any of the other three. There were enough examples in our fieldwork where greater calculation of consequences would have been possible, but it was not sought, or even where calculation of consequences existed but was over-ridden by normative considerations of rule-following and identity preservation. Finnish and Swedish agencies chose to make little use of performance related pay, although it was legally available to them. Forest research in the United Kingdom was undertaken mainly through competitive tendering, because that was seen as appropriate in the UK environment, but forest research in Finland was largely allocated to METLA without overt competition, because that was regarded as the appropriate practice for that particular set of institutional relationships. For profit, commercial forecasting work undertaken by the NMIs was treated very differently in the United Kingdom and the Netherlands, although they were operating in the same international market.

In short, assuming that behaviour reflecting the logic of appropriateness is frequent and important does *not* entail that such behaviour is universal, or that it always trumps consequential logic.

Putting the TSPD model to work

Having laid out the theoretical ground we can now put the TSPD to work (although, of course, it has already been working extensively, if quietly, in Chapters 3 to 10). We believe, however, that models and theories are themselves best understood comparatively, and therefore we will put TSPD to work alongside a different type of theory. Of the many we could have chosen (see Chapter 1), we have decided to use bureau-shaping theory as the comparator. Bureau-shaping theory has two obvious merits in this respect. First, it comes from the diametrically 'opposite box' in March and Olsen's classification of theories (i.e. from functional rationality), and should therefore provide a strong contrast. Second, it has recently been used – carefully and at length – to analyse agencies (Dunleavy, 1991; James, 2003). So some of its strengths and weaknesses have already been clarified.

We will also add a third dimension to the comparison, by including the practitioners' ideal type – the 'tripod' of Chapter 2 – to the mix. As will become apparent, however, it is difficult and slightly artificial to compare it point-for-point with the two academic theories because it was not built for quite the same purposes. It is essentially a normative model with the purpose of specifying how agencies should be designed and managed, not a vehicle for explaining empirical diversity and untidiness.

It should go without saying (though we will say it anyway) that the object of the comparison is not for one model utterly to slay the others, but rather to see how far each will take us in explaining some of the features of agencies which seem to have emerged from research. We will therefore apply the two academic models, and the tripod model, in turn, to each of the findings which have already presented.

Finding 1: the variability of agencies

Users of the TSPD model would be most surprised to find anything other than high variability. Agency forms are predicted to vary according to both their primary task and their institutional context (constitutional, legal, cultural). This is, of course, precisely what a great deal of the evidence produced in Chapters 3 to 10 indicates. The two elements will themselves change over time – implying adjustments to agency form and steering practices – but at different speeds. The primary task may change quite quickly, especially under the impact of new technologies (the advent of satellites in weather forecasting, for example). The institutional context is likely to change more slowly, and some elements within it may derive from long-forgotten, and now possibly irrelevant historical circumstances (inefficient history).

It is less clear how users of the bureau-shaping model would explain this variability. Some variability could certainly be explained by the different relative prominence of executive/operational type work within ministries. Ministries with more operational work could be expected to be keener on creating agencies (so that senior officials could concentrate on the more satisfying and high-status policy work – James, 2003, p. 60). Some could be explained by the different relative proportions of core budget to bureau budget to programme budget to super programme budget which characterize different activities. One would expect, say, differences between a *delivery agency*, with a core budget that absorbed most of the bureau and programme budgets, and a *transfer agency*, where the core budget would be tiny relative to the bureau and programme budgets (Dunleavy, 1991, pp. 182–91). In the EUROPAIR research, for example, prisons would count as a delivery agency, social security as a transfer agency.

Thus the bureau-shaping perspective does allow for some variation. Whether it allows for the full range of variation which we have witnessed is, however, another question entirely. In Sweden the foundation of the agency system lay not in the desire of senior officials to do more policy work (*pace* the bureau shapers), but rather in a democratic eighteenth century attempt to limit the power of a hitherto autocratic king (Pierre, 2004). In Finland the agency reforms of the mid-1990s involved taking certain operational tasks *back* into the ministries, and in focussing some of the surviving agencies not on routine operational work but rather upon research and development and advisory tasks: almost a reversal of what mainline bureau-shaping would predict. In the Netherlands, like in the United Kingdom, agencies were seen as a new thing, but much of the debate there was about just how far out to place operational tasks – whether to allocate them to agencies or to the ZBO/MABs. However, as James concedes: '[t]he bureau-shaping perspective is not sufficient to explain why executive agency reform was preferred as a bureau-shaping strategy rather than certain alternative strategies', such as MABs or contracting out (2003, p. 53). Possibly, however, it could be adapted and extended in order to integrate more contextual variation. For example, Christiansen uses functional rational theory to incorporate the existence of formal and informal corporatism in Denmark (the same approach could probably be applied to, say, Sweden and the Netherlands – see Christiansen, 1998, especially p. 277).

The tripod model would be uncomfortable with the sheer variety we have encountered, but one could imagine some hard-nosed NPM reformers explaining this simply as slow learning – as a lag while the tortoises catch up with the hares. Eventually – from this view – the Dutch will see that their agencies will do better if they have far more explicit performance contracting. Eventually the Swedes will strengthen their ministries so that their 'principals' become more capable of steering their 'agents'. It is hard to argue with this kind of thinly disguised 'one best way-ism' other than to point out that this degree of international convergence has never been achieved in the past, and there is no particular reason to believe that it is being approached at the moment (Pollitt and Bouckaert, 2004). In the tripodists' favour, however, is the observation that there does seem to be at least a rhetorical trend in their direction. This is most clearly heard in core departments, especially finance. Thus we find the Finnish Ministry of Finance complaining that parent ministries are not strict enough in setting targets for their agencies and holding them to them. There are also some similar sentiments, slightly more *sotto voce*, in the Netherlands. And the core elements in the Swedish government seek to respond to both external criticisms from the OECD and internal criticisms that ministries lack the firepower to control the large, powerful and long-established Swedish agencies (Blondell, 1998; Molander, Nilsson and Schick, 2002). Whether this rhetoric is likely to lead to real changes, we beg leave to doubt. At the time of writing none of these three continental countries have legislation on the books that would fundamentally alter the capacity of central ministries, or the balance of power between them and their agencies.

Finding 2: in reality, the 'tripod' model is rare

As TSPD theorists we would expect the tripod ideal type to remain just that – largely an ideal. At base this is because the full conditions for the tripod are met in only a modest proportion of public activities. The task has, first, to have measurable and reasonably predictable outputs and, if possible, outcomes, so that the 'results' can be clearly seen by those who want to steer the agency. Then, second, it should be of low political salience so that politicians are seldom tempted to intervene in its autonomy. Further, third, it should be of small-to-modest budgetary consequences, because very big budget items cannot avoid being drawn into political debates about overall fiscal policy. A vehicle licensing agency or a patents office may meet these tests, but many of the tasks allocated to agencies do not. Prisons are too politically controversial, their outputs are measurable but their outcomes are not. Forestry is of medium political salience – because of its commercial significance in Finland and Sweden and because of the growing environmental lobby throughout Europe and North America. Social security is both big budget and politically controversial. Meteorology almost qualifies (modest budget, low political salience, accuracy of forecasts can be measured) but as Chapter 8 showed, its tripod has begun to wobble slightly under the impact of commercial competition and internationalization.

Bureau-shapers would also be less than surprised that the tripod does not always seem to work. To begin with, functional rationalists are acutely aware of the risk of information asymmetries between principal and agent. Therefore, in situations where outputs and/or outcomes cannot be easily observed (Wilson, 1989), more autonomy may not be a stable solution. Then, second, while the bureau-shaping model assumes that top officials in the ministries will want to shed routine operational work, it does not assume that these mandarins will want to seal themselves off absolutely, by some self-denying statute preventing all subsequent interference. On the contrary, one might posit that, if things seem to be going wrong in the agencies, top officials will gain by producing a new reform, a new policy for 'fixing' the trouble. That reform should not mean the taking-back of operational tasks into the ministry, but it might well involve other kinds of innovation, such as new monitoring or audit arrangements, more contracting out, and so on. This possibility is recognized by James (2003, p. 135) and seems to fit with a number of the developments witnessed during the fifteen years' history of the Next Steps programme.

The existential rarity of the tripod model is faintly embarrassing for its practitioner advocates. One explanation would be that given in the previous section – that good news spreads slowly, and that we must allow more time for the superiority of the disaggregation/autonomy/performance contracting combination to show through. According to this view, ten years or more is not yet enough: not a particularly convincing line or argument, one might think. A more subtle defence of the tripod would be to say that, first, the model was not suited to all functions, but mainly to large block of routinizable operational activity; and second, that, although progress was slow, the tripod did seem to be roughly the direction of intended travel in most countries. This is more credible but, of course, it leaves much of the variety we have identified unexplained.

Finding 3: extensive national path dependency

This finding is central to the TSPD model, but plays very little part in the bureau-shaping model. The latter, true to its neo-classical economic roots, usually aspires to a kind of history-free universality. Neither Dunleavy (1991) nor James (2003) attempt to use it for much comparative work, or to explain institutional developments over periods of more than a decade or so. Right at the end of his analysis James does briefly refer to the possibility of further research in OECD countries with 'similar levels of government development, that embarked on reforms directly influenced by the UK experience'. However, he quickly qualifies this proposal by referring to the way the consistency of hypotheses 'is likely to be limited by differences in the context of reform' (p. 147). Little more is said about how these contextual differences could themselves be theorized.

We should add, however, that while the bureau-shaping model says little of path dependency, other brands of functional rationality certainly do. Most famously, the Nobel Prize-winning economist Douglass North models path dependency (North, 1990). Further back, Granovetter laid some foundations in his much-cited article on 'embeddedness' (1985). There he argued that:

> while the assumption of rational action must always be problematic, it is a good working hypothesis that should not be easily abandoned. What looks to the analyst like non-rational behavior may be quite sensible when situational constraints, especially those of embeddedness, are fully appreciated. (Granovetter, 1985, p. 506)

More recently we have received several persuasive papers on path dependency which show, in explicitly political terms, institutional processes which 'exhibit increasing returns' – that is the costs of changing course grow over time (Pierson, 2000a, p. 252; see also Pierson, 2000b).

This line of analysis does not at all reject the logic of consequences, but it does argue that that is only part of the picture:

> Functional explanations of institutional origins and change are not wrong-headed, but they are radically incomplete. As a consequence, they suggest a world of political institutions that is far more prone to efficiency, far less encumbered by the preoccupations and mistakes of the past, than the world we actually inhabit. (Pierson, 2000b, p. 496)

In principle it would seem that there is scope to extend the bureau-shaping model by somehow coupling it to other parts of rational choice theory which deal more satisfactorily with issues of embeddedness and path dependency.

Within the TSPD approach – unlike bureau-shaping – modelling the contexts is a crucial step. As we have seen, the EUROPAIR project found that general system factors such as majoritarianism versus consensualism, and centralization versus decentralization, cast a considerable influence over the ways in which agencies were constituted and managed. More tentatively, we hypothesized that differences in dominant cultural values could also play a role, albeit more diffuse and less direct. Indeed, it could be argued (see earlier) that systemic and cultural factors help to define the 'situation', and the situation then signals that one type of logic (appropriateness; consequences) is likely to gain the upper hand.

National differences are a puzzle for advocates of the tripod model. Because it aspires to be a universal model for good performance, it does not deal in the currency of cultural and systemic differences. If these are mentioned at all it is as a kind of inexplicable 'otherness' which, unfortunately, has to be lived with.

Finding 4: the influence of primary tasks

Both the TSPD model and bureau-shaping have something to say about this. Within the TSPD approach we have developed interpretations which rest on variables such as political salience, budget weight, plus the observability and measurability of outputs and outcomes. The foundational text on bureau-shaping classifies agencies very differently – according to the proportionate relationships between their different types of budget. Thus (to indicate briefly – see Dunleavy 1991 for detail) there are:

- Delivery agencies (large core budgets)
- Regulatory agencies (small core and bureau budgets)

- Transfer agencies (small core budget, large bureau budget)
- Contracts agencies (modest core budget, large programme budget).

From a TSPD perspective these types of budgetary differences are interesting and suggestive, but not yet directly influential. For the bureau-shaper they are important because control over budgetary amounts is one of the variables that senior officials are assumed to want to maximize (James, 2003, p. 36; although Dunleavy makes the refinement that it is only the core budget which top officials are likely to be really interested in (1991, p. 208). But for the TSPD model the logic of appropriateness takes precedence: the nature and status of the actual primary task, plus the quality of relationships with colleagues – that is, issues of identity – are crucial. Perhaps this is not *so* different from bureau-shaping, in the sense that the latter certainly stresses the quality of work as a major motivating factor for top officials (Dunleavy, 1991, p. 202; James, 2003, p. 36). What is less clear, however, is how the relationship between work quality and budget size is supposed to operate for bureau-shapers. On this point James seems to give more weight to budget-size as a motivation than does Dunleavy (though both give less than the earlier rational choicers such as Niskanen).

The tripod model doesn't say much about the differences between tasks, except for the recognition that the prime target for agencification is routine operational work, which should, according to doctrine, be separated from policy work. One problem with this line of analysis, as our studies of particular agencies has made clear, is that while routine operational work exists, there is also a lot of central government activity which is certainly operational but at the same time somewhat unpredictable and/or of high political interest. Social security and prisons are both examples of this category. They are tasks where there are arguments for autonomization (sometimes for *greater* autonomy than agency status provides), but also arguments against. They are not 'pure' operations, but they are obviously not pure policy either.

Finding 5: performance indicators are now commonplace, fully fledged performance management much less so

The bureau-shaping model would not appear to have much to say about this, although the rarity of genuine, tripod-like performance management could be explained in terms of information asymmetries (see Finding 3). From a TSPD perspective the explanation for the limited use of PIs in many cases would have two steps to it. First, in consensus cultures, measures would be likely to be used more as contributions to discussion than as strict targets (more as 'tin-openers' than as 'dials' – see Carter, Klein and Day 1992). Second, some tasks simply would not lend themselves to accurate measures of outputs or outcomes, or, if measurement were possible, its meaning could readily be deeply disputed. In these cases one would not expect PIs to play a core role in decision-making. Here one is put in mind of the prolonged, but (thus far) largely inconclusive, debates, in Finland, Sweden and the United Kingdom, about measures of recidivism for prisons.

Tripodists would presumably bemoan our findings as 'slow progress'. Eventually, they might argue, PI sets will be developed into true performance contracting. Time will tell. Sceptically, we note that essentially similar exhortations to 'really make performance measurement work' have been around in Finland for at least 10 years and in the United Kingdom for a similar period, but progress on the ground has been modest, and core departments and audit offices are still making more or less the same criticisms.

Finding 6: volatility in agency statuses and boundaries

This is a tricky issue for both models. If history is efficient (functional rationality) then why should particular tasks be constantly on the move, now slightly more autonomous, now less so, now in an agency, now drawn back into a ministry or put further out to a MAB or privatization? For TSPD (history-dependent) how can all this movement be reconciled with the idea of a stable path?

The bureau-shaping model does not centrally address this issue. James does have a brief section on the privatization of certain agencies in which he interestingly records that these moves 'further out' were often propelled by internal (staff) suggestions rather than external pressure (2003, p. 135). On the whole, however, he sees recent changes as minor adjustments within a 'broadly stable set of executive agencies' (p. 135). Elsewhere within the functional rationalist empire the presumption would presumably be that what we were witnessing here was an ongoing process of adjustment between principals and agents, with the former constantly seeking better information and control, and the latter seeking to maximize income and/or discretion. Certainly technological changes (new computer systems; new timber harvesting equipment; new systems of electronic surveillance in prisons) could alter the production functions of agencies and lead to moves by both agents and principals to safeguard their positions with respect to such innovations. So we cannot say that the functionalist rationalist theories would be unable to model continuing change, even if the particular works we have examined do not make much of this point.

For history-dependent institutionalists the finding that the details of organizational structures were quite volatile over time is not in fact that difficult to explain. Both main elements in the model – task and path – allow for change. Task characteristics change with social, economic and technological changes, and these may lead to consequent organizational adjustments. Thus weather forecasting has become a business, in which specialized forecasts can be sold to a variety of customers, and this has led to a string of organizational changes for NMIs (Chapter 8). The Dutch have sold off some of their commercial activities. The Swedes have had to develop elaborate accounting firewalls so as to protect themselves against accusations of cross-subsidization; and so on. In social security, under fiscal pressures, the task has been widely reconceived as now having to do not merely with providing people with basic livelihood, but also encouraging them to seek work ('workfare'). This has led to organizational change in a number of countries, usually in the direction of coupling the organizational units responsible for paying unemployment benefit more closely to those organizations responsible for assisting the unemployed to find work (Chapter 9).

The second element in the model – path dependency – may at first sight seem an inherently conservative component: always a damper on change, increasing returns to staying the same. In our view, however, this would be an oversimplification. What the path dependent logic suggests is that a system of organizations *will go on behaving the same way as before where the costs of exit rise over time* (Pierson, 2000a, p. 252). But – and this is our complicating thought – in systems where organizational change is easy to accomplish, the 'path' may be precisely one characterized by persistent change. Low cost organizational change then becomes part of the standard repertoire for dealing with all manner of problems: if in doubt, reorganize! A comparative analysis of public management reform shows that such reform is indeed far easier in some systems (e.g. New Zealand, the United Kingdom) than others (Belgium, Germany). The characteristics of the constitutions and the political systems in centralized, majoritarian, common law states make them easier sites for major reforms of public administration than decentralized, multiparty *rechtsstaat* regimes (Pollitt and Bouckaert, 2004). The historical record since 1980 clearly shows that many areas of the UK public sector have undergone serial reorganization, and that the overall depth and volume of such change in on a different scale from, say, Germany or, indeed, Finland, the Netherlands or even Sweden. The Next Steps programme was simply part of this, and we should not be surprised if it is being constantly tinkered with and re-reorganized. That is the UK 'path'. The political costs of standing still, of saying, in effect 'no more reorganization is needed – we are going to let things lie' outweigh the (low) political costs of announcing yet another reorganization.

This is an argument for a degree of UK exceptionalism. It therefore has to be acknowledged that we have also found on-going change in the other three countries covered by the EUROPAIR project; perhaps not as much as in the United Kingdom, but significant nonetheless. This can be explained mainly by task features (see above), although it would probably also be true to say that the broad expectation that every government will have some sort of public service reform programme – that is a standard part of a normal manifesto for government – has grown somewhat in all countries. With these qualifications, however, we would hold to the general picture that the overall *volume* of change has been lower in the three continental countries than the United Kingdom, and that the *pace* of change has certainly been more modest.

Practitioners might argue that volatility is little more than short term adjustments – learning that not all functions fit comfortably into the tripod format. They could point to the fact that only a few activities have been brought 'closer back in' in the United Kingdom, and that, despite the volatility, the overall trend has remained strongly towards greater autonomy. This is a reasonable point to make, but in our view it somewhat underestimates the volume and complexity of the organizational changes we have documented. For example, commercial and environmental pressures have forced continuous change onto NMIs and national forestry bodies, in some instances dividing them up, pushing some further out (trading status for the UK MET Office) and sucking others further in (the renationalization of the Swedish forestry company). In both the United Kingdom and the Netherlands important components of social security have been drawn tighter in to the ministerial centre. Meanwhile there have been significant debates in both Finland and the Netherlands about increasing the autonomy of the prison service. We view all this as slightly more than just short-term adjustments.

Finding 7: performance indicators are seldom used to clarify major value trade-offs

Bureau-shaping theory was not built to explain this kind of phenomenon, and it doesn't. Our TSPD model doesn't really speak to this very much either. It is tempting to resort to a simpler, older type of explanation, based on political logic. The explanation would run like this: first, these major value trade-offs (profit versus the environment; punishment versus rehabilitation) are rather uncomfortable for politicians. Whatever balance they strike, they will find a considerable body of critics seeking to push them in one direction or another, because there is no social consensus on these issues. Second, therefore, the more the precise balance that is taken can be either distanced from politicians and/or obfuscated, the better. If the precise balance remains obscure, then politicians remain free to claim that it is 'about right', stressing different elements to different audiences in the classic manner (the forestry minister's speech to the timber association is unlikely to be identical to his speech to the world conference on the environment). What we may expect, therefore, is that, first, such decisions will be distanced from ministers and 'technicized', and that PI systems will not be designed to show in any exact way what the trade-off is. And that seemed to be precisely what we found. For example, the environmental unit in the Finnish state enterprise for forestry explained very clearly that the conservation/exploitation balance was decided *inside* the organization, and that this saved ministers the difficulty of being personally identified with the decision (interviews, Metsahallitus, 5 September, 2001). Similarly, it quite suits ministers to allow prison governors to decide whether inmates can have TVs in their rooms, or how much training they should receive. If the mood of the mass media swings, and the TVs suddenly become a political issue then the minister can intervene and ban them – presenting him/herself as correcting an imbalance which was not of his/her making. An interesting case was the system used by the Dutch forestry ZBO, *Statsbosbeheer*, which actually packaged up and priced each environmental measure and placed this before the parent ministry asking them, in effect, if they were prepared to pay for it. Very little trace of this internal documentation could be found in the organization's annual report; even if the trade-off was decided in detail, those details remained an internal matter.

Within the performance-contracted tripod model PIs should certainly be employed to illuminate and guide major strategic choices. So this is another respect in which reality falls disappointingly short of the ideal type. Once more, the model cannot really offer an explanation; it can simply call for more focus, more training, more effort.

Finding 8: UK exceptionalism – the 'rude mechanicals' of Europe?

We have already discussed this issue at some length (see Findings 3 and 6 earlier) but there is perhaps a little more to say. Depending on perspective, one can see the difference in the way the UK agencies regard and use PIs as either sturdy British pragmatism ('if we are going to have them, let's use them properly') or symptomatic of a kind of NPM authoritarian managerialism (PIs as another way for those at the top of the management hierarchy to exercise control). Either way, it seems to be a cultural feature, a matter of somewhat different norms and values in the UK public sector as compared with the more consensual, more collective, less hierarchical continentals (see Table 3.1). If cultures change only slowly, and there are increasing returns to cultural conformity, then such a difference could be seen as being part of the UK 'path'.

However, we would not want to exaggerate either the precision or the importance of this finding. In the EUROPAIR research we have recorded no more than widespread impressions and accounts of how PIs are used: one would need a more intensive, comparative micro-study to confirm our suspicions of difference. One would certainly also need a far more fine-grained analysis of particular organizational cultures: the work of Hofstede is suggestive but very general. Finally, it is perhaps more significant that we found well-established PI sets virtually everywhere – in every country and sector – than that we found some differences in use between one location and another.

This last point could provide some small comfort for tripod advocates – evidence that, slowly, the gospel was spreading. UK exceptionalism could then be interpreted as a sign of virtue – someone has to lead the way. How the leadership of the United Kingdom could be explained, however, would be another question, and one that would fall largely outside the terms of the model itself.

Finding 9: embeddedness in international networks and/or markets

This is not a feature that is particularly well explained by either the bureau shaping model or the TSPD model. The latter could be said to have some slight purchase on the issue, since it is a characteristic of certain tasks that they necessarily involve international arrangements, most obviously meteorology (because part of the data has to come from beyond national boundaries, and current satellite technologies are only available through international arrangements) and forestry (because timber is and always has been traded extensively between countries). However, that does not take us very far.

What is clear from our fieldwork is that international arrangements frequently incorporate mixtures of co-operative and competitive elements. Both types of dynamic may act to constrain the ability of domestic ministries to 'steer' their agencies. Once an agency has signed up to an international agreement on some environmental or scientific standard, then that becomes a fixed point in its operations – more difficult for its ministry to shift. Furthermore the ministry may lack the expertise accurately to forecast what all the consequences of a particular technical or procedural standard may be. The relevant expertise may exist only within the agencies themselves, or in professional international standards organizations (Brunsson and Jacobsson, 2000). On the other hand international competition may also weaken the ministry's hand. In both the United Kingdom and Finland we found evidence that movements in international timber prices had to be accepted by ministries as legitimate reasons why their forestry agencies/enterprises should fall short of financial targets.

While such international influences are obviously significant, it is hard to know quite how to theorize them. There may be some value in conceptualizing the world of agencies as being not a dyad (agency plus parent ministry) nor yet a triad (agency plus ministry plus ministry of finance) but rather as a quadrille (the triad plus international networks and commitments). However, we have not yet been able to take this line of thinking further forward.

The tripod model has little to say about international networks. It is essentially a model from the era of 'high NPM', when the focus was on improving the efficiency of individual organizations rather than on issues of networking and joining-up different organizations (Pollitt, 2003, chapters 2 and 3). From this perspective the international arena is conceived as a place for practising benchmarking and learning best practice – in other words for perfecting the model.

An overview of TSPD and bureau-shaping

While many of the specifics of the two academic models have been dealt with in the preceding sections, some more general features also merit comment. In particular, the *scope* and *precision* of the two models differ significantly. In brief, the scope of TSPD is greater (or, at least, somewhat different), but its precision is less.

On scope, the bureau-shaping model seems to have been developed mainly to explain why certain types of organizational change were originally chosen. The core idea is that top civil servants will choose to off-load executive tasks so as to leave themselves with more interesting and congenial work (subject to certain political constraints). Dunleavy and James have less to say about how the executive tasks are managed *after* the autonomization, and they also have not much to say about *previous*, historical rounds of reorganization. There is some discussion of the problems that might be faced after agencification, but this does not seem to be central to their concerns. TSPD, by contrast, has been developed through the inductive study of agencies in action. It is concerned *both* with why agencies were originally created *and* with how they are managed and steered. The historical, 'path' element is held to shape what is created, and both the path and the task characteristics are then hypothesized to influence how agencies are steered (or not, as the case may be).

On precision, the bureau-shaping model yields some fairly specific predictions (James, 2003, p. 36). TSPD, however, is slightly more vague. In outline it proposes that the historical path and the characteristics of the primary task(s) will be influential on form *and* on steering arrangements, but precisely *which* elements of path and task are crucial remain to be filled in. In the present study we have specified some of these (majoritarian versus consensualist; high political salience versus low, etc.) but this is all still quite tentative and, in different contexts, different scholars could pick different variables as more or less important.

Last, but not least, it is clear that both models are quite data-hungry, albeit for different kinds of data. The bureau-shaping model may appear to run happily on the basis of a few assumptions about the preferences of top officials and the constraints exercised by politicians, but that is only the start. To test the model in detail would be formidably demanding. One would need to be able to compare different bundles of policy work time and budget (the two variables top officials are assumed to desire) under different political constraints:

> the expected elasticity of demand, defined as the percentage change in quantity demanded divided by the percentage change in 'price', could be compared to that found in the data from observations of officials. However, the evidence needed for such a detailed empirical

evaluation would be very difficult to obtain, requiring a very fine-grained analysis of officials' work over a long time period ... .

(James, 2003, p. 31)

In short, the information requirements for the fully fledged testing of a model of functionally rational actors are very large, and usually impossible, in practical terms, to satisfy (see also Pollitt *et al.*, 1998, pp. 96–7).

TSPD also requires a lot of data. Its practitioners must identify the main characteristics of the relevant political and administrative systems – both the structural features (constitutions, patterns of centralization/decentralization) and the dominant cultural norms. Then they must arrive at an understanding of the main technical, financial and political characteristics of the primary task. Without these specifics, they cannot produce explanations. Perhaps the only thing that could be said in favour of the TSPD is that most of this data is more readily available than are the preference functions of senior officials (which are what is required for the empirical verification of rational choice theories).

Concluding observations

We have come to the end of a long road, involving a large but untidy literature and particular visits to a couple of dozen organizations scattered across four countries. We have tried to bring some order to this landscape, but without doing excessive damage to its rich variety. Some of that variety is remarkably stable: the Swedish agency system is still there, after more than two centuries, as is the centralized British system of two warring parties (after more than a century) and the strong Dutch tradition of quiet, consensual negotiation and consultation. These embedded structures and cultural norms shape and constrain most reforms and reorganizations, and, further, they colour daily life for senior managers in many state agencies.

Neither are the tasks performed by agencies infinitely malleable. It strikes us as mildly extraordinary that some texts on public management can discuss particular organizational structures and processes at length without ever specifying the particular activities to which they are supposed to apply. That management tools, techniques and forms of organization are sometimes thus abstracted seems to us to be a risky way of proceeding. In examining the management of agencies we have been regularly reminded that tasks do matter: that in a sense they impose their own demands on forms of organization and measurement. Some things (trees, climatic change) operate on longer time scales than others (social security payments). Some things are easier to measure than others (the accuracy of a weather forecast, or the speed of payment of a benefit, as compared with the ultimate effects of prison on the lives of discharged prisoners). Some operations are, on the large scale of national expenditure accounts, expensive (social security) while others are far less noticeable (meteorology). Some activities regularly hit the political headlines (social security fraud, escapes by high-profile prisoners) while others roll along with only the occasional spurt of media exposure (forestry, meteorology). All these factors affect the relationship between ministries and semi-autonomous state agencies, and influence the ways in which senior agency managers think and behave.

Yet, despite all these constraints of path and task, the story we have told has been one of constant change, some of it quite dramatic (the Next Steps was, in scale terms at least, a huge exercise), much of it more technical or administrative. Society is changing, producing a different mixture of types of criminal and thereby forcing prisons to review their practices. Economies are changing, bringing governments under pressure to maximize employment and restrain welfare spending, with direct consequences for the flotilla of agencies that pay benefits and assist jobseekers. Technologies are changing, enabling a handful of satellites to generate more and better weather data than thousands of land stations could previously supply, so that national meteorological offices have been pushed further and further towards international arrangements – both co-operative and competitive. And finally, thinking about management has been changing – sometimes at a dizzying rate. PIs are now standard features, and our agencies are today grappling with accruals accounting, benchmarking, the use of balanced scorecards, new HRM techniques and demands for ever-greater external accountability.

Thus the pressures for change are manifold. What we see, however, is the remarkable degree to which these pressures, even when they are broadly similar in character across different countries, get translated into different local solutions. The 'big ideas' of the ideal type agency – disaggregation, autonomy, performance management – have thus been parlayed into all the various forms described in previous chapters. Whether one marvels at the wide international reach of generic NPM ideas, or one rejoices at the fantastic variety of its adaptations and distortions, is perhaps ultimately a matter of taste. Our preference lies more with the particular and the peculiar, but such variety, we would argue, can itself be classified and explained.

Appendix: The EUROPAIR Research Project

Introduction

EUROPAIR was the title of an international academic research project focused on performance management in agencies and other 'autonomized', 'arms length' public bodies. The project was supported by a grant from the UK Economic and Social Research Council. Research assistance and finance was also provided by Erasmus University Rotterdam. The project was led by Professors Christopher Pollitt (Erasmus University Rotterdam) and Colin Talbot (originally University of Glamorgan, subsequently University of Nottingham). Other core members were Dr Janice Caulfield (originally University of Glamorgan, subsequently University of Hong Kong) and Amanda Smullen (Erasmus University Rotterdam). Temporary members in the early stages were Karen Bathgate and Adrian O'Reilly (both of University of Glamorgan).

Research aims

EUROPAIR was an in-depth study of a matched set of agencies in four countries – Finland, the Netherlands, Sweden and the United Kingdom. The idea was to be able to compare the management arrangements for roughly the same primary tasks (e.g. running prisons, paying social security benefits) in all four countries. Field work got underway early in 2000, and was concluded in September 2002.

At the outset, there were six key questions:

- How was 'performance' conceived of and measured in the agencies concerned?
- How, by whom and for what was performance data used?
- To what extent were performance measurement systems integrated with other main management systems (e.g. budgeting, planning)?
- To what extent was there learning from other organizations, either in the same country or in other countries, and how did this learning take place?
- To what extent was it possible to trace the development of the agency's performance over time?

However, as the project got underway it was broadened somewhat, and linked to other agency research that the team was simultaneously engaged in. The broadening did not mean that any of the above questions were abandoned, but rather that some broader concerns were added, especially:

- What were the main characteristics of the relationships between each agency and its parent ministry, and between each agency and the respective Ministry of Finance/Treasury?

- Were there any other 'stakeholders' that had a significant influence on the performance management systems used by agencies (e.g. major customers, national audit offices)?

Research methods

There was very extensive study of the internal documents and systems of the agencies concerned. Subsequently more than 90 semi-structured interviews were carried out using a common interview schedule across the different participating organizations (see summary of schedule at the end of this appendix, and list of organizations in the *Acknowledgements* section). Published (public domain) materials relating to agency performance were also analysed, and their use traced through other, related organizations such as 'parent' departments, legislatures, audit offices, and others. There was also a good deal of email communication with officials in the various agencies and ministries concerned, clarifying and updating points identified during the interview programme.

Interview schedule

[This schedule was used in all the interviews with agency personnel, but not all questions were used at every interview. Sometimes a selection would be made, depending upon the time available for the interview, and the particular field of responsibility of the interviewee. Interviewees were almost always offered the possibility of non-attribution. Some chose this form of anonymity, and others chose to permit us directly to identify them in our published quotations.]

General introductory questions

1. How long have you worked here?
2. Where did you work previously?

How is 'performance' conceived of and measured in the sample of agencies studied?

3. If I say to you 'the performance of X' [name agency here], what are the first aspects that spring to mind?
4. What are the most important measures or indicators, from the point of view of agency staff?
5. Have there been any significant recent changes in the way in which performance is thought about here?
6. Have these changes been reflected in the measures and indicators?
7. Who determines what the current set of performance measures should be? [Where appropriate, pursue this with supplementary questions aimed at establishing how far the agency effectively sets its own indicators or, alternatively, how far indicators are imposed on it from outside.]

How far, by whom, and for what is the performance data used?

8. Is performance data much discussed within the agency?
9. Who makes the most use of it inside the agency?

10. Who (if anyone) makes the most use of it outside the agency? [Supplementary: can you give an example of its use?]

Is the performance data validated?

11. Are there internal checks on the accuracy of the data?
12. Are there external checks on the accuracy of the data?
13. How far do you think the performance data reflects the really important aspects of the agency's 'real' performance?

To what extent are performance measurement systems integrated with financial management systems? Where this integration is low, what are the reasons for that?

14. In general, how closely is the performance measurement system linked in with the other main management systems in the agency?
15. What kind of links are there with financial systems? [If weak, then why?]
16. What kind of links are there with planning systems? [If weak, then why?]
17. What kind of links are there with Human Resource Management (HRM) systems? [If weak, then why?]

What has been learned from other agencies, both in the same country and in other countries?

18. Do you think the agency has learned much from other organizations? [If yes, which ones?]
19. Where ideas have been borrowed from other organisations, what have been the factors promoting their adoption?
20. Is there much contact with similar bodies in other countries? [If yes, how do these contacts take place and what do they concern?]

What can be said concerning changes in agency performance over time? Are 'things getting better' and, if so, why and in what ways?

21. Does the data permit you to trace aspects of the agency's performance back over time? [If so, what aspects and for how long back?]
22. What aspects of the agency's performance are improving? [Supplementary: if they cite any, ask them what data shows the improvement?]
23. What aspects of the agency's performance are declining? [Supplementary: if they cite any, ask them what data shows the improvement?]

External/contextual influences on performance

24. What are the main external influences on how well the agency performs? [Supplementary: through what process do these influences operate?]
25. Which other organizations and groups do you have most contact with?
26. What is the nature of those communications – what is supplied or exchanged, and why?
27. Has the network of external relations (questions 24 and 25 above) changed much in the last 10 years? [If so, how and why?]

Notes

5 Sweden

1. Throughout this chapter the term agency not authority is adopted to describe the central independent bodies in Sweden. This is in part to recognize the Swedish government's view that these bodies are in many ways equivalent to the agencies being created in other countries, because they do actually have similarities to changes in other countries and to avoid the confusion of using other terms for example, such as authority.
2. These figures were provided by Åke Fagrell in the Employers Agency (Arbetsgivarverket).
3. My thanks go to Petter Peterson, Advisor in the Swedish Agency for Administrative Development, for his assistance in this paragraph.

6 The United Kingdom

* These are exceptional cases. In both cases the revenue departments were established in law by Parliament during the seventeenth and eighteenth centuries in order to keep the Monarch's hands out of the Revenue's 'tills'.

10 Social Security

1. Most recently, the CTSV has been brought back into the Dutch ministry.
2. The transformation of the Benefits Agency into Jobcentre Plus began in 2001 and was expected to take three years in its implementation.
3. Although Sweden was neutral during the conflict, it suffered social upheavals experienced elsewhere and post-war agitation for change. In Finland, an agency was established before the war which was an insurance corporation but was brought into the state fold in the 1950s with a wider mandate.
4. All information collected from the County Boards is online. The AMS experienced some local bureaucratic resistance to a uniform system – 'a sub-culture in the county' – creating minor problems with data collection.

References

Abma, T. and Noordegraaf, M. (2003) 'Public managers amidst ambiguity: towards a typology of evaluative practices in public management', *Evaluation*, 9(3) July, pp. 285–306.

Alexander, P. and Agency Policy Review Team (2002) *Better Government Services – Executive Agencies in the 21st Century* (The Agency Policy Review – report and recommendations), London: Cabinet Office.

Algemene Rekenkamer (1995) *Verslag 1994; deel 3: Zelfstandige bestuursorganen en ministeriele verantwoordelijkheid*, Tweede Kamer, veraderjaar 1994–95, 24 130, (nr3) Den Haag, Sdu.

Algemene Rekenkamer (2000) *Supervision of the State Forest Service* website English summary of a report published by the Netherlands Court of Audit on 16 March 2000 (http://www.rekenkamer.nl/en/summary/supervisionsstateforest.htm).

Algemene Rekenkamer (2002) *Verantwoording en toezicht bij rechtspersonen met een wettelijke taak deel 3*, Sdu uitgevers, 's-Gravenhage.

Allix, M. (2002) *An Overview of Agencies in France and Italy*, unpublished paper written during a course of Ph.D study within the BSK, Erasmus University Rotterdam.

Andersson, C. (2001) *Ambetsmannastat och Demokrati*, Stockholm: Scorerapportserie 2001:14.

Andrén, N. (1961) *Modern Swedish Government*, Stockholm: Almqvist and Wiksell.

Anton, T. (1980) *Administrative Politics: Elite Political Culture in Sweden*, Boston: Martinus Nijhoff Publishing.

Araújo, J. (2002) 'NPM and the change in Portuguese central government', *International Public Management Journal* 5(3) pp. 223–36.

Aristotle (1962) *Meteorological*, Cambridge, MA: Harvard University Press (translation by H.D.P Lee).

Association of Finnish Local Authorities (1995a) *Total Quality Management in Municipal Service Provision*, Helsinki: Association of Finnish Local Authorities.

Association of Finnish Local Authorities (1995b) *Quality in the Procurement of Municipal Services*, Helsinki: Association of Finnish Local Authorities.

Aucoin, P. (1996) 'Designing agencies for good public management: the urgent need for reform', *Choices* (IRPP) 2(4) April, pp. 5–20.

Axelrod, R. and Cohen M.D. (1999) *Harnessing Complexity*, New York: The Free Press.

Bardach, E. (1998) *Getting Agencies to Work Together: The Practice and Theory of Managerial Craftsmanship*, Washington DC: Brookings Institution.

Benefits Agency (1999) *Annual Report and Accounts 1989–99*, HC580, London: The Stationary Office.

Benefits Agency, UK Department of Social Security (2000) *Performance and Expenditure Report 2000/01* (December, Period 9).

Bergmark, A., Thorslund, M. and Lindberg E. (2000) 'Beyond benevolence – solidarity and welfare state transition in Sweden', *International Journal of Social Welfare* 9, pp. 238–49.

Blondell, J. (1998) *Budgeting in Sweden*, Paris: OECD.
Blondell, J. (2001) *Budgeting in Sweden*, Paris: OECD.
Boin, A. (2001) *Crafting Public Institutions: Leadership in Two Prison Systems*, Boulder: Lynne Rienn Publications.
Burch, M. (1995) *The British Cabinet System*, New Jersey: Prentice Hall.
Bogt, H. ter (1999) 'Financial and economic management in autonomised Dutch public organisations', *Financial Accountability and Management*, 15(3 and 4) August/November, pp. 329–48.
Boston, J., J. Martin et al. (1996) *Public Management – The New Zealand Model*, Auckland: Oxford University Press.
Bouckaert, G., Ormond, D. and Peters, G. (2000) *A Potential Governance Agenda for Finland*, Research Report No. 8, Helsinki: Ministry of Finance.
Bovens, M. and Plug, P. (1999) *Accountability at a Distance: Reconciling Political Accountability and Administrative Autonomy*, paper presented at the International Institute of Administrative Sciences Conference, Sunningdale, UK: 12–15 July.
Bovens, M. and Zouridis, S. (2002) 'From street-level to system-level bureaucracies: how in formation and communication technology is transforming administrative discretion and constitutional control', *Public Administration Review*, 62:2 pp. 174–84.
Boyne, G. et al. (2003) *Evaluating Public Management Reforms*, Buckingham: Open University Press.
Bozeman, B. (1987) *All Organizations are Public: Bridging Public and Private Organizational Theories*, San Francisco: Jossey-Bass.
Bradshaw, J. (1992) 'Social Security', in D. Marsh and R.A.W. Rhodes (eds) *Implementing Thatcherite Policies*, Buckingham: Open University Press.
Bromwitch, M. and Lapsley, I. (1997) 'Decentralisation and management accounting in central government: recycling old ideas?' *Financial Accountability and Management*, 13:2 pp. 181–201.
Brunsson, K. (1995) 'Puzzle pictures: Swedish budgetary processes in principle and in practice', *Financial Accountability and Management*, May, 11(2) pp. 111–25.
Brunsson, K. (1998) 'Non-learning organizations', *Scandinavian Journal of Management*, 14(4) pp. 421–32.
Brunsson, K. (2002) 'Management or politics – or both? How management by objectives may be managed: A Swedish example', *Financial Accountability and Management* May 18(2) pp. 189–209.
Brunsson, N. and Jacobsson, B. (2000) *A World of Standards*, Oxford: Oxford University Press.
Brunsson, N. and Olsen, J. (1993) *The Reforming Organization*, London: Routledge.
Caiden, G.E. (1991) *Administrative Reform Comes of Age*, New York: Walter de Gruyter.
Butler, D., A. Adonis et al. (1994) *Failure in British Government – the Politics of the Poll Tax*, Oxford: Oxford University Press.
Burch, M.H., I (1995) *The British Cabinet System*, New Jersey: Prentice Hall.
Campbell, C. and G. Wilson (1995) *The End of Whitehall: Death of Paradigm?*, Oxford: Blackwell.
Carpenter, D. (2001) *The Forging of Bureaucratic Autonomy – Reputations, Networks and Policy Innovation in Executive Agencies 1862–1928*, Princeton: Princeton University Press.

Carter, N., Klein, R. and Day, P. (1992) *How Organizations Measure Success: The Use of Performance Indicators in Government*, London: Routledge.
Caulfield, J. and Larsen, H.O. (eds) (2002) *Local Government at the Millennium*, Opladen: Lesk and Budrich.
(Chair of Commission) Taylor, M. (2001) *Building Better Partnerships*, London: IPPR.
Chancellor of the Duchy of Lancaster (1997) *Next Steps Agencies in Government: Review, 1996*, CM3579, London: The Stationary Office.
Chapman, R.A. (1997) *The Treasury in Public Policy Making*, London: Routledge.
Christiansen, P. (1998) 'A prescription rejected: market solutions to problems of public sector governance', *Governance*, 11(3) pp. 273–95.
Christensen, Tom, Per Lægreid and Lois R. Wise (2002) 'Transforming Administrative Policy', *Public Administration*, 80(1) pp. 153–78.
Cohen Committee (1997) *MDW-werkgroep: markt en overheid*, Den Haag ('MDW workgroup – market and government').
Common, R., N. Flynn et al. (1992) *Managing Public Services – Competition and Decentralisation*, Butterworth: Heinemann.
Comptroller and Auditor General (1995) *The Meterological Office Executive Agency: Evaluation of Performance*, London: National Audit Office.
Comptroller and Auditor General (1998) *Benefits Agency: Performance Measurement*, London: National Audit Office.
Comptroller and Auditor General (2000) *Good Practice In Performance Reporting in Executive Agencies and Non-Departmental Public Bodies*, London: National Audit Office.
Considine, Mark (2001) *Enterprising States: The Public Management of Welfare-to-Work*, Cambridge: Cambridge University Press.
Council of Europe (1983) *Prison Management*, Strasbourg: Council of Europe.
Cowen, T. and Parker, D. (1997) *Markets in the Firm – A Market-Process Approach to Management*, London: Institute of Economic Affairs.
Curran, B and Gunasekera, D. (2003) 'Partnership in the provision of public goods: The case of the Meteorological Services', *Canberra Bulletin of Public Administration* (16) February.
Davidson, A. (1989) *Two Models of Welfare: The Origins and Development of the Welfare State in Sweden and New Zealand, 1888–1988*, Doctoral dissertation, Uppsala, ACTA Universtitatis Upsaliensis.
Deakin, N. and Parry, R. (2000) *The Treasury and Social Policy*, London: Macmillan.
De Boer, E. and Peeperkorn, M. (2003) 'Idereen moet inleveren, ook het poldermodel', *de Volkskrant*, 20 September, p. 25 ('Everyone must deliver – even the Polders model').
De Bruijn, H. (2001) *Managing Performance in the Public Sector*, London: Routledge.
De Frisching, A., C. Blairs et al. (1997) *Prison Service Review*, London: HM Prison Service.
Derksen, W. and Kortsen, A. (1995) 'Local government: a survey', pp. 63–86 in W. Kickert and F. van Vught (eds) *Public Policy and Administration Sciences in the Netherlands*, London: Prentice Hall/Harvester Wheatsheaf.
de Soto, H. (2000) *The Mystery of Capital*, London: Bantam Press.
Department of Health and Social Security (1985) *The Reform of Social Security: Programme for Action*, London: HMSO.
DiIulio, J.J. (1987) *Governing Prisons*, New York: The Free Press.

DiIulio, J.E. (1994) *Deregulating the Public Service: Can Government be Improved?*, Washington, DC: The Brookings Institution.
Doumer, S. and Schreuder, H. (1998) *Economic Approaches to Organizations* (2nd edition), New Jersey: Prentice Hall.
DS 2000:63. (2000) *Ekonomisk Styrning*, Stockholm: Finansdepartementet.
Dunleavy, P. (1991) *Democracy, Bureaucracy and Public Choice: Economic Explanations in Political Science*, Hemel Hempstead: Harvester Wheatsheaf.
Dutch National Agency for Correctional Institutions (2001) *Facts in Figures*, den Haag, Dutch National Agency for Correctional Institutions.
The Economist (2002) 'Modelmakers: a survey of the Netherlands', 4 May, pp. 3–5.
Efficiency Unit (1988) *Improving Management in Government: The Next Steps* (The Ibbs Report), London: HMSO.
Ehn, P. (2001) *'Lite sunt fornuft.' En beskrivning av Vesta-projektet I regeringskansliet*. Stockholm: Socre Rapport Serie 2001(9).
Einerhand, M., Eriksson, I. and van Leuvensteijn, M. (2001) 'Benefit dependency and the dynamics of the welfare state: Comparing Sweden and the Netherlands', *International Social Security Review* 54.
Ervasti, Heikki (2001) 'Class, individualism and the Finnish welfare state', *Journal of European Social Policy*, 11(1) pp. 9–23.
Esping-Andersen G. (ed.) (1996) *Welfare States in Transition: National Adaptations in Global Economies*, London: Sage.
Esping-Andersen G. and Korpi, W. (1984) *From Poor Relief Towards Institutional Welfare States: The Development of Scandinavian Social Policy*, Stockholm: The Swedish Institute for Social Research, Report 5.
ESV. (1999) *Informella kontakter I samband med regleringsbrev och årsredovisningar*. Stockholm: ESV 1999:19.
ESV. (1999) *Myndigheternas syn på resultatstyrningen*. Stockholm: ESV 1999(20).
ESV. (2001) *Accrual Accounting in Swedish Central Government*, Stockholm: ESV 2001(8).
Finland (2000) The Social Insurance Institution (KELA). 'Outcome Orientation in the Development of Management Methods at KELA', Social Security and Health. Research: Working Chapters No. 17.
Finnish Meteorological Institute (2003) *Annual Report 2000*, Turku, Finnish Meteorological Institute (published in English, as well as Finnish and Swedish).
Finnish Meteorological Institute (2000) *Annual Report 1999*, Turku, Finnish Meteorological Institute (published in English, as well as Finnish and Swedish).
Flynn, N. (2002) *Public Sector Management* (4th edition) Harlow: Financial Times/Prentice Hall.
Forest Enterprise (1998) *Forest Enterprise: Annual Report and Accounts 1997–98*, Edinburgh: The Stationary Office.
Forest Enterprise (1999) *Annual Report and Accounts: Forest Enterprise 1998–1999*, HC800, Edinburgh: The Stationary Office.
Fortin, Y. (1996) 'Autonomy, Responsibility and Control', in *Performance Management in Government*, Paris, PUMA/OECD Occasional Paper 9, 33–42.
Fortin, Y. and Van Hassel, H. (2000) (eds) *Contracting in the New Public Management*, Amsterdam: IOS Press.
Fraser, Sir A. (1991) *Making the Most of Next Steps: The Management of Ministers' Departments and their Executive Agencies* (the Fraser Report) May, London: HMSO.

Freebairn, J.W. and Zilman, J.W. (2002a) 'Economic benefits of meteorological services', *Meteorological Applications*, (9) pp. 33–44.
Freebairn, J.W. and Zilman, J.W. (2002b) 'Funding meteorological services', *Meteorological Applications*, (9) pp. 45–54.
Friedman, R. (1989) *Appropriating the Weather*, Ithaca: Cornell University Press.
Fry, G. (1981) *The Administrative 'Revolution' in Whitehall*, London: Croom Helm.
Fry, G.K. (1993) *Reforming the Civil Service*, Edinburgh: Edinburgh University Press.
Fukuyama, F. (1995) *Trust – The Social Virtues and the Creation of Prosperity*, London: Penguin Books.
Fulton Committee (1968) *Committee on the Civil Service – Report*, London: HMSO.
Gains, F. (1999) *Understanding Department – Next Steps Agency Relationships*, Ph.D thesis, Department of Politics, University of Sheffield.
Gains, F. (2004) 'Adapting the agency concept: variations within "Next Steps"', in C. Pollitt and C. Talbot (eds) *Unbundled Government*, London: Taylor and Francis, pp. 53–74.
Garrett, J. (1972) *The Management of Government*, Harmondsworth: Penguin.
Goffman, E. (1974) *Frame Analysis*, Harmondsworth: Penguin.
Goffman, E. (1961) *Asylums: Essays on the Social Situation of Mental Patients and Other Inmates*, New York: Doubleday.
Goldsworthy, D. (1991) *Setting up Next Steps*, London: HMSO.
Gould, Arthur (1993) *Capitalist Welfare Systems: A Comparison of Japan, Britain and Sweden*, London: Longman.
Graham, A. and Roberts, A. (2004) 'The agency concept in North America: failure, adaptation and incremental change', in C. Pollitt and C. Talbot (eds) *Unbundled Government*, London: Taylor and Francis, pp. 140–64.
Granholm, H. (1999) 'Forest policy becoming international', in Reunala, A. *et al.* (eds) *The Green Kingdom: Finland's Forest Cluster*, Otava: Keuruu, pp. 256–65.
Granovetter, M. (1985) 'Economic action and social structure: the problem of embeddedness', *American Journal of Sociology*, 91(3) pp. 481–510.
Greer, P. (1994) *Transforming Central Government – The Next Steps Initiative*, Buckingham: Open University Press.
Greve, C., Flinders, M. and Van Thiel, S. (1999) 'Quangos – what's in a name? Defining quangos from a comparative perspective', *Governance*, 12(1) January, pp. 129–46.
Gustafsson, L. 'Renewal of the public sector in Sweden', *Public Administration*, Summer, 65(2) pp. 179–91.
Gustafsson, L. and Svensson, A. (1999) *Public Sector Reform in Sweden*, Malmö: Liber Ekonomi.
Hajlmarsson, A. (2001) *Financial Management and Control of Public Agencies*, Paris: SIGMA.
Halman, L. (2001) *The European Values Study: A Third Wave: Source Book of the 1999–2000 European Values Study Surveys*, Tilburg, WORC: Tilburg University.
Hänninen, H. (1999) 'Many actors influencing forestry policy', in Reunala, A. *et al.* (eds) *The Green Kingdom: Finland's Forest Cluster*, Otava: Keuruu, pp. 240–55.
Harden, I. (1992) *The Contracting State*, Buckingham: Open University Press.
Harden, I. and Lewis, N. (1986) *The Noble Lie – The British Constitution and the Rule of Law*, London: Hutchinson.
Harrinvirta, Markku Olavi (2000) *Strategies of Public Sector Reform in the OECD Countries: A Comparison*, Helsinki: Finnish Society of Sciences and Letters.

Harrison, A.E. (1993) *From Hierarchy to Contract*, Policy Journals.
Heady, F. (2001) *Public Administration – A Comparative Perspective* (6th edition), New York: Marcel Dekker Inc.
Heclo, H. and Wildavsky, A. (1981) *The Private Government of Public Money*, (2nd edition), Basingstoke: Macmillan.
Heidenheimer, A.J., Heclo, H. and Teich Adams, C. (1990) *Comparative Public Policy: The Politics of Social Choice in America, Europe, and Japan* (3rd edition) New York: St. Martins.
Hemerijk, A. and Visser, J. (1997) *A Dutch Miracle: Job Growth, Welfare Reform and Corporation in the Netherlands*, Amsterdam: Amsterdam University Press.
Hennessy, P. (1990) *Whitehall*, London: Fontana.
Hennessy, P. (1991) *Cabinet*, Oxford: Blackwell.
Hennessy, P. (1995) *The Hidden Wiring – Unearthing the British Constitution*, London: Gollancz.
HM Prison Service (2003) *HM Prison Service Annual Report and Accounts (HC 885)*, London: The Stationary Office.
Hofstede, G. (2001) *Culture's Consequences: Comparing Values, Behaviors, Institutions and Organizations Across Nations*, Thousand Oaks, CA: Sage.
Hogwood, B., Judge, D. and McVicar, M. (2000) 'Agencies and Accountability', in R. Rhodes (ed.) *Transforming British Government: Volume 1: Changing Institutions*, Basingstoke: Macmillan.
Holkeri, K. and Summa, H. (1996) *Contemporary Developments in Performance Management: Evaluation of Public Management Reforms in Finland: From ad hoc Studies to a Programmatic Approach*, paper presented to PUMA/OECD, Paris, November.
Holkeri, K. and Nurmi, J. (2002) *Quality, Satisfaction and Trust in Government: The Finnish Case*, paper presented to the Conference of the European Group of Public Administration, Potsdam, 4–7 September.
Holland, J.H. (1995) *Hidden Order – How Adaptation Builds Complexity*, Reading, MA.: Addison Wesley.
Home Affairs Select Committee (1997) *The Management of the Prison Service (Public and Private) (HC 57)* London: The Stationary Office.
Home Office (1998) *Prisons – Probation Review Final Report*, London: Home Office.
Hood, C. (1998) *The Art of the State: Culture, Rhetoric and Public Management*, Oxford: Oxford University Press.
Hood, C. and Jackson, M. (1991) *Administrative Argument*, Dartmouth: Aldershot.
Hood, C. et al. (1999) *Regulation Inside Government*, Oxford: Oxford University Press.
Hyndman, N. and Eden, R. (2002) 'Executive agencies, performance targets and external reporting', *Public Money and Management*, 22:3 pp. 17–24.
Hyndman, N. and Anderson, R. (1998) 'Performance information, accountability and executive agencies', *Public Money and Management*, 18(3) pp. 23–30.
James, O. (2001) 'Evaluating executive agencies in UK Government', *Public Policy and Administration*, 16(3) pp. 24–52.
James, O. (2003) *The Executive Agency Revolution in Whitehall: Public Interest versus Bureau-Shaping Perspectives*, Basingstoke: Palgrave.
James, O. (2004) 'Agencies and Joined-up Government in the UK' in C. Pollitt and C. Talbot (eds) *Unbundled Government*, London: Taylor and Francis, pp. 75–93.
Jenkins, K., Caines, K. et al. (1988) *Improving Management in Government: The Next Steps*, London: HMSO.

Johansson, S. (2000) *Management Effectiveness and Institutional Credibility: Assessment of Management Effectiveness of Protected areas in Finland*, paper presented at the International Conference on the Design and Management of Forest Protected Areas, Bangkok, 8–11 May.

Jordan, G. (1992) 'Next Steps Agencies: From Managing by Command to Managing by Contract?' *Aberdeen Papers in Accountancy and Finance Management*, Aberdeen: University of Aberdeen.

Joustie, H. (2001) 'Performance management in Finnish state administration', in *Public management in Finland*, Helsinki: Ministry of Finance, pp. 18–19.

Juslin, H. and Kärnä, J. (1999) 'Forest certification: marketing or forest policy?', in Ruanala, A. *et al.* (eds) *The Green Kingdom: Finland's Forest Cluster*, Otava: Keuruu, pp. 288–93.

Kautto, M., Heikkila, M., Hvinden, B., Marklund, S. and Ploug, N. (eds) (1999) *Nordic Social Policy: Changing Welfare States*, London: Routledge.

Keeling, D. (1972) *Management in Government*, Hemel Hempstead, Allen & Unwin.

KELA (1999) *Statistical Yearbook of the Social Insurance Institution, Finland*, Helsinki: KELA (*Kansaneläkelaitoksen tilastollinen vuosikirja*).

Kemp, P. (1993) *Beyond Next Steps: A Civil Service for the 21st Century*, London: Social Market Foundation.

Kemp, P. (1996) Interview with Author.

Kickert, W. (2001) 'Public management of hybrid organizations: governance of quasi-autonomous executive agencies', *International Public Management Journal*, 4(2) pp. 135–50.

Kickert, W. (2000) *Public Management Reforms in the Netherlands: Social Reconstruction of Reform Ideas and Underlying Frames of Reference*, Delft, Eburon.

Kickert, W. and van Vucht, F. (eds) (1995) *Public Policy and Administration Sciences in the Netherlands*, London: Prentice Hall/Harvester Wheatsheaf.

Kickert, W. and in 't Veld, R. (1995) 'National government, governance and administration', pp. 45–62 in W. Kickert and F. van Vucht (eds), *Public Policy and Administration Sciences in the Netherlands*, London: Prentice Hall/Harvester Wheatsheaf.

King, D. (1999) *In the Name of Liberalism: Illiberal Social Policy in the United States and Britain*, Oxford: Oxford University Press.

Kingsbury, S., Kingsbury, M. and Mieder, W. (1996) *Weather Wisdom. Proverbs, Superstitions and Signs*, New York: Peter Lang Publishing Inc.

Kiviniemi, M., Oittinen, R., Varhe, S., Niskanen, J. and Salminen, A. (1995) *Public Services go on the Market: Finnish Experiences and Views of New Public Enterprises and Companies*, Helsinki: Ministry of Finance.

Koninklijk Nederlands Meteorologisch Instituut (2000) *Jaarverslag 1999. Een eeuw in de weer*, KNMI, De Bilt.

Koninklijk Nederlands Meteorologisch Instituut (1999) *Jaarverslag 1998: In het teken van de regen*. KNMI, De Bilt.

Korsten, A. and van der Krogt, T. (1995) 'Human resources management', in W. Kickert and F. van Vught (eds) *Public Policy and Administration Sciences in the Netherlands*, London: Prentice Hall/Harvester Wheatsheaf, pp. 233–48.

Kraak, A. and van Osteroom, R. (eds) (2002) *Agentschappen: innovatie in bedrijfsvoering: een resultaatgericht besturingsmodel bij uitvoeringsorganisaties van de rijksoverheid*, Den Haag, Sdu.

Lane, J-E. (2000) *New Public Management*, Aldershot, Ashgate.

Larsson, T. (1995) *Governing Sweden*, Stockholm: Statskontoret.
Larsson, T. (2001) *Governing Sweden*, Stockholm: Statskontoret.
Leander, K. (1995) 'The normalization of Swedish Prisons' in V. Ruggerio, M. Ryan and J. Sim (eds) *Western European Penal Systems*, London: Sage.
Learmont, G.S.J. (1995) *Review of Prison Service Security in England and Wales and the Escape from Parkhurst Prison on Tuesday 3rd January 1995*, London: HMSO.
Leeuw, F. (1995) *The Dutch Perspective: Trends in Performance Measurement*, paper presented at the International Evaluation Conference, Vancouver, 1–5 November.
Le Grand, J. and Bartlett, W. (eds) (1993) *Quasi-Markets and Social Policy*, London: Macmillan.
Levy, J. (1999) 'Vice into Virtue? Progressive Politics and Welfare Reform in Continental Europe', *Politics and Society*, 27 pp. 239–73.
Lewis, D. (1997) *Hidden Agendas: Politics, Law and Disorder*, London: Hamish Hamilton.
Light, P.C. (1997) *The Tides of Reform – Making Government Work 1945–1995*, New Haven: Yale University Press.
Lijphart, A. (1984) *Democracies: Patterns of Majoritarian and Consensus Government in Twenty-one Countries*, London: Yale University Press.
Lijphart, A. (1999) *Patterns of Democracy: Governance Forms and Performance in 36 Countries*, New Haven: Yale University Press.
Lindbeck, A., Molander, P., Persson, T., Petersson, O., Sandmo, A., Swedenborg and Thygesen, N. (1994) *Turning Sweden Around*, Cambridge: The MIT Press.
Lipsky, M. (1980) *Street-level Bureaucracy – Dilemmas of the Individual in Public Services*, New York: Russell Sage Foundation.
Loughlin, J. and Peter, B.G. 1997 'State traditions, administrative reform and regionalization', pp. 41–62 in M. Keating and J. Laughlin (eds), *The Political Economy of Regionalism*, London: Frank Cass.
Lundkvist, Kristina. (2001) *Accrual Accounting in Swedish Central Government*, ESV 2001(8) Stockholm.
Lundell, B. (1994) *Sverige : Institutionella ramar förvaltningspolitiken* in Lærgreid, P. and Pedersen, O. (eds), *Forvaltningspolitik I Norden*. Jurist og Økonomforbundets Forlag.
Lynn, L., Heinrich, C. and Hill, C. (2001) *Improving Governance: A New Logic for Empirical Research*, Washington, DC: Georgetown University Press.
Mabbett, D. and Bolderson, H. (1999) 'Devolved social security systems: Principal-agent versus multi-level governance', *Journal of Public Policy* 18 (2) pp. 177–200.
Manning, Nick and Ian Shaw (1998) 'The Transferability of Welfare Models: A Comparison of the Scandinavian and State Socialist Models in Relation to Finland and Estonia', *Social Policy and Administration* 32(5) December, pp. 572–90.
March, J.G. and Olsen, J. (1998) 'The institutional dynamics of international political orders', *International Organization*, 52(4) Autumn, pp. 943–69.
Metcalfe, L. and Richards, S. (1990) *Improving Public Management* (2nd edition), London: Sage.
Metsähallitus (2000) *Metsähallitus in 1999*, Vantaa, Metsähallitus.
Metsähallitus (2002) personal email communication to C. Pollitt, 3 September.
Ministerie van Financiën (1998) *Verder met resultaat: het agentschapsmodel 1991–1997*, De Haag, (Dutch) Ministry of Finance.

Ministerie van Financiën (2001) *Instellingsprocedure baten-lastendiensten* (editie 2001), Den Haag (unpublished) ('Procedure for establishing asset-and-liability services').

Ministerie van Financiën (2002) *Evaluatie agentschappen*, Den Haag, Ministerie van Financiën.

Ministerie van Verkeer en Waterstaat (2002) *De besturingsrelaties tussen het Department for Transport en het Highways Agency: een verkenning*, Den Haag, Directie Organisatie en Informatie, July.

Ministry of Agriculture and Forestry (1999) *Finland's Forests – Jobs, Incomes and Nature Values*, Helsinki: Ministry of Agriculture and Forestry.

Ministry of Finance (1992) *Selvitys tulobudjetoinnin arvioinnista vuosina 1990–1993* (A report of the evaluation of result-oriented budgeting in the years 1990–1993; English summary available), Helsinki, Ministry of Finance.

Ministry of Finance (1993) *Government Decisions in Principle on Reforms in Central and Regional Government*, Helsinki: Ministry of Finance.

Ministry of Finance (1997) *Public Management Reforms: Five Country Studies*, Helsinki: Ministry of Finance.

Ministry of Finance (1998) *High-Quality Services, Good Governance and a Responsible Civil Society: guidelines of the Policy of Governance: Background Material*, Helsinki: Ministry of Finance.

Ministry of Finance (2000) *Performance Budgeting in Sweden – Outline of a Reform Programme*, Stockholm: Ministry of Finance.

Ministry of Justice (2000) *Public Administration in the Service of Democracy – An Action Programme*, Stockholm: Ministry of Justice.

Mintzberg, H. (1983) *Structure in Fives*, New York: Prentice-Hall International.

Mol, N. (1995) 'Quality improvement in the Dutch Department of Defense', in C. Pollitt and G. Bouckart (eds) *Quality Improvement in European Public Services: Concepts, Cases and Commentary*, London: Sage, pp. 103–28.

Molander, P., Nilsson, J-E. and Schick, A. (2002) *Does Anyone Govern? The Relationship Between the Government Office and the Agencies in Sweden*, report from the SNS Constitutional Project, Stockholm, SNS.

Moores, G. (2001) 'Framework for Assessing Performance: Outcome-oriented Management', Paper delivered to the International Social Security Association Conference, Taormina 29–30 November.

Morgan, G. (1996) *Images of Organisation* (2nd edition), London: Sage.

Muncie, J. and Sparks, R. (eds) (1991) *Imprisonment – European Perspectives*, New York: Harvester Wheatsheaf.

Murray, R. (2000) *Human Resource Management in Swedish Central Government*, Stockholm, Statskontoret (unpublished paper).

National Audit Office (1995) *The Meteorological Office Executive Agency: Evaluation of Performance*, HC 693 Session 1994–95, 25 August 1995, London: National Audit Office.

National Audit Office (1998) *Benefits Agency: Performance Measurement*, HC952, London: HMSO.

National Audit Office (1999) *Government on the Web*, HC87, London: The Stationary Office.

National Audit Office (2000) *Good Practice in Performance Reporting in Executive Agencies and Non-departmental Public Bodies*, HC272, London: The Stationary Office, 9 March.

Nebeker, F. (1995) *Calculating the Weather*, San Diego: Academic Press.
Newsam, S.F. (1954) *The Home Office*, London: George Allen and Unwin Ltd.
Nordlund A. (2000) 'Social policy in harsh times: social security development in Denmark, Finland, Norway and Sweden during the 1980s and 1990s', *International Journal of Social Welfare* 9, pp. 31–42.
North, D. (1990) *Institutions, Institutional Change and Economic Performance*, Cambridge: Cambridge University Press.
O'Connor, J. (1973) *The Fiscal Crisis of the State*, New York: St. Martin's Press.
OECD (1997) *In Search of Results: Performance Management Practices*, Paris, PUMA/OECD.
OECD-PUMA (1999). *Performance Contracting – Lessons from Performance Contracting Case Studies: A Framework for Public Sector Performance Contracting*, Paris: OECD.
OECD (2002a) *Public Sector Modernisation: A New Agenda*, (CCNM/GF/GOV92002)1, paper presented to a seminar of the OECD Global Forum on Governance, held at the London School of Economics, 2/3 December 2002.
OECD (2002b) *Distributed Public Governance: Agencies, Authorities and other Government Bodies*, CCNM/GF/GOV/PUBG (2002)2, paper presented to a seminar of the OECD Global Forum on Governance, held at the London School of Economics, 2/3 December.
OECD (2003) *Public Sector Modernization: Changing organizations*, GOV/PUMA (2003)19, Paris, 28 October.
Office of Public Services Reform (2002) *Better Government Services: Executive Agencies in the 21st Century* (http://www.civilservice.gov.uk/agencies).
Oikeusministerio (2000) *Vuotta 2001 Kosevat Tulostavoitteet Ja Tulosneuvottelut*. Helsinki, Oikeusministerio.
Osborne, D. and Gaebler, T. (1992) *Re-inventing Government: How the Entrepreneurial Spirit is Transforming the Public Sector*, Reading, Mass.: Addison-Wesley.
O'Toole, B. and Jordan, G. (eds) (1995) *Next Steps: Improving Management in Government*, Aldershot, Dartmouth.
Ouchi, W.G. (1981) *Theory Z – How American Business can Meet the Japanese Challenge*, New York: Avon Books.
Performance and Innovation Unit (2000) *Wiring it up – Whitehall's Management of Cross-cutting Policies and Services*, London: Cabinet Office.
Peters, G.B. and Bouckaert, G. (2004) 'What is available and what is missing in the study of quangos?' in Pollitt, C. and Talbot, C. (eds) *Unbundled Government*, London: Taylor and Francis, pp. 22–49.
Pierre, J. (ed.) (1995) *Bureaucracy in the Modern State: An Introduction to Comparative Public Administration*, Aldershot, Edward Elgar.
Pierre, J. (2004) 'Central agencies in Sweden: a report from Utopia' in C. Pollitt and C. Talbot (eds) *Unbundled Government*, London: Taylor and Francis, pp. 203–14.
Pierson, P. (2000a) 'Increasing returns, path dependence, and the study of politics', *American Political Science Review*, 94(2) June, pp. 251–67.
Pierson, P. (2000b) 'The limits of design: explaining organizational origins and change', *Governance*, 13(4) October, pp. 475–99.
Pierson, P. (ed.) (2000c) *The New Politics of the Welfare State*, Oxford: Oxford University Press.

Pliatsky, L. (1992) 'Quangos and agencies' *Public Administration*, 70(4) pp. 555–63.
Pliatzky, L. (1989) *The Treasury Under Mrs Thatcher*, Oxford: Blackwell.
Ploug, N. and J. Kvist (eds) (1994) *Recent Trends in Cash Benefits in Europe*, Copenhagen: Danish National Institute of Social Research.
Pollitt, C. (1984) *Manipulating the Machine*, Hemel Hempstead: Allen and Unwin.
Pollitt, C. (2000a) 'Is the Emperor in his underwear? An analysis of the impacts of public management reform', *Public Management*, 2(2) pp. 181–99.
Pollitt, C. (2000b) 'How do we know how good public services are?', in G. Peters and D. Savoie (eds.) *Governance in the 21st Century*, Montreal and Kingston: McGill-Queen's University Press.
Pollitt, C. (2002) 'Clarifying convergence: striking similarities and durable differences in public management reform', *Public Management Review*, 4(1) pp. 471–92.
Pollitt, C. (2003) *The Essential Public Manager*, Buckingham: Open University Press.
Pollitt, C., Birchall, J. and Putman, K. (1998) *Decentralising Public Service Management*, Basingstoke: Macmillan.
Pollitt, C. and Bouckaert, G. (2000) *Public Management Reform: A Comparative Analysis*, Oxford: Oxford University Press.
Pollitt, C. and Bouckaert, G. (2004) *Public Management Reform: A Comparative Analysis* (2nd edition), Oxford: Oxford University Press.
Pollitt, C., Caulfield, J., Smullen, A. and Talbot, C. (2001) 'Agency fever? Analysis of an international fashion', *Journal of Comparative Policy Analysis*, 3, pp. 271–90.
Pollitt, C. and Talbot, C. (eds) (2004) *Unbundled Government: A Critical Analysis of the Global Trend to Agencies, Quangos and Contractualisation*, London: Routledge/Taylor and Francis.
Ponting, C. (1986) *Whitehall: Tragedy and Farce*, London: Hamish Hamilton.
Powell, W. and DiMaggio, P. (eds) (1991) *The New Institutionalism in Organizational Analysis*, Chicago, Ill: University of Chicago Press.
Premfors, R. (1991) The 'Swedish Model' and public sector reform, *West European Politics* 14(3) pp. 83–95
Premfors, R. (1983) 'Governmental commissions in Sweden' *American Behavioural Scientist*, 26(5) pp. 623–42.
Premfors, R. (1998) 'Reshaping the democratic state: Swedish experiences in a comparative perspective', *Public Administration*, 76(1) pp. 141–59.
Premfors, R. (1999) 'Organisationsförändringar och förvaltningspolitik: Sverige' in P Laergraid et O Pederson (red), *Fra opbygning til ombygning I staten*. Københaven, Jurist – og Økonomforbundets Forlag.
Prime Minister and Minister for the Civil Service (1994) *The Civil Service: Continuity and Change*, (Cm 2627) London: HMSO.
Prime Minister and Minister for the Civil Service (1995) *The Civil Service: Taking Forward Continuity and Change*, (Cm 2748) London: HMSO.
Prince, M. (2000) 'Banishing bureaucracy or hatching a hybrid? The Canadian Food Inspection Agency and the politics of reinventing government', *Governance*, 13(2), April, pp. 215–32.
Prop. (1996–1997) *Förslag till slutig reglering av statsbudgeten*, II, Stockholm.
Puoskari, P. (1996) *Transformation of the Public Sector*, Helsinki: Ministry of Finance.
Regeringskansliet (2000) *The State Budget Procedure*, Stockholm: Regeringskansliet.
Reunala, A., Tikkanen, I. and Åsvik, E. (eds) (1999) *The Green Kingdom: Finland's Forest Cluster*, Otava: Keuruu.

Richards, D. (1997) *The Civil Service under the Conservatives 1979–1997 Whitehall's Political Poodles?* Brighton: Sussex Academic Press.
Ridley, F.F. (ed.) (1968) *Specialists and Generalists*, London: Allen and Unwin Ltd.
Romakkaniemi, P. (2001) 'Access to Finnish public sector information and its services', in *Public Management in Finland*, Helsinki: Ministry of Finance, pp. 4–7.
Rose, R. and Davies, P. (1994) *Inheritance in Public Policy*, New Haven: Yale University Press.
Ross, F. (1997) 'Cutting public expenditures in advanced democracies; the importance of avoiding blame', *Governance: An International Journal of Policy and Administration* 10, pp. 175–2000.
RRV (1993) *Resultstyrning I regleringsbrer*, Stockholm: RRV.
RRV (1994) *Den Statliga budgetprocessen och resultatstyrningen*, Stockholm: RRV 1994:32.
RRV (1998) *The Swedish State Budget*, RRV 1998:42.
Rubin, I.S. (2000) *The Politics of Public Budgeting* (4th edition), New York: Chatham House Publishers.
Sahlin-Anderssen, K. (2001) 'National, international and transnational constructions of New Public Management', in T. Christensen and P. Lægried (eds) *New Public Management: the Transformation of Ideas and Practice*, Aldershot: Ashgate, pp. 43–72.
Sandebring, H., Ryne, G. and Tonderski, A. (2000) *Commercialisation of Hydrometeorlogical Services: Analysis of the Process at SMHI*, Unpublished paper, Norrköping.
Savolainen, R. (1999) 'The Finnish system of government and central administration', in J. Selovuori (ed.) *Power and Bureaucracy in Finland, 1809–1998*, Helsinki: Edita, pp. 119–44.
Schama, S. (1996) *Landscape and Memory*, London: Fontana.
Selovuori, J. (ed.) (1999) *Power and Bureaucracy in Finland, 1809–1998*, Helsinki: Edita.
SFS (1987) *Verksfördning*, 1100, Stockholm.
SFS (1995) *Verksfördning*, 1332, Stockholm.
SFS (1996) *Förordning om myndigheters årsedovisning*, 19, Stockholm.
Sint, M. (1994) *Verantwoord verzelfstandigen* (committee report), Den Haag.
Smullen, A. (2004) 'Lost in translation? Shifting interpretations of the concept of "agency": the Dutch case', in C. Pollitt and C. Talbot (eds) *Unbundled Government*, London: Taylor and Francis, pp. 184–202.
Skogsvårdsstyrelsen (1998) *Skogsstyrelsens årsredovisning av Skogsvårdsorganisationens versamhet 1998*, Stockholm, Skogsstyrelsen (Annual report on forest management organization's activities).
Smullen, A.; Van Thiel, S. and Pollitt, C. (2001) 'Agentschappen en de verzelfstandiging paradox', *Beleid, Politiek en Maatschappij*, 28(4) pp. 190–201, ('Agencies and the paradox of autonomy').
Smullen, A. and Van Thiel, S. (2002) 'Agentschappen: eenheid in verscheidenheid', pp. 36–44 in Kraak and Oosteroom (eds) *Agentschappen: innovate in bedrijfsvoering*, Den Haag, Sdu.
Social Insurance Institution, Finland (KELA) Social Insurance Institution, Finland (2000) 'Outcome Orientation in the Development of Management Methods at KELA' *Working Papers No.17* (Helsinki).
SOU 1979:61 *Førnyelse gen omprøvning*.

SOU 1983:39. Politisk styrning – administrativ självständighet.
SOU 1985:40. Regeringen, Myndigheterna och Myndigheternas ledning.
SOU 2000:61 Utvärding och vidareutveckling av budgetprocessen.
SOU 2002:14 Granskning på medborgarnas uppdrag.
State Audit Office (Finland) (2001) *The Adjustment of Personnel in the Prison Administration*, VTV (State Audit Office).
Staatsbosbeheer (2000) *Jaarverslag 1999* (Annual report, 1999), Driebergen, Staatsbosbeheer.
Staatsbosbeheer (2001a) *Staatsbosbeheer: Everything Nature Has to Offer*, (brochure), Driebergen, Staatsbosbeheer.
Staatsbosbeheer (2001b) *Planning and Control in Nature and Woodland Management: A New Approach*, Driebergen, internal Staatsbosbeheer document.
Statskontoret (2002) *Prognos för SMHI – Myndighet, bolag eller både och?*, 2002(3) *Ekonomie-Print AB*, Stockholm.
Summa, H. (1995) 'Old and new techniques for productivity promotion: from cheese-slicing to a quest for quality', in A. Halachmi and G. Bouckaert (eds) *Public Productivity Through Quality and Strategic Management*, Amsterdam: IOS Press, pp. 155–65.
Sundström, G. (2001) *Ett Relativt blygsamt förslag*, Stockholm: SCORE Rapportserie 2001(2).
Sveriges Meteorologiska och Hydrologiska Institut (2000) *Årsredovisning 1999*, Impress, Linköping.
Sveriges Meteorologiska och Hydrologiska Institut (2001) *Årsredovisning 2000*. Abrahamsons Trykeri, Karlskrona.
Swedish Institute (2001) *Forestry and the Forest Products Industry*, Fact Sheet 129, Stockholm: Swedish Institute, November.
Swedish National Audit Office (2000) *Performance Audits of the Legal System 1990–1999*, Stockholm: RRV.
Talbot, C. (1996) *Ministers and Agencies: Control, Performance and Accountability*, London: CIPFA.
Talbot, C. (1996) Ministers and agencies: responsibility and performance, *Second Report – Ministerial Accountability and Responsibility HC313-ii*. Public Service Select Committee. London: HMSO. II (Memoranda of Evidence).
Talbot, C. (1996) 'The Learmont Report – who is responsible for prisons?', *Prison Service Journal*, March, pp. 30–6.
Talbot, C. (1996) 'The Prison Service: a framework of irresponsibility?', *Public Money & Management*, 16(1) pp. 5–7.
Talbot, C. (1997). 'UK Civil Service personnel reforms: devolution, decentralisation and delusion', *Public Policy and Administration*, 12:4, pp. 14–34.
Talbot, C. (1999) 'Public performance – towards a new model?', *Public Policy and Administration*, 14:3, pp. 15–34.
Talbot, C. (2001). 'UK public services and management 1979–2000: evolution or revolution?', *International Journal of Public Sector Management*, 14(4) pp. 281–303.
Talbot, C. (2004) 'Executive agencies: have they improved management in government?', *Public Money & Management*, 24(2) pp. 104–11.
Talbot, C. and Caulfield, J. (eds) (2002) *Hard Agencies in Soft States? A Study of Agency Creation Programmes in Jamaica, Latvia and Tanzania*, a report for the Department for International Development, UK, Pontpridd: University of Glamorgan.

Talbot, C., L. Daunton, et al. (2001) *Measuring Performance of Government Departments – International Developments*, Llantilio Crossenny, Public Futures (for the National Audit Office).

Taliercio, R. (2004) 'The design, performance and sustainability of semi-autonomous revenue authorities in Africa and Latin America', in Pollitt, C. and Talbot, C. (eds) *Unbundled Government*, London: Taylor and Francis, pp. 264–82.

Tarchys, D. (1983) 'Kampen mot Krångel och onödig byråkrati' in I. Ryden (ed.) *Makt och vanmakt: lärdamor av sex borgerliga regeringsår*, SNS, Stockholm.

Thain, C. and M. Wright (1996) *The Treasury and Whitehall – The Planning and Control of Public Expenditure, 1976–1993*. Oxford: Clarendon Press.

Tiihonen, S. (1996) *The Administration of the Summit in Finland* (conference paper).

Timmins, N. (2001) *The Five Giants – A Biography of the Welfare State*, London: HarperCollins.

Treasury and Civil Service Committee (1990) *Eighth Report: Civil Service Management Reform: The Next Steps, Vol. 1 and 2* (HC 494), London: HMSO.

Trosa, S. (1994) *Next Steps: Moving On* (the Trosa Report), London: Cabinet Office, February.

Trosa, S. (1995) *Moderniser l'administration: comment font les autres?*, Paris: Les Editions d'Organisation.

UK MET Office. (2000) *Annual report 1999–2000*, London: UK Met Office.

UK MET Office. (2003) *Annual report 2002–2003*, London: UK Met Office.

United Kingdom, Department of Social Security (2001) 'New Names, New Start: Government Steps Up "High Street" Services', Press Release No. 2001/143.

Vagg, J. (1994) *Prison Systems – A Comparative Study of Accountability in England, France, Germany and The Netherlands*, Oxford: Clarendon Press.

Van der Veen, R. and Trommel, W. (1999) 'Managed liberalization of the Dutch welfare state: a review and analysis of the reform of the Dutch social security system, 1985–1998', *Governance: An International Journal of Policy and Administration*,12(3) July, pp. 289–310.

Van Swaaningen, R. and de Jonge, G. (1995) The Dutch Prison System and Penal Policy in the 1990s: from Humanitarian Paternalism to Penal Business Management', in V. Ruggiero, M. Ryan and J. Sim (eds) *Western European Penal Systems*, London: Sage, pp. 24–45.

Van Thiel, S. (2001) *Quangos: Trends, Causes and Consequences*, Aldershot: Ashgate.

Van Thiel, S. (2004) 'Quangos in Dutch government', in C. Pollitt and C. Talbot (eds) *Unbundled Government*, London: Taylor and Francis, pp. 167–83.

Van Thiel, S. and van Buuren, M. (2001) 'Ontwikkeling van het aantal zelfstandige bestuursorganen tussen 1993 en 2000: zijn ZBO's "uit" de mode?', *Bestuurswetenschappen*, 55:5, pp. 386–404. ('The development of the number of autonomous bodies between 1993 and 2000: are ZBOs out of fashion?').

Vedung, E. (1992) 'Five observations on evaluation in Sweden', in Mayne, J., Hudson, J., Bemelmans-Videc, M. and Conner, R. (eds) *Advancing Public Policy Evaluation: Learning from International Experiences*, Amsterdam: Elsevier.

Verhaak, Frans O.M. (1997) 'Shifting Frames of Reference in Dutch Autonomisation Reforms', in Kickert, W.J.M (ed.) *Public Management and Administration: Reform in Western Europe*, Cheltenham: Edward Elgar.

Vos, E. (2003) Agencies and the European Union', in L.Verhey and T. Zwart (eds) *Agencies in European and Comparative Law*, Intersentia Publishing, pp. 113–47.

Weiss, P. (2002) *Borders in Cyberspace: Conflicting Public Sector Information Policies and their Economic Impacts* (www.aedue.org/aeduedocuments/weiss).
Weller, P., Bakvis, H., et al. (eds) (1997) *The hollow Crown – Countervailling Trends in Core Executives*, Basingstoke: Macmillan.
White, R. (2001) 'The evolving public-private meteorological partnership', *Bulletin of the American Meteorological Society*, vol. 82(7), pp. 1744–37.
Whitley, R. (1988) 'The management sciences and management skills', *Organization Studies*, 9(1) pp. 47–68.
Whitley, R. (1989) 'On the nature of managerial tasks and skills: their distinguishing characteristics and organization', *Journal of Management Studies*, 26(3) pp. 209–24.
Wildavsky, A. (1992) *The New Politics of the Budgetary Process* (2nd edition), New York: Harper Collins.
Wilks, S. (1996) 'Sweden' in N. Flynn and F. Strehl (eds) *Public Sector Management in Europe*, Hertfordshire: Prentice Hall, pp. 23–49.
Wilks, S. (1995) 'Reform of the national budget process in Sweden', *International Journal of Public Sector Management*, 8(2) pp. 33–43.
Wilson, J.Q. (1989) *Bureaucracy: What Government Agencies do and Why they do it*, New York: Basic Books.
Wilson, J.Q. (1994) 'Can the bureaucracy be deregulated? Lessons from government agencies', in J. DiIulio (ed.) *Deregulating the Public Service: can Government be Improved?*, Washington, DC: The Brookings Institution, pp. 37–61.
WMO. (1989) *Technical Regulations: General Meteorological Standards and Recommended Practices*. WMO report no. 49 vol. 1, Geneva.
WMO. (1989) 'Quality control' In *Guide on the Global Observing System*, WMO report no. 488, Geneva.
WMO. (1996) *Exchanging Meteorological Data. Guidelines on Relationships in Commercial Meteorological Activities*, WMO report no. 837, Geneva.
WMO. (1999) *Guide to Public Weather Services Practices*, WMO report no. 834, Geneva.
Yamamoto, K. (2004) 'Agencification in Japan: renaming, or revolution?', in Pollitt, C. and Talbot, C. (eds) *Unbundled Government*, London: Taylor and Francis, pp. 215–26.

Index

Aaltonen, Esko 125
ABD (*Algemene Bestuursdienst*) 66
Abma, T. 25
abuses of power 83
accountability 39, 65, 68, 71, 130, 236
  civil service 100
  compromised 4
  formally imposed 37
  implied 229
  individual 8, 101
  insufficient 22
  more clear requirements badly needed 60
  new public management principles to enhance 221
  no basis for enforcement 89
  strengthening mechanisms of 229
  see also public accountability
accounting 16, 167
  'businesslike' techniques 165
  see also accruals accounting
accreditation systems 166
accruals accounting 53, 69, 71, 87, 94, 110
  proposal to extend to ministries 73
adaptation 17
Administrative Act (Sweden 1987) 94
Administrative Development Agencies
  Finland 55
  Sweden 164
'administrative DNA' 33–4, 35, 38
administrative systems 43, 52–4, 66–7, 81–4, 102–4
adversarial systems 98, 101
advisory councils/boards 63, 160
Afghanistan 152
agencification 3, 4, 12, 21, 32, 34, 71
  commitment to 73
  financial and accounting flexibilities 76

foundation for programme 69
ideal type of 41
increasingly cumbersome regulations 74
reality and success 43
recent international wave 13
agency theories 12–18
agentschappen 10, 22, 71, 73, 165, 219, 226
Agriculture and Forestry Ministry (Finland) 59, 185, 187, 189–90, 201, 202–3, 211, 212
Agriculture Ministry (Sweden) 193
Agriculture, Nature Management and Fisheries Ministry (Netherlands) *see* LNV
Aho, Esko 56
Algemene Rekenkamer 22, 69, 74, 167
amalgamations 68, 69
AMS (Swedish National Labour Market Board) 92, 218, 219, 224, 240
  classic tripartite governance structure 225
  computer-based placement system 235
  County Labour Boards and 223, 225, 227, 232, 235
  Employment Service 232, 234, 238
  performance reports 241
  public/private nature 232
  reformed 229
  salaries 236
  Unemployment Insurance Division 223, 232, 233, 239
Amsterdam 187
Anglophone/Anglo-Saxon biases 12
annual reports 87, 92–3, 154, 180, 187, 196, 199, 201–2, 202, 206
anti-competitive practices 162–3
Anton, T. 81
Araŭjo, J. 21
Arctic 159, 186

Aristotle 147
armies 9
arms-length bodies 7, 36, 219
Armstrong, Sir Robert 100, 104
AssiDomän 191, 193
Aucoin, P. 22
audit 140, 144, 167, 180, 202, 235–6
Australia 64, 126, 128
Australian Meteorological Institute 148
autonomization 34, 37–8, 75, 77, 109–11
 elaborate conditions for 73
 external 73
 high, hard to sustain 217
 management 88
 proposals for 69
 reforms 219, 228
 substantial 219
autonomy 9, 10, 23, 24–5, 32, 77, 219, 220, 226, 228
 challenge to 229
 considerable 66
 constitutional 221
 financial 16, 73–4
 high level of 218
 implied 36
 local prisons management 129
 managerial 19, 37, 60, 61, 76, 94–5, 109, 110, 111
 operational 78
 organizational 188
 parliament-based 223
 policy 41
 statute defining 71
 substantial, fought for and won 31
 theoretical 22
aviation sector 159, 164, 166, 169, 175

'badge engineering' 107
'balanced scorecard' tool 232, 233
Balkende, Jan Peter 63, 77
Balogh, Thomas 102
Bardach, E. 23
benchmarking 232
Benefits Agency (UK) 217, 218, 219, 220, 230, 233
 annual spend 222

area directorates 227
critique of formulation of some targets 234
HR management information system 236
non-financial performance data routinely furnished by 231
performance targets 229
planning process 237–8
portrayed as a 'one stop shop' 224
responsibility 223–4, 225
semi-autonomy 225
unique management structure 225–6
 see also Jobcentre Plus
Benn, Tony 101
Beveridge reforms 98
Bichard, Michael 108
biodiversity 186, 192, 198
Blair, Tony 183
block grants 132
Blondell, J. 91
Bolderson, H. 224
'Boss' (business control system) 167–8
Boston, J. 15
Bouckaert, G. 7, 49, 52, 83, 87
Boyne, G. 14
Bradshaw, J. 220
Britain *see* United Kingdom
British Civil Service 6, 32, 34–5, 38, 99, 101–2
 exposed to sustained criticism 104
 no formal constitutional or legal basis 100
 numbers drastically reduced 105
 personnel practices 110
 reforms 68, 105
 security of tenure 103
 see also Parliamentary Treasury and Civil Service Committee
British Empire 126
Broadmoor 129
Brunsson, K. 86, 87, 88, 92
budgets/budgeting 139–40, 222
 accrual system 70
 annual allocation 9
 automatism in 84, 86

budgets/budgeting – *continued*
  carry-over from one year to the next 110
  combined operational and programme 222
  convenient instrument of political control 86
  cuts 221
  'frame' 94
  in-year variations 132
  performance 70
  reforms 86, 87, 88, 91
  results-oriented 55, 60, 62
  running costs 55, 233
  targets formalized in 177
'bureau shaping' model 220, 261, 262, 263–5
bureaucracy 30–1, 34, 61
  career 103
  deregulation of 38
  inefficient 64
  political control of 86
  troublesome and unnecessary 84

Cabinet Office (UK) 68, 103, 112
calculation 250
Canada 7, 10, 22, 33
  prisons 126, 132, 139
capital accounting 110
'captures' 4
Carter, N. 258
Caulfield, J. 20
centralization 50, 61, 97, 104, 110, 219
  resisted 63
Centre Party (Finland) 50
certification 200–1, 202
Charter Mark system 113
Child Support Agency (UK) 111, 113
Christian Democrats
  Netherlands 63, 65
  Sweden 80
Christiansen, P. 253
Civil Aviation Service/Authority (Sweden) 83, 170
civil servants
  agency employees have same legal status as 77
  educational background of 83
  grades unique to organization or functions 108
  highest/top 66, 68, 102
  percentage working in agencies 76
  rational self-interest of 18
  see also senior civil servants
civil service 53, 83–4
  distinction between public service and 82
  general reforms 77
  massaging numbers 20
  trust in 65
  see also British Civil Service
'clan culture' 104
coalitions 49, 51, 65, 77, 99, 124
  centre-left 63
  centre-right 63, 68
  'purple' (left-right) 63
  reforming 50
coercive isomorphism 33
collaboration 151, 153
  international 149
collective bargaining 94
collective responsibility 8
collective rule 82
collectivism-individualism 27, 51–2, 64
commercial activities
  forestry 189
  meteorology 149, 150, 155, 161–6, 170, 174–5, 176
Commission on the History of Central Administration (Finland) 58
commission system 84
common law 7, 184
Communist Party (Finland) 50
compensation 207
competition 105, 153
  national authorities 151
  rise in, for commercial contracts 149
  unfair, cross-subsidized 211
  viable 150
competitive bidding 132
computer troubles 235
consensual approach 50, 51, 54, 61, 63, 66, 80, 81, 98

Index 289

consensual approach – *continued*
  extreme ideologies not dominant in 68
  individual accountability 101
Conservatives
  Finland 50
  Sweden 63, 80
  UK 97, 98, 99, 103, 124, 136, 159, 219–20
Considine, M. 220
consociational system 63
Constitution Act (Finland 1919) 49
constitutional monarchy 80, 99
Constitutions
  British 99–100
  Finnish 49, 60
  Swedish 37, 80, 82, 83, 85, 86, 89, 91
consultancy 53, 55
consultative councils 63
contracting-out process 132–3
contracts 23–4, 40
  absence of the term 91
  internal 171
  management 233
  one-sided 40
  performance 24
  set of principles for designing 14
contractual
  relationships/arrangements 10, 32, 39–40, 42,
  most difficult tasks to handle through 24
contractualization 34, 39–41
Contributions Agency (UK) 100
cooperation 142
'core departments' 73
corporatism 63, 64, 204, 219, 223
  classic 221
Corrections Canada 132, 139
corruption 38
Council of Europe 125
County Labour Boards (Sweden) 223, 224, 225, 227, 232, 235
Cowper, Jeremy 108
creative activity 73
cronies 4
cross-subsidization 73, 168, 196, 211

Crown Prerogative 100
CSA (Finnish Criminal Sanctions Agency) 117, 131, 143, 146
CTSV (Dutch Social Security Supervision Board) 217, 226, 270
cultures 16
  administrative 25, 28, 81, 184
  bureaucratic 61
  'gifted amateurism' and generalism 104
  institutional 27
  national 155, 184, 210
  organizational 135, 144
  performance indicator 76
  political 61, 64, 101
  politico-administrative 50–2, 54, 80–1, 101–2, 210
  service 86
Curran, B. 148, 149
Custodial Clinics 129
customer focus 170
Customs & Excise *see* HM Customs & Excise
cutbacks/cuts 6, 69, 73
  and decentralisation 70
Czechoslovakia 125

Day, P. 258
death penalty 119
De Boer, E. 66
decentralization 50, 54, 55, 56, 61, 85, 129, 217, 219, 223
  extensive 81
  fashionable format for 69
  high level of 238
  implementation of 70
  legislated 220
  unitary 63, 80
decision-making 34, 54, 67–8, 104–5
  collective 64, 80
  developing feedback loops to 231
  discretionary 38
  extensive and objective information in 81
  municipal 55
  political 57, 90
  priorities of work in NMIs 155

decision-making – *continued*
  shift from political sphere to bureaucracy 84
  substantiated 142
defence 159, 169
Defence Meteorological Board (UK) 178
Defence Ministry (Finland) 193
delegated authority 77
democracy 211
  arguments about 84
  consensual 204
'democratic deficit' 89
Den Haag 73, 76, 119, 187
Denmark 125, 127
Department of Work and Pensions (UK) 219
deregulation 94
Derksen, W. 70
developing countries 14, 20, 38
devolved management 229
DiIulio, J. J. 129
dilettantism 102
DiMaggio, P. 20
disabled people 95
disaggregation 8, 10, 32, 34–7, 38, 205, 217
  structural 60, 61, 76, 88, 89–90
discretion 10, 24, 26, 34, 42, 77
  management 95
  tremendous scope for 38
  unofficial 38
dissagregation 107
distributed public governance 7
dividends 160
divorce 36–7
DJI (Dutch National Agency for Correctional Institutions) 118, 129, 133–5, 136
  objectives 136
doctoral degrees 154
doctrines 33–4, 41
  government-wide 73
  most fundamental building blocks 42
Doumer, S. 14
downsizing 20, 56, 175
  large scale 76
DS 88, 91, 94

DSS (UK Department of Social Security) 107, 220, 222, 230, 240
  see also Department of Work and Pensions
'dual system' 64
Duchy of Lancaster 6
Dunleavy, P. 14, 255, 256, 257, 264
'Dutch disease' 219
'Dutch economic miracle' 69
Dutch Employers Council 165–6

ECMWF (European Centre for Medium Range Forecasting) 157
ECOMET (economic interest group) 150, 151, 161
economic approaches 13, 16
economic crisis 54
education 98, 137, 138, 139
  high trust ratings to 64
Eduskunta (Finnish legislature) 50
effectiveness 17, 20, 69, 84, 231
  cost 228
efficiency 16, 18, 19, 169, 231
  annual reports 236
  drive for 68
  driving up 109
  enhanced 23, 221
  focus on 228
  greater concern with 69
  greater measurable 74
  improvements in 14
  improving 105
  increased 20, 75, 132
  maximized 198
  search for 17
efficiency gains 70
'efficiency scrutinies' 105
EFI (European Forest Institute) 187
egalitarianism 81, 101
elections 63
Electricity Grid (Sweden) 83
elites 81
embeddedness 15, 262–3
empirical evidence 19–24
employer organizations/associations 73, 219, 225
employment insurance 223
employment opportunities 98

employment policies 94, 95
Employment Service (UK) 217
endangered species 207
Enforcement of Sentences Administration Act (Finland 2001) 131
England 191, 192, 193
 Forestry Commission relations with ministries 213
England and Wales 126
Enschede 65
enterprise management 217
Environment Ministries
 Finland 190, 198, 199
 Netherlands 66, 177
 Sweden 164
environmental differences 184
equality
 'before the law' 83
 gender 93, 95
 high levels of 221
equity losses 14
Estonia 187
ESV (Swedish Financial Management Authority) 80, 93
établissements publiques (France) 8–9, 10, 11
ethnic diversity 122
ethnic minority staff 137
EU (European Union) 49, 53, 157, 161
 Commission, 'externalisation' of tasks 6, 7
 Common Agricultural Policy 187
 directives 150
 newsprint exports from Sweden 186
 regulations 162
 upheavals caused by entry into 221
EUROPAIR Research Project 247, 252, 256, 260, 262, 267–9
European Meteorological Institutes 150
European Meteosat 149
evaluation 56, 57, 74–5, 76, 77
 continuous 142
exceptionalism 247, 260, 262
expertise 20, 21, 90

FCC (Finnish Competition Council) 162–3
Federation of Finnish Forest Industries 191
Finance Ministries 178
 Finland 52, 53, 54, 56, 57, 60, 62, 143, 144, 171, 225, 237, 240
 Netherlands 70, 71, 73, 74, 77, 165, 209–10
 Sweden 84, 87, 93, 138–40, 159, 209, 225
financial control procedures 74
financial freedom 71, 87
financial reporting 87, 93
Finland 4, 7, 8, 49–62, 64, 77
 agency reforms (1994–96) 76
 career civil service 83
 forestry 59, 184, 185, 186, 189–91, 194, 197, 202, 208; *see also* METLA; *Metsähallitus*
 individualism 101
 meteorology 147, 168, 176; *see also* FMI
 power-distance index 101
 prisons 119, 120, 121, 122, 124–5, 126, 127, 128, 129, 140–4; *see also* CSA
 public employment figures 66
 reforming pre-existing agencies 31
 results-oriented management 69
 role differences 49
 social security 217, 220, 222, 225, 238; *see also* KELA
First World War 152, 160
fiscal positions 13–14, 69
Fish, Michael 179
'Five Giants' 98
flexibility 32, 93, 162, 208
 employment policy 94
 'end year' 110
 enhancing 20
Flynn, N. 25
FMI (Finnish Meteorological Institute) 154, 157, 159, 166, 171, 178, 181
 commercial activities 161, 162–3
 law describing tasks of 160
 performance indicators 178
FMI (UK Financial Management Initiative) 105, 106

Fogden, Mike 108
FORECA 162, 163
Forest Enterprise (UK) 186, 189, 191, 192, 193, 195, 197, 202, 205, 209
  certification 201
  Forest Holidays 196
  objectives 199–200
  performance data 213
Forest Research (UK) 192, 193, 196-7
forestry 8, 90, 183–215
Forestry Commission (UK) 192, 193, 194, 196, 197
  main targets 206
  regulation 203
  relations with ministries 213
  standard promulgated by 201–2
  strong forestry ethic 212–13
Fortuyn, Pim 63, 65
Fowler Reviews of Social Security (UK 1985) 219–20
frame budget 94
France 8–9, 10, 11, 101
'Fraser figure' reporting 177
fraud 65, 233
Freebairn, J. W. 148, 150
Friends of the Earth 187–8
Frisching, A. de 119, 129
FSC (Forest Stewardship Council) 200–1, 202
Fulton Committee (UK 1968) 32

Gaebler, T. 19
Gains, F. 21–2, 23
gedogen 66
gender 92, 95, 221
geographical differences 186
Germany 6, 10, 50, 221
global economic upheavals 14
goal-orientation 74, 75
Goffman, Erving 5, 118
golden eagles 206–7
good practice 21
Gothenburg 131
governance arrangements 112, 224–7, 228
governing boards 68, 90
government 126
gradualism 61

Granovetter, M. 15, 255
Great Depression (1930s) 97
'Great Efficiency Operation' (Netherlands 1990) 69
'Green Book' reports 143
Greenpeace 187–8, 198
Groningen revolt (1971) 119
Groupes d'interets publiques (France) 8
Gunasekera, D. 148, 149

Hadley Centre for Climate Prediction and Research 159
Hajlmarsson, A. 93
Hameenlinna penitentiary 125
Hänninen, H. 191
Harden, I. 36
health care/services 64, 98
Heidenheimer, A. J. 222
Hennessy, P. 102, 106
hierarchy 8, 13, 38, 39, 101
  avoided 81
HIRLAM (High Resolution Limited Area Model) 157
HM Customs & Excise (UK) 31, 41, 100, 106, 112
HM Treasury (UK) 102, 103, 106, 112, 196, 209
  enormous power exercised by 111
  new approach to controlling ministries spending 109
  Public Service Agreements between departments and 237
  relations with forestry bodies 213
  tight control from 110
  see also Parliamentary Treasury and Civil Service Committee
HMPS (HM Prison Service, UK) 118, 126, 128, 131, 132, 133, 135, 136, 137, 138
  current objectives 136
  performance indicators 135, 136
Hofstede, G. 25, 27, 29, 49, 51, 64, 81, 101
Hogwood, B. 15, 21, 23
Holkeri, Harri 55
Holkeri, K. 52
Home Office (UK) 126
  Immigration and Nationality Department 106, 107

Index 293

Home Office (UK) – *continued*
  prisons a sub-department within 129
  re-offending a 'policy' matter for 138
homogeneity 23, 81
Hong Kong 32
Hood, C. 25, 33, 34, 38, 41
House of Commons/House of Lords (UK) 99
housing 98
Howard, John 65, 117, 125
Howard, Michael 124, 136
HRM (Human Resource Management) 56, 70
human rights 141
HWS (Holland Weather Services) 161, 164
'hybrid' organizations 15
hydrology 157, 175
hypotheses testing 13, 15

IACs (Japanese Independent Administrative Corporations) 10, 22
ICTs (Information and Communication Technologies) 25, 26
ideal-type agencies 30–46
ideologies 68
implementation process 57, 58
  decentralization 70
  successful, informal contacts instrumental to 90
improvement ethic 17
incentives 14–15, 175, 220
  economic 24
  financial 219
  performance 239
'independence principle' 82, 89
indicators
  economic 167–8, 169, 208
  efficiency 169
  quality 76, 170
  see also performance indicators
individual freedom 64
individualism 81, 101
  collectivism and 27, 51–2, 64
individuality 142

Industry, Employment and Education Ministry (Sweden) 160, 191, 193, 212
Industry, Trade and Commerce Department (Sweden) 225
inequality 27, 40, 51
informational asymmetries 40, 257
  acute 179
Inland Revenue (UK) 31, 41, 100, 106
'insider' process 53
institutionalism 248, 249
  historical 13
institutionalization 177
integral management 68
interaction 142
interest groups 142, 150
Interior Ministry (Finland) 52, 54
internal markets 39
International Meteorological Organisation 148
internet 149
interpretive theories 13, 16–18
in 't Veld, R. 63, 64, 66
IRA prisoners 119
Iraq 152
'islands of excellence' 20
ISO approaches 53, 166, 200, 201
IT projects 235
Italy 10, 50, 101

Jäätteenmäki, Anneli 50
Jackson, M. 33, 34, 38, 41
Jamaica 3, 7, 31
James, O. 14, 19, 23, 237, 252, 254, 255, 257, 258, 264–5
Japan 3, 7, 8, 22, 162, 164
  agency-type reforms 33
  IACs 10, 22
Jobcentre Plus (UK) 217, 219, 224, 270
Joensuu 187
joint stock companies 55, 58, 59
joint ventures 161
Joustie, H. 60
Juslin, H. 200, 201
justice 141
Justice Ministries
  Finland 131

Justice Ministries – *continued*
  Netherlands 129, 134
  Sweden 94, 95, 130–1
Juvenile Institutions 129

Kärnä, J. 200, 201
KELA (Finnish Social Security Institute) 217, 218, 221, 225, 229, 231, 234, 242
  annual volume of statistics 235–6
  contractual/partnership arrangement with local authorities 227
  dedicated funding 237
  high autonomy 240
  parliament-based autonomy 223
  performance agreements first introduced into 232
  Quality Programme 232
  spending 222
  unique status 228
  wide functional responsibilities 223
Kemp, (Sir) Peter 39, 40, 112
Keynesian economic policies 103
Kickert, W. 15, 22, 63, 64, 66, 68, 69, 73, 75
Kingsbury, S. 147
Kiviniemi, M. 52
Klein, R. 258
KNMI (Royal Dutch meteorological office) 73, 156, 159, 178, 181
  board 161
  commercial activities 161, 165, 166
  performance measures 167, 172, 176–7, 177–8
  public tasks 160, 164
  research and quality of production 174
Korea 7
Korsten, A. 70
KPIs (UK Key Performance Indicators) 106, 111–12, 113, 135–8, 141
Kraak, A. 74
KVV (Swedish Prison and Probation Service) 118, 123, 130, 131, 140
  performance targets 138–9

Labour party/government (UK) 97–8, 136, 224
Lane, J.-E. 14, 19, 24
Larsson, T. 79, 80, 82, 90
Latvia 22, 31, 42
legal differences 184
legislatures 21
  unicameral 50, 80
legitimacy 20, 57
  search for 17
leisure centres 9
Lewis, Derek 18, 21, 130, 131, 135, 136, 137, 138
Liberal Democrats (UK) 98
liberalist economic doctrine 221
Liberals
  Netherlands 63
  Sweden 80
  UK 97
Lipponen, Paavo 54, 55
Lloyd George, David 101
LNV (Dutch Agriculture, Nature Management and Fisheries Ministry 191, 193, 194, 196, 203
local authorities 103, 220
  contractual/partnership arrangement with 227
Local Employment Services Committees (Sweden) 225
logic 250, 251
  deductive 13
Loughlin, J. 83
loyalty 27, 51
LPF party (Netherlands) 63
Lubbers, Ruud 68, 69, 74
Luce, Richard 34–5
Lundell, B. 83

Mabbett, D. 224
MABs (More Autonomous Bodies) 9, 10, 24, 106, 194, 253
majoritarian systems 97, 98
'managed liberalisation' 217
management practices 75
management reforms 52, 53, 54, 55, 62, 67–70, 104–6
  hardly ever discussed 68
management strategy 24, 25, 58
March, James 248, 249–50, 251

Index

'market strategies' 85
media 159
  communications 149, 163
  contracts 164, 176
  intense questioning by 179
  mass 101
Meteoconsult 164, 165
meteorology 82, 90, 147–82
  see also NMIs
METLA (Finnish Forest Research Institute) 189, 190, 193, 196, 197
Metsähallitus (Finnish Forest and Park Service) 8, 187, 190, 191, 192–3, 195, 197, 199, 203, 208, 211, 261
  encouraged to make profits 213
  environmental goals 198
  Natural Heritage division 199, 205, 206–7
  PEFC 201
  trust between ministry and 210
micromanagement 22
mimetic isomorphism 20, 33
ministerial responsibility 64
Ministry of Agriculture, Fisheries and Food (UK) 192
Ministry of Defence (UK) 160, 161, 169
'mission' 23
mobile telephones 149, 162, 163
modernization 20
Molander, P. 14, 22, 89, 91
monocratic arrangements 56
monopoly 22
MPs (Members of Parliament) 15, 211
MTMs (market-type-mechanisms) 39, 69, 105
multinational companies 162, 164
multi-party systems 63
Muncie, J. 117
municipalities
  Finland 52, 54, 55, 58, 59
  Netherlands 67, 70

Napoleonic Code countries 7, 184
National Audit Offices 180
  Finland *see* VTV
  Netherlands *see* Algemene Rekenkamer
  Sweden *see* RRV
  UK 21, 234, 235
national boards 52, 58, 59, 61, 76
'national characteristics' 184
National Coalition (Finland) 50
national health 223
National Health Service (UK) 103, 129
National Institute for Economic Research (Sweden) 93
national insurance 98
national parks 198
National Property Board (Finland) 191
national sovereignty 57
'national treasures' 101
National Weights and Measures Laboratory (UK) 41
Nationale Spoorweg 8
Nebeker, F. 152, 153–4
'neo-institutionalist' school 17
Netherlands 3, 4, 7, 8, 19, 36, 61, 63–78
  agency formation 39
  agency-type reforms 33
  civil service 6
  financially orientated reform 86
  forestry 184, 185, 186–7, 198, 200, 209–10, 211; *see also* LNV
  individualism 101
  meteorology 147, 148, 157; *see also* KNMI
  moderately autonomous organizations 31
  power-distance index 101
  prisons 120, 121, 122, 124, 125, 126, 127, 128; *see also* DJI; VDPI
  quangos 21
  railway service 8
  role differences 50
  social security 217, 223, 224, 228, 230; *see also* CTSV; SVB; SVR
  see also under agentschappen; VBTB; ZBOs
New Deal 31
New Labour governments (UK) 97

New Zealand 4, 7, 13, 19, 39
  anti-government attitudes 64
  Crown Entities 6, 9
  implementation process 57
  organizations with extensive
      autonomy 31
Next Steps programme (UK) 10,
    14, 37, 39, 40, 58, 107, 108,
    208–9
  autonomy 77
  general accounts of 106
  inception of 105, 109
  largest of the agencies 219
  one of the first experiments 219
  one of the most prominent
      features 111
  percentage of civil servants in
      agencies 76
  prison service a quasi-autonomous
      agency under 130
NGOs (non-governmental
    organizations) 187, 194
  international 201
NIE (New Institutional Economics)
    13, 18, 39
NMCs (National Meteorological
    Centres) 157
NMIs (National Meteorological
    Institutes) 147–8, 156, 259
  basic tasks 157
  classified as craft
      organizations 154
  collaboration between 153
  commercial activities 149, 150,
    151, 155, 161
  decision-making priorities of work
      in 155
  dependency on non-government
      sources of funding 150
  infrastructure expense 153
  legal status 160
  main customers of 159
  organizational status 151
  overseeing performance of 154
  shared characteristics among 180
  tasks closely associated with
      national security 152
  see also FMI; KNMI; SMHI;
      UK MET

Nobel Denton 162
Noordegraaf, M. 25
Nordic public enterprises 10
normality 141
  search for 17
norms 6, 15
  alternative 17
  collective 28
  cultural 51, 265
  historically embedded 17
  local 16, 17
  organizational 27
  scientific 151
Northern Ireland 99, 126
North, Douglass 255
Norway 125, 127
NPM (New Public Management)
    philosophies 14, 149, 204
Numerical Weather Prediction
    Models 157
  see also NWPI
Nuurmi, J. 52
NWPI (Numerical Weather Prediction
    Index) 169, 172

ocean and defence stations 169
oceanography 157, 175
Oceanroutes 162
OECD (Organization for Economic
    Cooperation and Development)
    19, 60, 66, 253
  Distributed Public Governance (2002)
      3, 6, 30, 35, 37, 39, 92, 240
  Public Sector Modernization (2003)
      3, 4, 7
offending behaviour programmes
    136–7, 138
Office of Public Services Reform
    (UK) 22
old-aged pensions 219
Olsen, Johan 248, 249–50, 251
'Operational Strategy' (UK) 235
ordinances 89, 90, 92, 94–5
organization theory 13
organizational change 18, 68, 175
organizational structures 24
Osborne, D. 19
Ouchi, William 104
overheads 109

Parliament Act (Finland 1928) 49
Parliamentary Treasury and Civil
    Service Committee (UK) 37, 39,
    40, 112
Passport Agency (UK) 113
path dependency 21–2, 61
    see also TSPD
patterns of institutions 126–31,
    156–66, 189–94, 221–7
PDI (power-distance index) 27–8,
    51, 101
Peeperkorn, M. 66
peer oversight 154
PEFC (Pan-European Forest
    Certification) 201
penal policy 123, 124
Pension Insurance Act (Finland
    1956) 218
Pension Service agency (UK) 224
performance 32, 39, 90, 133–41, 160
    budgeting 70
    financial 92, 189
    follow-up of 93
    holding managers to account
        for 19
    important element in
        contractualization 40
    monitoring 161
    perceptions 17–18
    poor/bad 113, 178, 179
    rewards for 87, 113
    see also following entries prefixed
    'performance'
performance-based organization'
    initiative 43
performance contracting 76, 77, 88,
    91–3, 111–13, 225
performance indicators 60, 75, 76,
    78, 177, 204–5, 233
    defining 231
    different challenges to designers
        of 203
    final decisions about 178
    financial 171
    key 209
    most important 174, 207–8
    now commonplace 257–8
    seldom used to clarify major value
        trade-offs 261–2

top-down pressure for 230
very detailed list of 232
who makes most out of 180,
    211–13
see also KPIs
performance management 57,
    166–72, 185, 198, 202,
    204–1, 233
    fully fledged 257–8
    generic techniques, international
        dissemination of 233
    implementing 227–41
    introduction into agencies 228
performance measurement 68, 70,
    143, 148, 151, 153, 161, 167, 169,
    170, 172, 231–3
    accessibility 168
    collecting and publishing 166
    customer focused 175
    determining 177, 178
    greater emphasis on 217
    mainstreaming 236–8
    non-financial 76
    satisfaction with 176
performance-related pay 56, 62,
    169, 236
performance reporting 21, 40–1, 42,
    177, 235–6
performance targets 60, 138–9,
    178–9, 229, 233–5
    contradictory nature of 234
    environmentally prudent approach
        to forestry 198
    how set 177, 206, 209
    key 233
Peters, B. G. 83
Peters, G. B. 7
PFI (Private Finance Initiative) 132–3
Pierre, J. 3, 15, 79, 81, 83, 90
Pierson, P. 255, 256, 259
Plant Production Inspection Centre
    (Finland) 59
Poland 125
Polders model 66
policy
    changing 123–6
    forestry 185
    official rhetoric 44
    split between operations and 41

policy – *continued*
  state agencies responsible for
    administration of 81
  'welfare-to-work' 224
policymaking 64, 80, 81
  successful, informal contacts
    instrumental to 90
  split between policy
    implementation and 41
political control 86, 91
political interference 68
  lessening 19, 21
  prevention of 217
  protecting administrative agencies
    from 83
political steerability 20
politicisation 221
politico-demographic patterns 97
politics
  'primacy of' 70, 71
  relationship between
    administration and 102
  role of review in 80
Poll Tax (UK) 105
Pollitt, C. 6, 9, 15, 22, 83, 87, 184,
    249, 265
Portugal 3
Postbank 68
postmodernist variants 13
'post-War consensus' 98
Powell, W. 20
Premfors, R. 83, 85, 87, 217
Prince, M. 15, 21
principal-agent theory 14, 39, 40,
    138, 224, 225
principles 141–2
Prison Commissioners (UK) 129
prison riots 118, 119, 124, 131
prisoner escapes 118, 119,
    137, 139
  high profile 113, 138
prisons 41, 43, 111, 117–46
  autonomy in running 25
  overcrowding and
    under-funding 108
  privately run 9, 132
privatization 68, 69, 83, 105
  belief in 220
  largely disappeared from UK 197

  no great enthusiasm for 56
  via local government 221
probation 123, 126, 127–8, 130, 131,
    141, 142
procedural rules 26
professionalism 142, 147
profitability 198
Progressive Liberal Party
    (Netherlands) 63
proportional representation 63, 80
prosperity 221
provinces 67, 70
PSPE data analysis 66
public accountability 40, 41, 70, 231
  lack of 74
public expenditure 68
  implications for 221
Public Health and Environment
    Ministry (Netherlands) 66
'public interest perspective' 19
public opinion 64
Public Service Agreements 240
PUMA (European Group for Public
    Administration) 53
punishment 119, 123, 127, 128
  strong ideological bias against 204
Puoskari, P. 54
purchasing and providing 41

quality indicators 170
  frequently lacking 76
quality measures 228, 232
quangos (quasi-autonomous
    non-governmental organisations)
    8, 21
  intermediary forms of 31
quasi-contractual
  relationships/arrangements 10,
    32, 39, 41, 42, 77
quasi-markets 219

railways 59
rampant capitalism 149, 197
Rampton 129
rational choice theories 13–15, 18,
    23–4, 256, 257
rationalization 226–7
'Rayner Scrutinies' 105, 106
Reagan, Ronald 53, 65

'Reaganomics' 68
re-aggregation 61
reality 16, 43
reasonableness 141
recession 220
rechsstaat 68, 83
recidivism 138, 139, 141
  heavily influenced by family
    circumstances 143–4
recreation 189, 197, 200, 205
'red tape' 38
reforms 21, 30, 31, 32–3, 58, 61, 79, 94, 236
  administrative 52, 68
  agency-type 39
  agentschap 165
  autonomization 219, 228
  budgetary 86, 87, 88, 91
  civil service 77, 105
  commitment to 85
  contemporary 45
  decentralization 220
  disaggregatory 38
  efficiency, market-like 229
  ethical standards in 65–6
  HRM 56
  impact on central apparatus 43
  justified 42
  potential trajectories of 85
  programme of evaluations of 57
  questioning of 74
  slow process in introducing 84
  social security 217, 218, 219
  structural 229
  welfare policy 98
  see also management reforms
Regional Forestry Centres (Finland) 192, 194
regionalization and rationalization 226–7
regulations 38, 94, 160, 203
  bending of rules and 66
  EU 161, 162
  increasingly cumbersome 74
  tightening of rules and 219
rehabilitation 119, 120, 123, 127, 128, 136
  costs for 139
  downplayed 124

drug 135
success of 138
reindeer 207
remand prisons 139
Renewal Programme (Sweden 1985) 85, 87
rents 98
re-offending 136, 138
research and development 6, 52, 56
resettlement 137, 138
resources 36, 37, 40
responsiveness 14, 85
results-oriented management 69, 208, 228
Reunala, A. 183
'reversal of control' 22
Rietveld (Dutch parliament) 133
Riksdag (Sweden) 80, 82
road traffic authorities 159
ROCE (Return on Capital Employed) 169
role differences 49–50
Rossby Centre 159
Rotterdam 187
Royal Mints
  British 112
  Dutch 69
RRV (Swedish National Audit Office) 86, 91, 92, 140, 232, 241
rule and rote 34
running costs 55, 109, 110, 150, 233
  privately managed prisons 132
Russia 187

salaries 94
Savolainen, R. 58
scandals 50, 68
Schama, S. 183
Schreuder, H. 14
Scotland 185, 186, 192, 213
  legal system and prison service 126
  Parliament 99, 193
Second World War 31, 97, 98, 152, 160
sectoralization 68
self-evaluations 232
self-interest 18, 103
Selovuori, J. 54, 58

senior civil servants   14, 15, 21
  enabled to avoid responsibility   20
  long-term participation of   54
  mainly lawyers   53
separation   36, 37, 41, 42, 107–8
  agency-type changes and   42
  greater formalization of   89
  structural   10, 19, 90
Service Charters (Finland)   56
service delivery   41
Service Delivery Agreement (UK)   233
SFS   89, 92, 94
sickness and disability payments   219
Sint, M.   73
Slavic prison/criminal policy   126
SMHI (Swedish Meteorological
    Institute)   82, 148, 158, 159,
    171, 172, 181
  accuracy of prediction   173
  administrative independence   160
  commercial activities   161, 163, 164
  customer focus   170
  good reputation   156
  important organizational
      changes   175
  office in Finland to increase market
      share   162
  performance measures   167–8, 169,
    170, 174, 177, 179
  structural changes   175, 176
  target levels   168, 178
  turnover figures   170
  uniqueness   157
SOAs (Canadian Special Operating
    Agencies)   10, 22
Social Affairs and Health Ministry
    (Finland)   217, 240
Social Affairs and Unemployment
    Ministry (Netherlands)   226
Social and Cultural Planning Bureau
    (Netherlands)   65
social constructivist theories   13,
    16–18, 28
Social Democrats
  Finland   50
  Netherlands   63, 65
  Sweden   80, 83–4, 85, 123
Social Insurance Institute (Finland)
    223, 238

social justice   221
social partners   219
'social planning'   83
social science approaches   13, 16,
    18, 28
social security   25, 74, 90,
    216–42
  high trust ratings to   64
socialization   51
SOPs (Standard Operating
    Procedures)   26
SOU   80, 83, 85, 91
Soviet Union (former)   125, 221
SPAR (staff planning and resourcing)
    accounting system   135–6
Sparks, R.   117
Special Hospitals   129
specialists   4
specialization   20, 34, 35, 41
  functional   218, 221
Spruce Bark Beetle   188
Staatsbosbeheer   186–7, 191–2,
    193, 195–6, 200, 210, 211, 213,
    215, 261
  elaborate planning system
      206, 209
  FSC certification   202
staff sickness   137
Staff Skills Index   169
stakeholder representation
    160–1, 225
'standard operating procedures'   38
standardization   95
standards   154, 201–2
  ecological, economic and
      social   200
  ethical   65–6
  see also ISO
Standards Committee (UK)   226
state expenditure   69, 222
state intervention   98
state-owned companies   55, 58, 59,
    83, 164, 191, 192, 194, 197
  agencies with commercial functions
      turned into   56
  joint stock   55, 58, 59
  modest   68
  off-budget   59
State Revision body (Sweden)   235

steering 9, 14, 16, 60, 66, 89
  active 22, 78
  barriers to 84
  democratic 61
  goal-oriented 39
  internal 211
  market 85
  new forms of 59
  performance-oriented 57
  proposals to improve 85
  quite precise 25
  results 77, 86, 91, 238
  strategic 41
Steering Committee for the Review of the Prison Service (UK 1997) 138
Strangeways riot (1990) 119, 124
Strasbourg 187
'street level bureaucrats' 38
structural separation 10, 19, 90
Summa, H. 52, 55, 60
Sundström, G. 84
supervisory boards 225
sustainable development/ sustainability 183, 200
SVB (Dutch Social Insurance Bank) 217, 218, 222, 224, 231, 238, 241
  annual efficiency report 236
  autonomy 226
  'balanced scorecard' 233
  budget indexed maximum 237
  establishment (1990) 230
  jurisdiction 223
  main performance targets set by 234
  regionally based 227
Sveaskog AB 191, 192, 193, 197
Svenska Skogsplantor 195
SVR (Dutch Social Insurance Council) 219, 226
SVS (Swedish National Board of Forestry) 188–9, 191, 194–5, 204, 205, 208, 212, 213
  private forest covered by 206
  protection of environment and production 199
  regulator and purveyor of priced advice services 203

units allowed to show profit only in international arena 197
Sweden 3, 4, 7, 32, 36, 64, 79–96
  agency autonomy/independence 9, 15
  civil service 6
  constitutionally defined boards 31
  forestry 184, 185, 186, 200, 201, 202, 211; *see also* AssiDomän; Sveaskog; Svenska; SVS
  Government Office 14
  individualism 101
  large agencies part of old-style government 61
  meteorology 147, 148, 172, 180; *see also* SMHI
  monitoring 22
  percentage of civil servants working in agencies 76
  policymaking 41
  power-distance index 101
  prisons 120, 122, 125, 126, 127, 128–9, 132, 141; *see also* KVV
  public employment figures 66
  reforming pre-existing agencies 31
  results-oriented management 69
  role differences 50
  social security 217, 220, 221, 224, 228; *see also* AMS
  specific reform ideas 68
  see also VESTA

Talbot, C. 6, 20
Taliercio, R. 14, 20
Tanzania 3, 7, 22, 42
target-orientation 142
targets 39, 62, 168, 169, 170
  financial 205, 208, 209, 210
  formalized 177
  management-set 206
  non-financial 209
  quality 232
  setting and seeking 77
  specific 137
  very detailed list of 232
  see also performance targets
Tarschys, D. 84
task-based cases 43

task specific factors   23
   see also TSPD
taxation   31, 73, 98
technical competence   51
technocratic approach   54
terrorist prisoners   126
Thailand   7
Thatcher, Margaret   53, 65, 98, 101, 104, 105, 106, 197
Thatcherism/Thatcherite social policy   68, 220
third-party voting   97, 98
Tidaholm riots (Sweden 1994)   119
Tiihonen, S.   53
Tilt, Richard   130
Tories *see* Conservatives (UK)
'total institutions'   118
tourism   149, 185, 197, 198, 200
   and recreation   189, 205
TQM (total quality management) approach   53
trade associations   191
trade unions   219, 228
Trading Funds   110, 159–60, 175
Traffic and Infrastructure Ministries
   Finland   160
   Netherlands   160, 165
training   75, 93
transfer of power   70
transparency   142, 150, 163, 168
   lack of   104
   reduced   4
Transport Ministry (Finland)   160
Transport (and Water) Ministry (Netherlands)   39, 71, 73, 160
tripod model   30, 33, 34, 60, 107, 253–5, 263, 257
trust   64, 65, 210
TSPD (Task-Specific Path Dependency)   18, 249, 250, 251–3, 255, 256, 257–8, 260, 262, 263–5
turnover   170
Twelfth World Meteorological Congress (1995)   151
two-party systems   97

UK MET Office   153, 157, 174, 181, 260
   commercial activities   161, 162, 175
   comparing accuracy with other MET offices   172
   complaint within UK Competition Commission   162
   customer focus   170
   Defence Meteorological Board   161
   employees described as scientists   154
   failure of TV weather forecaster (1987)   179
   forecasting model used by   169
   important organizational changes   175
   performance measures   168–9, 178
   targets   169
   Trading Fund status   159–60, 175
   well known and well loved   156
unbundled agencies   42
'unbundling of government'   31, 32
unemployment   220, 224
unemployment insurance   218, 223
unicameral legislatures   50, 80
unitary states   49, 63, 80
United Kingdom   7, 19, 36, 60, 73, 97–114
   agency formation   39
   agenda setting   92
   anti-government attitudes   64
   citizen trust   65
   claims and criticisms   4
   exceptionalism   247, 260, 262
   forestry   184, 185, 208, 210; *see also* Forest Enterprise; Forest Research; Forestry Commission
   implementation process   57
   interference   22
   internal contracts   40
   largest five agencies   41
   majoritarian approach   61
   meteorology   147, 148, 166, 167, 177, 180; *see also* UK MET
   ministry/agency relationship   8, 21, 23
   moderately autonomous organizations   31
   performance indicator culture   76
   prisons   119, 120–1, 122, 124, 126, 127, 129–30

Index

United Kingdom – *continued*
  privatization largely disappeared from 197
  public employment figures 66
  Public Service Agreements 77, 233, 237
  regulation inside government 38
  role differences 50
  social security 217, 219, 228; *see also* Benefits Agency; DSS
  staffing and spending 3
  state bodies to private ownership 68
  substantial statutory boards 31
  unbundled agencies 42
  see also British Civil Service; Cabinet Office; Fulton Committee; HM Customs & Excise; HM Treasury; HMPS; Inland Revenue; KPIs; National Audit Offices; National Weights and Measures; Next Steps; Office of Public Services Reform; Whitehall
United Nations 183
  Rio Conference (1992) 187
United States 6, 7, 36–7
  agencies and policy autonomy 41
  anti-government attitudes 64
  externally imposed restrictions and regulations 109
  federal agencies 15
  GPRA (Government Performance and Results Act) 41
  important federal functions 31
  performance contracting 42
  prisons 126, 132
  rational choice variants 13
  reforms 31, 33, 68
  role differences 50
  weather satellites 153
user-responsiveness 19
utility maximizing actors 13
Utrecht 187

Vagg, J. 119
values 141, 154
  alternative 17
  local 16, 17
  national 155
  'nature' 185
  variations in 27
Van Osteroom, R. 74
Van Thiel, S. 14, 19, 21, 22, 71, 74
Vanhanen, Matti 50
VBTB (Dutch performance budgeting) 70, 134
VDPI (Dutch national association of prison warders) 129
VESTA (Swedish workgroup) 87–8
volatility 258–60
Vos, E. 21
voucher schemes 85
VTV (Finnish State Audit Office) 144

wage subsidization 233–4
Wales 185, 192, 193, 213
  Welsh Assembly 99, 193
weather forecasts *see* meteorology
welfare states 32, 98–9
  end to 'golden era' of 221
  expensive, labour-intensive services 68
  growing burdens 14
White, R. 149, 150
Whitehall 43, 101, 102, 103–4, 106, 108
  one of the largest budgets in 219
Whitemoor maximum security prison 119
Whitley, R. 183
Wildlife and Countryside Act (UK 1985) 193
Wilson, James Q. 15, 23, 25, 26, 29, 30–1, 154
WMC (World Meteorological Centre) 157
WMO (World Meteorological Organization) 148, 150, 151, 153, 154
WNI (Weather News Incorporated) 162
Woodland Assurance scheme (UK) 202
Woolf, Lord Justice 124, 125
World Bank 32

WSI (Weather Services International) 162
WWF (World Wildlife Fund) 187–8

Yamamoto, K. 22

ZBOs (Dutch Independent Administrative Bodies) 8, 10, 11, 14, 75, 253
  agencies exist in the shadow of 77
  creation of 69, 70, 71, 73, 74
  initial priority for 228
  insufficiently accountable to centre 22
  number fallen 69
  payment of benefits transformed into 219
  privatisering 68
  public accountability 70, 74
  staff figures 66
  see also Staatsbosbeheer
Zillman, J. W. 148, 150